Reading Stanley Elkin

*For Eleanor Welch Bailey
and Joseph W. Bailey*

Contents

Preface

In his review of Stanley Elkin's *The Living End*, Frank Kermode wondered why Elkin's characteristic literary admixture of "sour, manic prose," linguistic extravagance, and "comic terror" has not gained him a wider audience, and he regretted that the work showed little promise of altering that circumstance. The targets of *The Living End*, Kermode contended, "seem somewhat too large and easy," and then he added, "but only on cursory inspection; the fine print will stand a lot of attention from anyone who thinks he could get hooked on a taste so wild and bitter."[1] The existence of this book is proof enough of one reader's having gotten hooked; what the study must demonstrate is that the "fine print"—not only of *The Living End*, but of all Elkin's work, early and late—is, as Kermode suggested, deserving of careful critical attention.

Elkin's work has been subjected to enough critical scrutiny at this point—discussions of his fiction by Raymond Olderman[2] and Thomas LeClair[3] in the mid-1970s and Doris Bargen's full-length study (1980)[4] having established his novels' accessibility to rigorous and detailed analysis—that there is no need to justify its extended examination here. But there remains a tendency among critics and reviewers to assume that, however much they admire or enjoy it, his fiction is ultimately shapeless, self-indulgent, uncontrolled—in short, inartistic. A deliberate, thoroughgoing confutation of that view is one of the primary objectives of this book.

Two different assumptions underlie this attitude toward Elkin's work. One is that it is too funny to be serious. The predominantly

Preface

comic purposes of his fiction, Elkin's detractors contend, tend to dissipate the formal energies of his work, the narrative tensions necessary to effective fiction being so continually released as to make his books feel excessively loose, relaxed. A related, perhaps corollary, argument holds that because his work gravitates toward self-contained scenes and humorous sketches, it is episodic, lacking in formal coherence and structure. ("The Brooks that comes to mind with Elkin," as one reviewer neatly summed up this position, "is not Cleanth but Mel."[5]) And, most recently, the objection has frequently been raised that Elkin has come increasingly to value language (language-for-its-own-sake is the popular term) in excess of its worth, letting an ostentatious and gimmicky syntax and diction dictate the course of his stories and novels, sacrificing coherence to mere expressiveness and form to poetic exuberance.

It will be the burden of the entire work to establish the speciousness or irrelevance of such objections to Elkin's art, but it may be worthwhile to sketch out the gist of my responses briefly here. To begin with the final objection, we will see that one major development in Elkin's fiction has indeed been its progressively greater interest in and self-consciousness about language, an issue that actually represents the primary thematic concern of the novellas in *Searches and Seizures* and of the opening novella of *The Living End.* This does not, certainly, deny that Elkin's language has become more and more distinctive, intricately poetic, and tirelessly evocative; it is only to suggest that his work has come increasingly to dramatize the evolution of his own attitude toward language and to inquire seriously into the meaning of the gesture of extreme language. The significance of language in Elkin's fiction will be discussed in detail in the chapters dealing with *Searches and Seizures* and *The Living End,* but the conclusion of those arguments can be glimpsed in William Gass's comment on Elkin's description of merchandise stacked on a department store counter in *A Bad Man:* "Nothing but genre blindness," Gass insists, "could prevent us from seeing that there is no warmer, wealthier poetry being written in our time."[6]

The argument that his work is marred by its episodic nature assumes that Elkin is trying—and failing—to write plot-centered fiction, that his attempts at conceiving consonant, resonant stories and

Preface

novels possessed of beginning-middle-end sequentiality and solid, satisfying narrative-level resolutions are somehow constantly going awry. *The Franchiser* clearly demonstrates how little Elkin is concerned with cohesion of this narrative-level sort. The chapter dealing with that novel sets out to show that it is rendered coherent more through metaphor and analogy than through plot, its consonance achieved through the convergence of parallel scenes and the intertwining of patterns of reduplicative imagery. Implicit in this book and informing its every page is my assumption—which the second chapter attempts to substantiate—that, although his earlier work seems to align itself naturally with the plot-centered fiction of contemporaries like Philip Roth and Saul Bellow, there has always been an anti-realist tendency in Elkin's work, a tendency that ties it more closely to the fiction of Thomas Pynchon, Robert Coover, and Donald Barthelme than to the tradition of social realism that underlies the American Jewish novel. To perceive the evolution of Elkin's fiction in any other way obliges one to declare *The Living End* an inexplicable divergence from Elkin's habitual mode, rather than to see it (as the work's penultimate chapter does) as an extension and culmination of tendencies discernible in his work from *Boswell* and *Criers & Kibitzers, Kibitzers & Criers* forward.

Is Elkin's fiction—to consider the initial objection last—overwhelmed by its own extravagance of humor? Is there an excess of the comic in his work? Certainly—but then, there is an excess of practically everything in his work: of pathos, poetry, and hilarious dialogue, of outlandish situations and rhetorical tours de force, of puns, funny stories, and spirit-crushing insights, of improbable tales and visionary similes, of paradigms and picaresque quests and eccentric, fully imagined people, places, and things—and of catalogues like this one. Elkin's is a fiction of excess, a fiction of abundance and artistic generosity. To recognize this is to understand that the real tension underlying all his work, whatever its shape once it has been transformed, is that of the imagination refusing to allow invention to flag—that of the creative mind's insistence that new pleasures and insights can still be wrung from the old materials and the old words if enough energy and vision are brought to the task. This aspect of Elkin's art can be discussed only in uncomfortably in-

tuitive and impressionistic terms, but before we leave inspiration behind to concentrate on qualities (form, deliberate execution,
metaphoric cohesion) that Elkin's work is reputed to lack, we should
note that it is only because of that surface exuberance and generosity
of invention that his work invites critical analysis in the first place.
Explication must be the mode and method of our undertaking, then,
and if the vast majority of the passages cited in the following pages
are trotted out to provide evidence of pattern or to demonstrate coherence, a few others will be quoted as much for the simple pleasure
of quoting them, as a reminder of the extra-structural joys of language and invention which are the animating dynamic behind all of
his fiction.

The manuscript of this book in various stages of preparation
benefited from the encouragement and suggestions of J. Kerry
Grant, Geoffrey Green, Marjorie Perloff, Max F. Schulz, Paul Seydor,
Ann Lowry Weir, Eleanor Welch Bailey, and Lucretia Bailey Yagh-
jian. Stanley Elkin read it, too, and in at least one case he told me
why I was wrong. Jackson I. Cope recommended that I make a dissertation, and then a book, out of what I thought about Elkin, and his
assumptions concerning the careful reading of literary texts inform
its every page. St. Lawrence University provided support for the
manuscript's preparation as well as an atmosphere extraordinarily
conducive to the task. And Frances Weller Bailey read and reread
and revised and proofread and proved how mistaken Elkin's Boswell
is in his contention that "You had to go it alone to make it mean
anything."

NOTES

1. Frank Kermode, " 'Love and Do as You Please," review of
The Living End by Stanley Elkin, *New York Review of Books,* 1 August 1979, p. 46.

2. The first important discussion of Elkin's work appeared in
Raymond M. Olderman, *Beyond the Waste Land: The American
Novel in the Nineteen-Sixties* (New Haven: Yale University Press,
1972), pp. 53-71, 175-81 et passim.

Preface

3. Thomas LeClair, "The Obsessional Fiction of Stanley Elkin," *Contemporary Literature* 16: 2 (1975): 147-62.

4. Doris Bargen, *The Fiction of Stanley Elkin* (Frankfurt: Verlag Peter D. Lang, 1980).

5. Geoffrey Stokes, review of *The Living End* by Stanley Elkin, *Village Voice*, 20 August 1979, p. 82.

6. William Gass, *On Being Blue* (Boston: David R. Godine, 1976), p. 89.

1

The Bully Poetics of Stanley Elkin

We begin with Push the Bully, protagonist and narrator of the short story Elkin has characterized as his best, "A Poetics for Bullies."[1] Push qualifies as a representative Elkin protagonist not because he exhausts the characteristics of the central figures who would succeed him in Elkin's fiction, but because he exemplifies and articulates more distinctly than any other early protagonists an attitude—a temperamental bias bordering upon philosophical stance—with which each of them is to some degree invested. "I'm Push the Bully," he proclaims in one of the two first-person narrations contained in the *Criers & Kibitzers, Kibitzers & Criers* collection, "and what I hate are new kids and sissies, dumb kids and smart, rich kids, poor kids, kids who wear glasses, talk funny, show off, patrol boys and wise guys and kids who pass pencils and water the plants—and cripples, *especially* cripples. I love nobody loved."[2] The pervasiveness of Push's rancor reflects its irrational basis, but he is no more apologetic about this than he is about the often ignoble motives that underlie his malevolence. When the mother of a boy he is bullying complains that he picks on her son only out of jealousy of the boy's red hair, Push readily admits the justice of her charge: "It's true," he explains, "I did wish I had his red hair. I wish I were tall, or fat, or thin. I wish I had different eyes, different hands, a mother in the supermarket. I wish I were a man, a small boy, a girl in the choir. I'm a coveter, a Boston Blackie of the heart, casing the world. Endlessly I covet and case" (p. 197).

Push's argument is with limitation, circumscription, with the

1

boundaries imposed upon his possibilities by the reality of his being only Push, and thus having only his own options and capacities. He defines himself, then, largely in terms of the spontaneous, gratuitous, irrational desires he feels but cannot gratify; he incessantly and obsessively wants to encompass more, have more, be more than his paltry single share of existence allows him to encompass, have, be. For all of his coveting and casing, however, Push is not so much dissatisfied with what he is as angry at all that he isn't. It is this logic, and the resentment that is its product, that he enacts through his bully's tactics, inflicting on his victims not pain but an awareness of their inadequacies congruent with his awareness of his own. He becomes infirmity's goad and deficiency's advocate, one whose self-appointed mission is to zero in on other kids' vulnerabilities, exploit their afflictions, stir their insecurities, and in general keep them as mindful of their flaws and insufficiencies as he is of his. Push forces gallons of water on a boy who suffers from hyperactive saliva glands, insisting that the affliction threatens to dehydrate him if he fails to drink enough; he mocks the obesity of fat boys and imitates the individual limps of cripples; he reminds an acne-scarred boy that the girls he wants to date find his appearance distasteful. He perpetuates all of these offenses out of an odd sense of solicitousness ("Who else cared about the fatties, about the dummies and slobs and clowns," he asks rhetorically, "about the gimps and squares and oafs and fools, the kids with a mouthful of mush, all those shut-ins of the mind and heart, all those losers?" [p. 206]) as ingenuous as it is unrelenting.

That there is a sense in which his bullying is carried out in his victims' best interests is established through his confrontations with the story's antagonist, a paragon named John Williams. Williams, the ultimate new kid in town who is immediately embraced by the same boys whom Push holds in subjection, is the bully's opposite in every respect. He doesn't want—he has. He doesn't bully—he comforts. He doesn't incite conflict, but fosters conciliation. He doesn't harp on deficiency, but seeks compensation for or amelioration of it. Whereas Push drives boys in upon themselves, forcing them into incessant confrontations with the drooling, overweight, crippled or otherwise debilitated individual self, Williams brings them out and

The Bully Poetics of Stanley Elkin

communalizes them, sharing stories of his adventures with them and involving them in games the successful participation in which no handicap can impede.

Push recognizes the enemy in John Williams quickly enough, but the bully's magic (the "sleight-of-mouth" and strategies of vulnerability exploitation) that he uses on other boys who similarly—if unintentionally—represent repudiations of his vision fails to have any effect upon this new adversary. His attempt at parodying Williams's precise, articulate speech produces only a mediocre simulacrum of that eloquence, as Push proves himself capable of mimicking effectively only his targets' flaws, not their virtues. His scrawling of the hated name on a wall seems to celebrate rather than curse it, and he doesn't even try the "match burn twice" or similarly routine deceits of the bully's repertoire on Williams, deeming them unworthy of the opposition. The bully's magic fails to work here because Williams is able to counter it with a stronger magic: the constructive, charismatic, communal magic of the hero, magic that brings together the many in the name of the one. Significantly, Push calls Williams "the prince" before he learns his name; this detail, in addition to a number of other aristocratic references that accumulate about Williams in the course of the story, suggests that "A Poetics for Bullies" is on one level a confrontation between nobility and the bully's democratic spirit, the noblesse oblige underlying Williams's treatment of the boys contending with the "one boy, one debility" egalitarianism of Push. This aspect of the boys' response to Williams is rendered dramatically in the story and is never really expounded upon; a helpful gloss on the relationship can be found, however, in the story which precedes "A Poetics for Bullies" in *Criers & Kibitzers, Kibitzers & Criers.*[3] "On a Field, Rampant" concerns a protagonist named Khardov, whose conviction is that he is the heir to the throne of an as yet unidentified European country; the story relates his search for the land of his supposed noble birth. He never finds that land—or at least his claims are nowhere recognized—but his disclosure in one country of his presumed identity nonetheless convinces some of the commoners, who respond by fixing "their looks of patient ecstasy upon him, their weak sad freight of disease and despair and hope and love. He could feel their senseless love mounting steadily, building, bursting in upon him like waters that have split their banks" (p. 195). The self-proclaimed monarch angrily rejects the obeisances of his would-be subjects. Williams, conversely, encourages the subjection of his entourage to himself, inviting their dependency, accepting their devotion and offering himself as their champion. It is this offense that the democratic Push cannot abide. ("Do you know what makes me cry?" he asks early in the story, "The Declaration of Independence. 'All men are created equal.' That's beautiful" [p. 197].)

Push prepares for the necessary confrontation with his antagonist, bullying him into a fight that Push fully intends to lose, believing that the defeat will prove Williams's frailty, his merely human inability to turn the other cheek. Predictably, Push's strategy fails. Williams is able to justify his brutalization of the bully as the just comeuppance due a tyrant. Williams graciously offers a hand to his felled opponent, a gesture that Push very nearly accepts, his palm itching to grasp the fellowship, peace, and release from self-absorption that this handclasp would mean. But, in a characteristically Elkinian moment, Push peremptorily rejects dependency for isolation, refuses rest in favor of need and resentment, turns down the offered assistance for no better reason than "All I know at last is what feels good" (p. 215). What feels good is the affirmation of the self in all of its inadequacy, insufficiency, and want. Following this climactic moment of rejected apostasy is an extended apologia, a declaration of the bully's credo that will be echoed throughout the pages of Elkin's subsequent fiction.

His anger mounting steadily as he assaults Williams and his followers with the full force of his antagonism, Push insists that the comforts of community are delusory, not redemptive, and that even a paragon like John Williams represents no serious counterargument to the inequities, deficiencies, and infirmities that characterize the lives of human beings. Push understands that the obeisance the boys pay Williams—like the self-abnegation offered up to the protagonist of "On a Field, Rampant" by the commoners—is merely their attempt to look away from the realities of the unitary, isolated self, to seek in an ideal a kind of rejoinder to and deliverance from their overwhelming feelings of inadequacy and powerlessness. That

The Bully Poetics of Stanley Elkin

self from which they seek release, drooling, crippled, or scarred as it might be, is not, in Push's ethic, to be bartered away for a bogus communal redemption in the name of an ideal. Thus he rejects the proffered friendship by insisting, "Push is no service animal. No. *No*. Can you hear that, Williams? There isn't any magic, but your no is still stronger than your yes, and distrust is where I put my faith" (pp. 215-16).

Having refused Williams his allegiance, Push sees immediately how markedly that denial has reduced his nemesis, corrupting his perfection and leaving him deficient, compromised. This unanticipated triumph exhilarates Push, inspiring him to launch into his (again, distinctly Elkinian) credo:

I feel a power in me. I am Push, Push the bully, God of the Neighborhood, its incarnation of envy and jealousy and need. I vie, strive, emulate, compete, a contender in every event there is. I didn't make myself. I probably can't save myself, but maybe that's the only need I don't have. I taste my lack, and that's how I win—by having nothing to lose. It's not good enough! I want and I want and I will die wanting, but first I will have something. This time I will have something. I say it aloud. "This time I will have something." I step toward them. The power makes me dizzy. It is enormous. They feel it. They back away. They crouch in the shadow of my outstretched wings. It isn't deceit this time but the real magic at last, the genuine thing: the cabala of my hate, of my irreconcilableness. [p. 216]

The uncompromising, all-enveloping affirmation of the self here is unmistakable, as is the unblushing celebration of the fact that to live is to want, and to never cease wanting. The debt to existentialist thought is equally apparent, especially in Push's assertion that he didn't make himself, probably can't save himself, but has nevertheless found someone he can affirm being. Less obvious here, however, is the significance of Push's reference to "the real magic at last," a line that echoes his previously cited, equally enigmatic assertion that "There isn't any magic." Push's first comment about magic, offered as he is confessing to the shabby obviousness of his bully's ploys, provides a context through which his subsequent references to magic can be understood. Embarrassed by his predictable repertoire of tawdry tricks, Push would prefer to wield the power of real sorcery, but "There is no magic. If there were I would learn it. I would find out the words, the slow turns and strange passes, drain the bloods and get the herbs, do the fires like a vestal. I would look for the main chants. *Then* I'd change things. *Push* would. But there's only casuistical trick. Sleight-of-mouth, the bully's poetics" (pp. 198-99).

"A Poetics for Bullies" concludes, then, in the assertion that there *is* a form of magic that transcends the claims of the aristocratic virtues of charisma, charm, grace, and ability. The "real magic" involves the uncompromising affirmation of self, the negation of and fanatical resistance to all that would circumscribe, limit, or impose boundaries upon the possibilities for expansion of the solitary, necessarily isolate, human self. "Casuistical trick" will have to suffice much of the time, "the bully's poetics" providing a kind of leverage in the absence of this more potent force. But occasionally the power of negation, the dynamic of the incontestable will, can emerge and transfigure the self through which it is operating, allowing it to subdue the world and accomplish miracles in the process. Accordingly, Push's final action confirms his possession of (or by) the "real magic." He performs a miracle, albeit one distinctly appropriate to the all-negating source of his sorcery's inspiration. His "real magic," in other words, is not that which brings life to dead lands or produces something where there was nothing; his magic, on the contrary, introduces nothing where there was something, transforms verdant fields to deserts. " 'I will have something,' " he repeats menacingly as he approaches Eugene of the hyperactive salivary glands: " 'I will have terror. I will have drought. I bring the dearth. Famine's contagious. Also is thirst. Privation, privation, barrenness, void. I dry up your glands, I poison your well.' " The others crowd around to view the prodigy and, indeed, Eugene's "throat is parched. There is sand on his tongue" (pp. 216-17).

Push's irascibility and intransigence, his opposition to forms of behavior typically considered virtuous, genteel, or superior, his unremitting need to affirm himself and his insistence upon making of negations the basis of that affirmation—these are the qualities that subsequent Elkin protagonists will most conspicuously share, with

The Bully Poetics of Stanley Elkin

Leo Feldman of *A Bad Man* and Alexander Main of "The Bailbondsman" becoming their quintessential embodiments. His fellow protagonists in *Criers & Kibitzers, Kibitzers & Criers* also display many of his principal traits. The unappeasable and essential anger that Push vents upon Williams and his entourage at the story's conclusion is echoed, for instance, in the wrath of Khardov, the protagonist of "On a Field, Rampant." A royal medallion, the possession of which has represented Khardov's primary claim to royal ancestry, comes to seem instead merely a prefiguring of his response to the failure of his quest for restoration. The lion it bears, "rampant, the claws bursting from the furred paws," embodies a "rage, like his own, concentrated on no object, irrelevant but steady, spraying the air like spit." Khardov comes to understand that the lion, positioned "at the edge of the shield as at the edge of the jungle—loose, lost, peripheral, partner to nothing" (p. 191), delineates his own situation, excluded from the aristocratic lineage his ego demands and possessed of a helpless, impotent fury at his consequent commonness. His irate rejection of the homage offered by the lowly folk who have accepted his pretensions to nobility reflects not only his distaste for their proffered obsequiousness, then; it reflects as well his recognition that the credence they have placed in his claim, much like that which he has placed in it, is based on the delusion that his anger is princely. He has learned, to the contrary, that his want of princeliness makes him angry. The lion's rage is not regal, in other words; the lion rages because it is peripheral to regality. As for Push, so for Khardov. Jealousy is their lot, insufficiency their condition, anger and resentment at this state of affairs their heritage. A realization arrived at by James Boswell in Elkin's first novel neatly summarizes the conclusions reached by both Push and Khardov: "It was incredible that anyone should ever get what he wanted," Boswell explains on the novel's next-to-last page, "and I experienced, sharp as pain, deep as rage, a massive greed, a new knowledge that it was not enough, that nothing was ever enough, that we couldn't know what was enough or want what was enough. It wasn't even a question of deserts. Everybody deserved everything."[4]

If anger is, as these protagonists clearly decide, the inescapable response to the human condition, it is not presented as utterly impo-

tent or unavailing. Push's anger, after all, culminates in his generation of "the real magic," his rage producing one concrete miracle
(the overmatched bully's subduing of his adversary) and one symbolic one (his drying up of Eugene's salivary glands). For Khardov,
too, anger is, if not redemptive, at least transfiguring; its power
lends him the kind of majesty denied him by his birth. That anger
and the aggressive force it generates are not only what much of
Elkin's fiction is about; they also constitute the underpinnings of an
aesthetic which his best work affirms and enacts. That aesthetic is
articulated, in analogical terms, in "A Poetics for Bullies."

It is difficult not to hear in Push's complaint that he has no
magic but only "casuistical trick. Sleight-of-mouth, the bully's poetics" echoes of the modern writer's familiar grouse against the in-
effectuality of his medium. (We might think of Humbert Humbert's
plaint to his nymphet: " 'Oh, Lolita, I have only words to play
with!' "[5]; we might recall the narrator of John Updike's "Leaves"
describing his literary gift as "a curious trick, possibly useless, but
mine,"[6] or the similar grumblings of narrators and characters in the
fiction of Barth, Barthelme, Beckett, or Fowles.) Push's deprecation
of his trade does, in fact, have approximate parallels in Elkin's discussion of his. In one interview Elkin expresses agreement with W.
H. Auden's contention that poems "never saved a single Jew from
the ovens,"[7] and his general tendency in public statements has been
to minimize the serious cultural contribution of his work and of fiction in general. Instead, he discusses fiction as a medium that, above
all, "gives language an opportunity to happen,"[8] one in which the
only things real to the writer are "sentences and metaphors and
syntax"[9]—the props, in other words, of the novelist's "casuistical
tricks." For Elkin, as for his protagonist, however, ordinary poetics
can produce extraordinary effects if the "sleight-of-mouth" is heterodox enough and the infusion of self behind it sufficiently potent.
This is what Elkin meant when he explained that his fiction "is not
trying to sell anybody anything. I am trying to upset the applecarts
of expectation and ordinary grammar, and you can only do that with
fierce language. You can only do that with aggression: the aggression of syntax and metaphor, the aggression, really, of actual, by God
metered prose."[10] Good prose for Elkin conducts an assault on the

The Bully Poetics of Stanley Elkin

reader's assumptions about existence, and his sense of the purpose of writing is very close to that articulated by Joan Didion in her essay, "Why I Write": the setting down of words on paper, she argues, represents "the tactic of a secret bully, an invasion, an imposition of the writer's sensibility on the reader's most private space."[11]

Verbal aggression is not, of course, Elkin's ultimate purpose in writing, any more than "casuistical trick" is Push's only resource in bullying. Both undertake the aggressive act in the faith that it will culminate in the achievement of "the real magic," in the transformation of the ordinary and familiar into the extraordinary and strange. In the same interview in which he discusses his use of "by God metered prose," Elkin proceeded to comment further upon the presence of aggressive language in his work, arguing that the extreme rhetoric is produced "not only to perform for us, to show its triplets and barrel rolls, but to introduce significance into what may otherwise be untouched by significance."[12] Something happens in the literary transaction that gives significance on the page to that which had none in the world, and if Elkin doesn't resort to the magic metaphor to describe that process here, he often does refer to it, throughout his career, when talking about fiction's purposes or discussing the strengths and weaknesses of the work of his contemporaries.

As early as 1959, Elkin, reviewing Peter Lisca's *Wide World of John Steinbeck,* argued that Steinbeck's real gift was dramatic rather than novelistic. Citing as evidence his "failure to develop an individual prose style," Elkin contended that Steinbeck managed to write a number of good books and a few great ones "without ever having learned *how* to say a thing, or at any rate without ever having the way he says things somehow intrinsically stamped on the things he says."[13] The review leaves little doubt as to Elkin's view of the effectiveness of such a signatureless prose style. In a 1967 review of *The Fixer,* by Bernard Malamud, Elkin returns to this idea, this time explicitly referring to the notion of literary magic. His objection to Malamud's novel is that "there is no 'language' in the book as such, none of the astonishing rhetoric of William Gass, say, or Leonard Cohen, or Norman Mailer. So rare, in fact, is anything like 'style' in *The Fixer* that when one reads of 'the responsible knock of the hammer,' it comes almost as an affront."[14] This stylistic reservation expressed, Elkin offers a general critique of the novel as a whole, defining his notion of "magic" in the process.

Let me say straight off that *The Fixer* is immensely moving, but that this quality is at once its supreme achievement and part of its downfall. For what moves us is "magic." ("Magic" is imprecise, but there is no other word for it.) What moves us is inconsistency, the heart's last-ditch obstinacy or its dark-horse generosities. We cry at musicals—as least I do—when someone with no particular reason to bursts into exuberant song....There is an inverse ratio between small cause for joy and joy's expression. We hail every hold-out with our tears and Yakov Bok is such a hold-out and we hail him. But it's still irrational. It's still magic.[15]

Elkin's objection to Malamud's novel comes to this: *The Fixer* moves us with its searing portrayal of a victim and his sufferings, but its commitment to affecting us in this way leaves its narrative momentum constantly gravitating toward moral and emotional tableaux, toward images of static, unquestionable truths that give the reader nothing to do but to agree that Bok is indeed sorely tried. (Bok suffers enormously under his burden of injustice and cruelty, and we come to expect to find his sufferings increasing as the novel proceeds; if, amid his sufferings, he were suddenly and inexplicitly to burst into laughter or song, Elkin is suggesting, that would excite our wonder and lead us away from static truth toward vital enigma.) The unavoidability of the truth of Bok's suffering is what compromises *The Fixer's* effectiveness for Elkin, the ubiquity of that truth's dramatization throughout the novel obviating any possibility of mystery or ambiguity or moral complexity, qualities that exist, he maintains, in inimical relation to images of preestablished and unambiguous truth. Elkin is arguing that the absence of rhetorical exuberance in *The Fixer* reflects the extent to which it is a novel dedicated to *recording* the truth, rather than to its *discovery*. Although possessed of the "magic" he seeks in fiction, Malamud's book takes too few expressive risks and is too sure about its own meaning to be utterly and convincingly "magical."[16]

The fiction that Elkin had published by 1967, when this review

The Bully Poetics of Stanley Elkin

appeared, was not so innocent of rhetorical flourish and stylistic ex-travagance as he claimed *The Fixer* to be, of course. Although the confident and deliberate poetic excesses of *The Living End* and *George Mills* were more than a decade away, Elkin was clearly al-ready favoring those "magical" moments when language tran-scends its own "casuistical tricks and sleight-of-mouth" and attains a crazy poetry that "introduces significance into what may other-wise be untouched by significance." In his earliest fiction such mo-ments generally take the form of ecstatic speeches delivered by characters responding to extraordinary circumstances: Boswell's dream monologue urging the members of his Club to forget their deaths and to concentrate instead on his, or Leo Feldman's testi-mony in his own behalf before a prison kangaroo court intent upon his execution. Gradually Elkin allowed the "aggression of syntax and metaphor" to permeate the narrative surface of his fiction, no longer reserving his "fierce language" for characters' speeches alone. As a result, his work from *A Bad Man* forward reflects an in-creasing tendency to disregard conventional distinctions between first-and third-person narrative modes, his narrators' voices coming to sound more and more like, and beginning to fade indistinguish-ably into, the voices of the protagonists whose stories they are telling.

Since that time Elkin has remained remarkably consistent in his preference for extravagant prose styles, both in his own work and in that of other writers, a fact conspicuously reflected by his com-ments about the stories he chose for inclusion in *The Best American Short Stories 1980.* What he admires most about these stories, he ex-plains, is the quality of the vision in which they conclude, a vision achieved through a "language of magic," through "the beautiful cool comfort of a language that makes it all better, the soiled history, the rotten luck," even when we know that in life the "magic and in-version and transcendence" the language enacts cannot hope to "make it all better." It's not life, however, but fiction that Elkin is talking about here, fiction with its conclusions and resolutions like "rhetorical sacraments" which lend solace ("art's and language's consolation prize") to the living, fiction which compensates for one of life's greatest failings: "But life's tallest order is to keep the feel-

Reading Stanley Elkin

ings up, to make the two dollars worth of euphoria go the distance. And life can't do that. So fiction does. And there, right there, is the real—I want to say 'only'—morality of fiction."[17]

However idiosyncratic the terms in which he couches them, and however individual their application in his fiction, Elkin's poetics derive from and owe a distinct debt to one familiar and unmistakable source. The writer whose work most directly influenced the formulation of Elkin's aesthetic presented himself as "a poet without education who possessed only instinct and a fierce conviction and belief in the worth and truth of what he was doing, and an illimitable courage for rhetoric (personal pleasure in it too: I admit it) and who knew or cared for little else."[18] William Faulkner's initial influence upon Elkin's work was, as Elkin has freely acknowledged, predominantly stylistic.[19] Sentences in such early stories as "Fifty Dollars" and "On a Field, Rampant" display many of the devices and qualities—syntactical intricacy, parenthetical elaboration and digression, cumulative modification, and fondness for abstract, Latinate words—so characteristic of Faulkner's prose.[20] Elkin's development of his own style gradually reduced the presence of Faulknerian echoes in his work, but if his prose became less Faulknerian, the poetics underlying it remained very much informed and inspired by the aesthetic of that "poet without education." Elkin articulated his understanding of that aesthetic in his Ph.D. dissertation, "Religious Themes and Symbolism in the Novels of William Faulkner," completed in 1961. Although he later came to disparage the successfullness of the thesis,[21] he nonetheless admitted that what it identified as the central Faulknerian theme—"the egocentric will pitted against something stronger that itself"—was, if not what Faulkner's fiction was all about, what his own fiction would be about.[22]

Elkin's approach to Faulkner's novels emphasized content rather than form, but he asserted early in the dissertation that one cannot be finally considered in isolation from the other. ("A writer's language is, in a way, a writer's commitment," he maintained, adding the important—and characteristic—qualification, "unless, of course, the writer's vocabulary is circumscribed to begin with, and in that case, the man probably would not *be* a writer."[23]

The Bully Poetics of Stanley Elkin

In the dissertation's third chapter, "Faulkner and the Religious Vocabulary," Elkin set out to delineate the link between Faulkner's diction and his perception of things, arguing that "even his style is religious," the language consistently evoking "the lost sense of wonder suddenly revived."[24] There are, quite clearly, similarities between a prose that revives a sense of lost wonder and Elkin's notion that extavagant rhetoric is required to "upset the applecarts of expectation and ordinary grammar," and Elkin's discussion of the religiosity of Faulkner's style further substantiates the parallel.

This tone of awe which Faulkner manages to work into, which, indeed, is part of his narratives, indicates, I think (when considered together with the lofty tone of his public declarations), the general awe in which he stands of the human spirit, and this general awe is, in one context at least, religious. It is my notion that Faulkner's style, his investment in sentence rhythms, his stockpiling of Latinate words, his tightly reined parallelisms and intricate negatives, and, finally, his massive hyperbole, are the result not of being, as he calls himself, "a failed poet" but of perhaps unconscious devoutness.... Faulkner's stylistic excesses represent a lush spirituality. Without being able to explain it more precisely, I see the hyperbolic grandeur of his style as an integral part of his religious vocabulary.[25]

No comparable religious vocabulary permeates Elkin's work, and "lushly spiritual" describes neither its character nor its effect. Whereas Faulkner's style gravitates toward a "hyperbolic grandeur" that owes at least some of its resonance to its evocation of Christian myth (or, more exactly, to Christian eschatology), Elkin's style is founded upon a distinctly secular American idiom comprised variously of shoptalk, salesman rhetoric,[26] and the accents of Jewish-American humor, its vocabulary colloquial rather than religious. The disparity between these stylistic starting points comes to seem less significant when we recognize that, in Elkin's view, Faulkner's "tone of awe" is personal rather than theological, individual rather than orthodoxly pious. The Christian mythology so often evoked in his work supports and informs but never creates the distinctive Faulknerian atmosphere of spiritual extremity, of ultimate things perceived and approached in ultimate terms. His Christian sources, Elkin argued, gave Faulkner culturally familiar precedents for the dramatization of those issues—questions of morality and mortality, of "the human heart in conflict with itself"—that commanded his profoundest attention, but it was finally his own private spiritual idiom that Faulkner was creating through the style, an idiom that used Christian analogues to articulate deeply held humanistic beliefs. "Because Faulkner's major theme is the discipline of suffering," Elkin wrote on his dissertation's last page, "it is only natural that the environment of his themes and symbols is religious, a metaphor for aspirations not toward God, perhaps, and certainly not toward Heaven, but toward some final affirmation of the self."[27]

The "final affirmation of the self" was, for Elkin, the point as well as the purpose of Faulkner's work, and the style he created served as a means of conceiving and enacting that self in all its complexity and spiritual depth through the medium of language. ("I think that style is the song that [a writer] sings," Elkin told an interviewer in 1975,[28] thus reaffirming the view of style that he had taken in his dissertation.) What Faulkner taught Elkin—or what Elkin took him to mean— was that a writer's work represents an affirmation of self only insofar as it is possessed of a distinctive literary voice, a characteristic syntactical way of organizing the world which necessarily evokes other voices and idioms but which is nonetheless one's own. (It is only fitting, then, that Elkin dated the beginning of his writing career from "On a Field, Rampant," the story in which, despite Faulknerian echoes, he claims to have discovered his style.[29]) What Elkin added to that lesson, out of either choice or necessity, was the personal insight that voice is ultimately more important than content,[30] that rhetorical extravagance is often its own—and its only—best argument. This is the point of "Perlmutter at the East Pole," the final story in *Criers & Kibitzers, Kibitzers & Criers,* in which an anthropologist who has traveled the world in search of the synthesis of all human knowledge terminates his quest in New York's Union Square. He rises to speak, lacking the synthesis but aware of the need to speak nonetheless; the story closes upon his salutation to the crowd, leaving his actual words unrecorded. This point is made as well by "A Poetics for Bullies," in which Push insists that all he has to express (because he has no charisma, no advantages—no real content of his own) is renunciation, his refusal to be reconciled and his "bully's sour solace."[31] But, he is quick to add, "It's enough. I'll make do" (p. 217).

"Making do" with minimal assets and compromised advantages is a necessity so common to Elkin protagonists as to practically define their condition. Character after character presents himself as being in some way deficient in personal substance. In *Criers & Kibitzers, Kibitzers & Criers* alone we find four stories ("I Look Out for Ed Wolfe," "The Guest," "A Poetics for Bullies," and "Perlmutter at the East Pole") that deal with characters attempting to compensate for tenuous or uncertain senses of self. The novels and novellas which follow this collection similarly depict men for whom identity is something contingent, extrinsically derived or jerry-rigged; they ultimately substitute deed or role for personality, style for self. For all his egocentricity, Leo Feldman, the title character of *A Bad Man*, experiences this sort of self-doubt, his insecurities expressed through Elkin's favorite mode of interior monologue cum third-person narrative:

"That Feldman," anyone might have said, "there's a man who's *alive*. As if eccentricity and a will to scheme like a bomb to go off had anything to do with life. As if aggression and the maneuvered circumstance did.

Look at him, his ringed, framed concentration like a kid seeking a lost ball in high grass. An aesthetic of disappointment, a life of wanting things found wanting, calling out for the uncalled for.[32]

Dick Gibson, the protagonist of Elkin's subsequent novel, arrives at an equally contemptuous estimation of himself, admitting that he has "an apprentice personality and one track soul," that he has "gotten every idea he has ever had from what they permitted to be spoken on the air," and that he is a man who "has nothing to confess ...his own slate is clean, his character unmarked, his history uneventful." [33] And Ben Flesh is most explicit about his experience of personal vacuity in *The Franchiser:* "Only some people, me, for example, are born without goals. There are a handful of us without obsession....I live without obsession, without drive, a personal insanity even....The loneliest thing imaginable. Yet I've had to live

Reading Stanley Elkin

this way, live this, this—sane life, deprived of the warrants of personality."[34]

The affirmation of self that Push comes to at the close of "A Poetics for Bullies" represents one thematic antipode of Elkin's fiction; at the opposite pole stands the negation of Ben Flesh, his lament for a life lived "deprived of the warrants of personality." Between these two thematic extremities are aligned the remainder of his protagonists, with their varying capacities for self-affirmation and self-effacement. James Boswell achieves an equivocal celebration of self in *Boswell*; Marshall Preminger achieves an unequivocal destruction of same in "The Condominium"; and so on. The extent to which these later works affirm the self will be a central concern in the ensuing chapters; I introduce the issue here only to provide grounding for one final speculation about the relationship between Elkin's pet theme ("There is only one psychological assertion that I would insist upon," he explained in a *Paris Review* interview. "That is: the SELF takes precedence"[35]) and his attitude toward his craft.

"A Poetics for Bullies," this speculation goes, represents a more extensive and illuminating analogue of Elkin's work and the energy behind it than our treatment has so far suggested. In Push's contemptuous description of his bully's repertiore we might glimpse not only an anticipation of subsequent protagonists' confessions of self-doubt and personal insubstantiality; we might see as well an expression of Elkin's doubt about the material he has to work with— not myth-generative country but faceless, interchangeable cities; not a complexly resonant past but a one-dimensional, banal present; not heroic questers but weightlifters and salesmen and disc jockeys; not the decline of dynasties but the deterioration of the hopes of lonely single men. Elkin cannot (and does not attempt to) compete with his literary mentor on the level of material, plot, or richness of situation; nonetheless, his tendency to deprecate his own work when comparing it to Faulkner's reflects both his awareness of the disparity between them and the habituality with which the comparison occurs to him. The level upon which Elkin can compete with, and compare himself approximately to, Faulkner is stylistic, for his work is necessarily more dependent upon style for its effects than Faulkner's ever was. The people and concerns of Yoknapatawpha County are elevated to some extent through their rendering via Faulkner's elaborately Latinate style, but readers nonetheless sense that, in Faulkner's eyes, much of the richness was inherent in the subject matter itself; his gift for plotting and dramatic expansion simply contribute additional dimensions to the work. Elkin, on the other hand, deliberately begins with the mundane, even the banal, and then relies almost entirely upon style to transform his unelevated subject matter into compelling and affecting narrative. His plots characteristically resolve themselves (insofar as they do resolve themselves) less through action than through language and metaphor. Even if Elkin's material is, in some sense, mundane (and he would very likely reject the judgment as irrelevant), even if that fact occasionally leads him to speak with diffidence about his fiction, the fiction itself is alive and extraordinarily vivid, sustained by his obvious love of language and illuminated by his delight in the manipulation of words and metaphors. Beginning, perhaps, with nothing more than what Leo Feldman calls an "aesthetic of disappointment" and a temperamental resistance to any power that would circumscribe the self or demand its obedience and subordinacy Elkin not only "makes do" in literary terms but often makes "magic," the deceits of language and metaphor in his work combining to effect "the real magic at last" while simultaneously creating the style that is the song of Stanley Elkin. Push's last words in "A Poetics for Bullies" sum up both his dedicated bully's ethic and his creator's unapologetic writer's aesthetic: *"I push through."*

NOTES

1. Thomas LeClair, "Stanley Elkin: The Art of Fiction LXI" (interview), *Paris Review* 66 (Summer 1976): 83-84. In a subsequently published interview Elkin admitted that "anybody who wants to understand my works should have to understand 'A Poetics for Bullies' first," because "Push in that story undergoes, willfully, all the stratagems of most of my protagonists" (Doris Bargen, "An Interview with Stanley Elkin," an appendix to her *The Fiction of Stanley Elkin,* p. 264).

2. Stanley Elkin, *Criers & Kibitzers, Kibitzers & Criers* (New

York: Random House, 1965), p. 197. Subsequent quotations from this edition are cited in parentheses in the text.

3. Elkin's comments on "A Poetics for Bullies" encourage its comparison with "On a Field, Rampant": "Actually," he told Thomas LeClair, " 'A Poetics for Bullies' is a companion piece to 'On a Field, Rampant,' the first story I wrote which was any good" (LeClair, "Elkin: The Art of Fiction," p. 83).

4. Stanley Elkin, *Boswell: A Modern Comedy* (New York: Random House, 1964), p. 444. Subsequent quotations from this work are cited in parentheses in the text.

5. Vladimir Nabokov, *Lolita* (New York: G. P. Putnam's Sons, 1958), p. 227.

6. John Updike, *The Music School and Other Stories* (New York: Alfred A. Knopf, 1966), p. 53.

7. LeClair, "Elkin: The Art of Fiction," p. 62.

8. Phyllis Bernt and Joseph Bernt, "Stanley Elkin on Fiction: An Interview," *Prairie Schooner* (Spring 1976): 16.

9. Scott Sanders, "An Interview with Stanley Elkin," *Contemporary Literature* 16: 2 (Spring 1975): 135.

10. Ibid., p. 133.

11. Joan Didion, "Why I Write," in William Smart, ed., *Eight Modern Essayists* (New York: St. Martin's Press, 1980), p. 333.

12. Sanders, "Interview," p. 133.

13. Stanley Elkin, review of *The Wide World of John Steinbeck* by Peter Lisca, *Journal of English and German Philology* 58 (January 1959): 157.

14. Stanley Elkin, review of *The Fixer* by Bernard Malamud, *Massachusetts Review* 8 (Spring 1967): 388.

15. Ibid., pp. 389-90.

16. Elkin's argument here closely resembles that of Mark Schorer, who argues in an influential essay, "Technique as Discovery," that "the final lesson of the modern novel is that technique is not the secondary thing it seems to [H. G.] Wells, some external machination, a mechanical affair, but a deep and primary operation; not only that technique *contains* intellectual and moral implications, but that it *discovers* them" (Hudson Review 1: 1 [Spring 1948]: 74). Robert Frost affirmed the same notion more succinctly in an interview: "No tears in the writer, no tears in the reader. No surprise in the writer, no surprise in the reader" (Richard Poirier, "Interview with Robert Frost," in *Writers at Work: The Paris Review Interviews,*

2nd series, ed. George Plimpton [New York: Viking Press, 1965], p. 32).

17. Stanley Elkin, "Introduction," *The Best American Short Stories 1980*, ed. Stanley Elkin and Shannon Ravenel (New York: Houghton Mifflin, 1980), pp. xviii–xix.

18. "To Bennett Cerf and Robert K. Haas," 10 January 1945, *Selected Letters of William Faulkner*, ed. Joseph Blotner (New York: Random House, 1977), p. 188.

19. Elkin admits his stylistic debt to Faulkner in his *Prairie Schooner* interview, explaining, "A story like 'On a Field, Rampant' has Faulknerian sentences in it. I suppose that everything I have ever written has Faulknerian sentences in it" (Bernt and Bernt, "Elkin on Fiction," p. 19).

20. Two distinctly Faulknerian sentences from early Elkin stories: "Jaunty, laughing, his face radiant with the stories he told (as though stories were kept there, in the mouth itself, piled on a confusion of layers that only his tongue could extricate, as on the ship he could direct with his hands which crates first to remove from the hold), his fingers tied invisible sea-knots to complement the music of his sure, beautiful voice, high for a man's" ("Fifty Dollars," *Southwest Review* [Winter 1962]: 42). "From the very beginning, there was the hope, not tarnished even now, on the cot in the shabby room, in the broken house, in the wounded neighborhood, in the strange city, in the alien country, in the unfamiliar hemisphere, in, at least, the unresponsive world—the hope, conviction even, that in a real way he had been a prince" ("On a Field, Rampant," *C & K*, p. 191).

21. Sanders, "Interview," p. 132.

22. LeClair, "Elkin: The Art of Fiction," p. 59.

23. Stanley Lawrence Elkin, "Religious Themes and Symbolism in the Novels of William Faulkner," Ph.D. diss., University of Illinois, 1961, p. 53.

24. Ibid., p. 49.

25. Ibid., p. 42.

26. "I was a very attentive listener to my father's stories and to my father's shop talk," Elkin told LeClair (p. 68). "This may be the real source of my style."

27. Elkin, "Religious Themes," p. 406.

28. Bernt and Bernt, "Elkin on Fiction," p. 19.

29. LeClair, "Elkin: The Art of Fiction," p. 58.

30. Bernt and Bernt, "Elkin on Fiction," p. 16.

31. Push is reminiscent of Mink Snopes as Faulkner describes him in *The Mansion*, a passage which Elkin cites in his dissertation: "Because patience was his pride too: never to be reconciled since by this means he could beat Them; They might be stronger for a moment than he but nobody, no man, no nothing could wait longer than he could wait when nothing else but waiting would do, would work, would serve him" (Elkin, "Religious Themes," pp. 176–77).

32. Stanley Elkin, *A Bad Man* (New York: Random House, 1967), p. 217. Subsequent quotations from this edition are cited in parentheses in the text.

33. Stanley Elkin, *The Dick Gibson Show* (New York: Random House, 1971), pp. 66, 229. Subsequent quotations from this edition are cited in parentheses in the text.

34. Stanley Elkin, *The Franchiser* (New York: Farrar, Straus & Giroux, 1976), p. 282. Subsequent quotations from this edition are cited in parentheses in the text.

35. LeClair, "Elkin: The Art of Fiction," p. 60.

2

A Desert Sensibility
in the Virgin Land

There is a presence, as elusive as it is pervasive, in much of Elkin's fiction, a reality with which all of his protagonists come into contact and in terms of which each must orient and define himself. That presence consists in what might variously be designated the ordinary, the routine, the normal—in what the protagonist of Elkin's first novel, *Boswell,* describes as "a texture of domesticity, thick as atmosphere, as complexly *there* as government—its highways, national parks, armies—implicit in a postage stamp" (p. 312). Outside of "the self takes precedence" theme discussed in the previous chapter, no single idea recurs more consistently in Elkin's stories and novels than that of the ordinary and of perceptions of the world opposed to it. Furthermore, the presence of no theme in his work more distinctly identifies Elkin with postmodern American writers such as Thomas Pynchon, Robert Coover, Donald Barthelme, and Max Apple, whose work reflects a similar penchant for the thematic juxtaposition of ordinary conceptions of the world and existence with more dramatic, portentous, and even supernatural perceptions of reality. Pynchon is dramatizing this opposition, for instance, when he has Oedipa Maas, the protagonist of *The Crying of Lot 49,* see that "behind the hieroglyphic streets there would be either a transcendant meaning, or only the earth."[1] The tension between the safe political predictabilities and vector analysis projections of the fastidious Mr. Brown and the anarchistic, liberating yet disquieting, spontaneous visions of the Cat in the Hat with his "Tricks and Voom and things like that"[2] in "The Cat in the Hat for President" reflects

21

Coover's interest in this basic thematic dichotomy, one underlying much of his work from *Pricksongs & Descants* through *The Public Burning.* Whereas both Pynchon and Coover tend consistently to designate a competing vision or a reality opposed to ordinary conceptions of existence in their work (Pynchon positing mysterious historical or physical patterns or sinister cabals as antagonists, Coover evoking mythic perceptions of the real as counters), Elkin, more like Barthelme and Apple, shifts the ordinary's adversary from one work to the next, opposing it with a desperate celebration of self in *A Bad Man,* with visions of mythic transcendence in *The Dick Gibson Show,* with the ravages of disease in *The Franchiser,* and so on. The pervasiveness of this thematic opposition throughout Elkin's fiction qualifies him as perhaps our most dedicated literary chronicler and critic of the American ordinary.

What makes the ordinary a difficult theme to discuss is that Elkin treats it alternately as an external reality and as a mental projection of one, as a concrete presence in the world and as a perceptual structure we carry in our heads which not only colors but actually dictates what we comprehend and how we comprehend it. The clearest illustration of this point can be found in the first section of *The Living End,* conveniently titled "The Conventional Wisdom." Ellerbee, the chapter's protagonist, is murdered and ascends to Heaven, where he finds everything—St. Peter with his key to the Pearly Gates, harp-playing angels floating by on fluffy clouds— exactly as the conventional wisdom has always pictured it, a veritable children's Bible image of paradise. Summarily dispatched to Hell, Ellerbee finds that it, too, is precisely as the popular imagination has conceived it. We gradually begin to understand that he has been sentenced to an eternity of living amidst the conventional wisdom, doomed to inhabiting a place that is as much an image in human consciousness as it is an actual locale. A number of Elkin's other protagonists experience parallel difficulties in distinguishing the ordinary world they inhabit from the one their minds project, and in this deliberate juxtaposition of the material and the mental, the actual and the perceptual, Elkin's literary purposes again coalesce with those of Robert Coover, whose fiction presents similarly "familiar mythic or historical forms to combat the content of those

A Desert Sensibility in the Virgin Land

forms and to conduct the reader...to the real, away from mystification to clarification, away from mystery to revelation."[3]

To be an Elkin protagonist, then, is to be constantly struggling against—or, in some cases, siding enthusiastically with—a mental projection of the world that assumes it to be safe, sound, well constructed, admirably suited to our needs, normal. Elkin takes no small pleasure in describing the various sources from which we derive our faith in the existential ordinary and which seem so incontestably to confirm its autonomous actuality. Radio, with its neat time segmentations and reassuring interruption of our silences, is one such source. And so Elkin gives us Dick Gibson, a cipher and embodiment of the Midwest American Standard view of reality, a radio personality whose voice becomes "part of the generalized sound of American life" and whose ideal, by his own admission, is to "have life be like it is on the radio—all comfy and clean" (pp. 84, 27). Another vehicle for the promulgation of the conventional view is popular music, references to which proliferate throughout Elkin's fiction. From the early story, "Perlmutter at the East Pole" (in which the protagonist boasts that all his brainstorms come from "popular music. That's where the ideas are" [*C&K*, p. 239]), to the 1976 novel *The Franchiser,* with its elaborate scaffolding of show-music motifs and Tin Pan Alley echoes, that music which is franchiser Ben Flesh's personal heritage ("Standards. Hits. Top of the charts. Whistled. Hummed. Carried on the common American breath" [*TF,* p. 341]) is the environment through which nearly all of Elkin's protagonists move, their ears preternaturally attuned to those lyrics that, in their assumption of life's ordinariness, affirm their view of the world and their place in it.

One other notable repository of the conventional wisdom is language—words, with their ability to give substance to and codify the normal. The Elkin characters who treat language as a primary means of expressing their intrinsic unexceptionalness, who use language as a badge signaling their solidarity with the typical and regular of America, are numerous. On a bus trip to new Jersey, Dick Gibson encounters a woman whose conversation consists almost entirely of knock-knock jokes, "little moron" stories, and corny one-liners, her explanation of this linguistic tic being " 'I thought that's the way people speak' " (*DGS*, p. 53). In his travels Ben Flesh picks up a hitchhiker who converses in public service announcements, advising Flesh that " 'Only you can prevent forest fires' " and reassuring him that he keeps the Rolaids he is chewing with the rest of his medicines, out of the reach of children (*TF*, p. 221). The most elaborate and significant episode in which language is purposefully manipulated to make it reflect the average and the everyday occurs in Elkin's second novel, *A Bad Man.* At the conclusion the protagonist, Leo Feldman, recalls a relationship he has had with one Dedman, a man uncomfortable with uncodified friendships and inarticulate camaraderie. What Dedman really wanted, Feldman understood, was a friendship that reduced both of them to mere images of each other, a bond that sacrificed difference and idiosyncrasy to the good of the relationship. Offended, Feldman turned on Dedman, mocking his notions of comradeship by insisting that they call each other "Ace" and "Chief" and that they speak to each other only in the good-buddies jargon of fraternity men, babbling " 'Way to *go,* big fella' " and " 'How're they hangin', Flash?' " at every opportunity.[4] Although Feldman's situation differs from that of the travelers whom both Gibson and Flesh meet, he is no less aware than are they of language's potential for expressing one's enlistment in the ranks of the average and the regular, a potential that he exploits by parodying it, using conventional forms to mock themselves and to mock as well the preposterous artificiality of the relationship they are intended to codify.

The ordinary, then, is delivered up in a number of forms in Elkin's fiction, but the message behind it is always the same. Another of Ben Flesh's hitchhikers, a man recently released from a twenty-year prison term, provides the most explicit defense of the ordinary to be found in the Elkin canon, while simultaneously identifying Flesh as a man who, like himself, has particular reasons to take this message to heart. " 'I been shut up with fellows like you decades,' " the ex-convict insists. "Crook, all crimes are crimes of passion. Adventure lays in the bloodstream like platelets.... Get a normality. Live on the plains. Take a warm milk at bedtime. Be bored and find happiness. Greys and muds are the decorator colors of the good life. Don't you know anything? Speed kills and there's cholesterol in excitement. Cool it, cool it. The ordinary is all we can handle" (*TF*, p. 220). The ordinary is the safe, the passionless, the mediated; it prevents those living within its bounds from losing touch with the human—defined in its most superficial terms—while it also insulates them against unfamiliar or disquieting experiences by providing preconceived explanations of all phenomena, and it assures them that the accommodations they make and the sublimations they achieve on its behalf will ultimately afford them longer, though more boring, lives.[5]

If it is in their concern with the investigation and illumination of the ordinary that Elkin's stories and novels most closely resemble the metafictional cum epistemological works of Pynchon, Coover, Barthelme, and Apple, it is in the nature of the opposition that some of his characters express toward it that his fiction diverges most perceptibly from the matter and manner of theirs. In protagonists such as Push the Bully, the Feldmans of "In the Alley" and *A Bad Man*,[6] and Alexander Main of "The Bailbondsman," Elkin presents the ordinary's antagonists and combatants: irascible, willful, tenacious, uncompromising protagonists for whom the self is the ultimate value and all external forces that attempt to define, restrict, or impinge upon that self are the enemy. A primary commitment in life for these characters, consequently, is the disruption of all bureaucracy, literal, or figurative—all forms of organization that subordinate the claims of the individual to their own collectivist imperatives and objectives.

Push admits his autonomy and isolation, recognizing his utter unsuitability to the world of charisma, grace, and privilege. But he affirms that solitary self nonetheless, insisting upon its constituent elements of "envy, jealousy, and need," boasting of "the cabala of my hate, of my irreconcilableness" (*C&K*, p, 217). Irreconcilable equally well describes Feldman, who refuses to submit to the role of dying man that the world would impose upon him in "In the Alley," rejecting an ordinary, dignified hospital death in favor of a "heroic death," one he can personally seek out and fully experience, no matter how tawdry or degrading its circumstances.[7] Outdoing both Push and Feldman in the purity of his dedication to irreconcilability is Leo Feldman, the protagonist of *A Bad Man*, Elkin's most extensive treatment of the "self takes precedence" theme. Feldman not only

Reading Stanley Elkin

rejects the mutual self-abnegation implicit in Dedman's offer of friendship; he also uses his department store basement to sell illegal products and services to the public. When arrested and jailed for this, he does everything in his power to disrupt the bureaucratic regimentation imposed by the prison's dictatorial warden, attempting to undermine its well-ordered codes of behavior and to dissolve the prisoners' united front, their collectivized identity. Similarly committed to the disruption of conventional orders is Alexander Main, partly because, as a bailbondsman, he profits from others' legal trespasses, but also because he has a taste for violation and contingency, a taste he articulates in toasting "Our times":

Here's to the complicated trade routes of the drug traffic, to microdot tabs of LSD, to folks' vengeant itchiness as the discrepancies bloom apace and injustices shake the earth like underground faults. Here's to moonshots and the confusion of priorities. To TV in the ghetto and ads in the glossies and whatever engines that raise expectations like the hard-on, and drive men up one wall and down the other. To hard times and our golden age of blood![8]

Main cultivates disorder less for its own sake than for the possibility it offers for action and self-assertion. Every fissure in the cultural superstructure provides him with access to power, creating an occasion for him to step between the law and the lawless and to exercise his judgment as to who should be released back into the society and who should remain in the state's custody. What Main is, then, is what Feldman and Push are, what the prison warden calls Leo Feldman: "a bad man"—a subverter of order and organization in the name of self, one who, in the world's view, will always stand accused of his own character, guilty of his own impulses. He is a man, in short, whose will, needs, and desires will ever be too strong for him to surrender possibility or allow all of the special and the extraordinary, the exceptional and the abnormal, to be routinized out of existence.

The character and quality of the opposition these "bad men" pose to the American ordinary reflects an influence nowhere to be found in the fiction of Elkin's fellow chroniclers of the American ordinary—Saul Bellow and, more generally, writers of the American-Jewish novel tradition of the 1950s and '60s. What Elkin and Bellow share, and what these four Elkin characters exemplify, is what Max Schulz has termed "radical sophistication," a refusal to see the basic polarities of human existence reduced to anything less than irreconcilability, and a conviction that the tension between communal demands and individual desires is one of the most inevitable and insoluble of these conflicts.[9] The notion that, as Moses Herzog explains in *Herzog,* man is capable of taking on his "bone-breaking burden of selfhood and self-development," that he need not utterly surrender his "poor, squawking, niggardly individuality,"[10] represents a point of thematic convergence linking the fiction of Elkin and Bellow. That link is further testified to by their shared preference for writing novels dominated by a male protagonist, usually designated in the work's title, around whom a number of less sharply characterized men and women orbit, serving less as characters than as projections of the choices the protagonist must make in his attempts to successfully balance personal needs with public responsibilities.

The extent of Elkin's literary indebtedness to Bellow's work is difficult to measure with precision, though Elkin's acknowledgment that Bellow is "probably the writer who has influenced me most deeply"[11] decreases the likelihood of that influence's being overestimated. Viewed in structural terms, *Boswell,* Elkin's first novel, is probably his most Bellovian work, its discursiveness and loosely picaresque form, as well as the extended philosophical meditations of its first-person narrative mode, recalling *The Adventures of Augie March* and *Henderson the Rain King.* Bellow's influence is also discernible in Elkin's early short fiction, the resolutions of both "Criers & Kibitzers, Kibitzers & Criers" and "I Look Out for Ed Wolfe" consisting of emotional epiphanies, catharses of compassion and human-relatedness reminiscent of the conclusions of Bellow's "The Old System" and *Seize the Day.* Elkin's general philosophical outlook has equally marked similarities to Bellow's. The ideas expressed in the following passage from Bellow's 1963 introduction to a collection of Jewish short stories reflect aesthetic and existential presuppositions that Elkin's work conspicuously enacts and affirms: "These stories have about them something that justifies them to the most grudging inquiry—they have spirit, originality, beauty. Who

Reading Stanley Elkin

was Babel? He was an accident. We are all such accidents. We do not make up history and culture. We simply appear, not by our own choice. We make what we can of our condition with the means available. We must accept the mixture as we find it—the impurity of it, the tragedy of it, the hope of it.[12]

Bellow's major influence on this writer for whom style means so much, however, is stylistic. If Faulkner gave Elkin an aesthetic of excess from which to begin, Bellow provided him with a stylistic model upon which to impose that excess. Perhaps the most effective way of pointing up the similarities between their styles (before proceeding to show why they seem so little alike) would be to cite as evidence one critic's attempt to describe Bellow's style. "There is always the sense of a living voice in [Bellow's] prose," Leslie Fiedler has argued.

Muted or released, his language is never dull, or simply expedient, but always moves under tension, toward or away from some kind of rich, crazy poetry, a juxtaposition of high and low style, elegance and slang, unlike anything else in English except *Moby Dick*, though at the same time not unrelated in range and variety to spoken Yiddish.

Since Bellow's style is based on a certain conversational ideal at once intellectual and informal, dialogue is necessarily for him a distillation of his strongest effects. Sometimes one feels his characters' speeches as the main events of the books in which they occur.[13]

Anyone familiar with Elkin's prose might wonder if this isn't a more apt description of his style than of Bellow's, save that "elegance" identifies a cultivated civility in Bellow's prose that Elkin's eschews, and "intellectual" does not really describe the nature of the thoughtfulness characteristic of Elkin's protagonists. Were it more accurately to describe Elkin's style, this passage would need an exponential multiplication of each of its terms, the liberal insertion of "very" and "extremely" and "excessively" at strategic points in its course. For the Elkinian inflation of tone, pitch, and language accounts for the fact that his style so infrequently echoes Bellow's despite the descriptive similarities. Elkin's style, like Bellow's, attempts to encompass formal and vernacular, elevated and vulgar planes of discourse through their assimilation into one elastic and expansive level of narrative. His novels, too, display a tendency to gravitate structurally toward characters' speeches, the cruxes of his work as often crises of rhetoric as crises of plot. Finally, dialogue provides his work with the model upon which the narrative line is predicted, the narrators of his novels coming to seem more and more continuations or extensions of the idioms of the central protagonists. Elkin's admission that "To the extent that I imitate anyone, I think I may—in dialogue—imitate Saul Bellow"[14] makes explicit what the comparison of any two of their early novels clearly demonstrates: that Elkin's own "rich, crazy poetry" (a crazier, if not richer, poetry than Bellow's own) was developed under Bellow's tutelage and influence, and that Elkin's primary debt to him is less thematic or philosophical than stylistic.

More difficult to resolve than the nature of Elkin's debt to Bellow's work is the issue of Elkin's relationship to the tradition with which Bellow is so conspicuously identified and to which Elkin has consistently and repeatedly disclaimed all allegiance. Elkin's apparently contradictory public comments about Bellow's influence upon his work (in one interview he admitted to imitating Bellow in dialogue, in another he called Bellow's influence "probably stronger than that of any other writer," while in a third he declared himself "a tremendous admirer of Saul Bellow's" but insisted that "our styles are really nothing like one another's"[15]) reflect an ambivalence toward this issue not unlike that which prompts him to equivocate about his enlistment in the ranks of the Jewish-American novelists; his work seems to provide one kind of evidence, his interviews another. The two issues are, quite clearly, sensitive ones for him. They are worth considering further not because it would be useful to be able to categorize him as a Jewish-American novelist, but because their clarification allows us to understand where his career began so that we might later appreciate how far it subsequently moved from that starting point. To decide whether Elkin initially belonged in the ranks of Jewish-American novelists of the 1950s and '60s, we begin (as one must always begin with Elkin) by considering the stylistic evidence, and we then proceed to discuss the "Jewish-Americanness" of his plots and themes.

One of the most persuasive and helpful descriptions of the characteristics of the Jewish-American prose style is offered by Irving Howe in his introduction to an anthology of Jewish-American stories. Howe's passage is worth citing at length here because of its potential for accommodating all three styles—Elkin's, Bellow's, and that of the Jewish-American tradition as a whole. The style, Howe argues, consists in

A yoking of opposites, gutter vividness with university refinement, street energy with high culture rhetoric;

a strong infusion of Yiddish, not so much through the occasional use of a phrase or word as through ironic twistings that transform the whole of language;

a rapid, nervous, breathless tempo, like the hurry of a garment salesman trying to con a buyer or a highbrow lecturer trying to dazzle an audience;

a deliberate loosening of syntax, as if to mock those niceties of Correct English which Gore Vidal and other untainted Americans hold dear, so that in consequence there is much greater weight upon transitory patches of color than upon sentences in repose or paragraphs in composure;

a deliberate play with the phrasings of plebeian speech, but often, also, the kind that vibrates with cultural ambition, seeking to zoom into regions of high thought;

in short, the linguistic tokens of characters who must hurry into articulateness if they are to be heard at all, indeed, who must scrape together a language.[16]

Howe's typography of the Jewish-American prose style closely resembles Fiedler's description of Bellow's style in a number of its details; thus it makes sense for him to locate "the climax and conclusion" of the style he is delineating in Bellow's prose. More important, this passage represents yet another example of a stylistic description of Bellovian prose that characterizes with equal accuracy Elkin's early style.

The ease with which Bertie of "The Guest" shifts in his lonely monologues from literary allusion through pop psychology to jazz lingo to serious philosophical contemplation to mystical nonsense and drug-induced visions epitomizes Elkin's delight in mixing modes of discourse in his work, in writing in a style that allows the

A Desert Sensibility in the Virgin Land

"yoking of opposites." His imitation of Bellow's dialogue, in fact, is attributable to its ability to accommodate disparate inflections and idioms: "That rich kind of Constance Garnett mix of the formal and the vernacular," he explained in an interview, "that's what Bellow does better than anyone else in the world, in dialogue. And that's something I try to do."[17] Actual Yiddish words and phrases very seldom appear in Elkin's fiction, but the grammatical forms that result from the grafting of Yiddish syntax onto English (and that underlie the effectiveness of so much modern Jewish-American comedy) are prevalent in his work, his humor early and late often depending upon the dislocations of cadence and inflection that typify Yiddishized English. We have already noted Elkin's willingness to include the sales pitch as one of the informing elements of his style; that style's "breathless tempo" is fashioned to overwhelm the reader's resistance, to inundate his certainties with a more complex and vital vision whose rhetorical effect is "to upset the applecarts of expectation and ordinary grammar" via "fierce language."[18] Elkin's sentences subordinate consistency and decorum to spontaneity and surprise; his primary effects are created less through careful development and accumulation than through sudden bursts of clarifying simile and metaphor. Finally, what trick is more familiarly and distinctly Elkinian than the playful manipulation of "phrases of plebeian speech"? What writer delights more in the contrivance of passages such as "I floated deliciously buoyant in a sea of self, with some blank check of forgiveness, forever beyond guilt" (*B*, p. 278)? Or consider "he had learned to live under threat, a quality of last-hired, first-hired dogging his steps and days" (*ABM*, p. 299), or "Build me of crystal, Lord. I would be Jesus Crystal. *In Excelsis Diode*" (*DGS*, p. 239), or—to cite one of the deity's speeches from Elkin's compendium of rhetorical tricks, *The Living End*—"where are My Rebels and organizers, My hotshot bizarrerie, all you eggs in one basket curse-God-and-diers? Where are you? My iambic angels in free fall, what's doing?"[19] Such phrases are the contrivances of a writer devoted to resuscitating language by reclaiming clichés, by restoring life to hackneyed verbal formulations through inverting them or wrenching them out of context or turning them into puns or parodically nominalizing them. In the accumulation of such passages is

Reading Stanley Elkin

much of what we think of as Elkin's style, that eccentric "language he has scraped together" in his fiction.

If Howe's description of the cardinal traits of the Jewish-American prose style has any validity, then, it is clear that Elkin's style has much in common with that style. A consideration of the themes of Elkin's early fiction reinforces the stylistic evidence linking Elkin's work to the Jewish-American literary tradition.

While Elkin's recent fiction has concerned itself only glancingly with the notions to which Jewish-American fiction typically addresses itself (those of the Jew's assimilation into, or rejection of, the majority American culture, and the possibility of the survival of a recognizable Jewish identity once that assimilation has been effected), such issues are much more central to his early work, which bears an occasional marked resemblance to that of Bernard Malamud and Philip Roth, two major contributors to the Jewish-American literary tradition in the 1950s and '60s. Elkin's Meyer Feldman ("The Sound of Distant Thunder") and Jake Greenspahn ("Criers & Kibitzers, Kibitzers & Criers") are urban shopkeepers beset by fears and agonies not unlike those suffered by the ghetto merchants of Malamud stories such as "The Last Seven Days," "Angel Levine," and "The Prison" (to cite only those stories that Elkin could have read before publishing his own). Feldman's epiphany at the close of Elkin's story (" 'All the beauty,' he sobbed, 'all the beauty' "[20]) is reminiscent of the Malamud protagonist's typical discovery of the supernatural at the core of the mundane and spirit-defeating reality he inhabits. Less obvious, perhaps, are the similarities between two stories published in 1959, Roth's "Goodbye, Columbus" and Elkin's "Among the Witnesses." Each story has as its protagonist a middle-class Jewish young man just out of the service who is attempting to postpone making any definite decisions about his future—attempting, that is, to declare a personal moratorium on his responsibility to define his position relative to the tensions between his culture and his heritage. Both characters find no such moratoria possible. Roth's Neil Klugman and Elkin's Richard Preminger reluctantly recognize and accept the social roles to which their cultural heritage commits them, abandoning their efforts to disengage themselves from their familial pasts.

A Desert Sensibility in the Virgin Land

That these stories share settings as well as a number of cultural presuppositions is obvious enough. The point of comparing them here is not to suggest that Elkin's early short fiction imitates Malamud's or Roth's, but to illustrate that some of his fiction located itself squarely and self-consciously within the bounds of the Jewish-American literary tradition, to which Malamud and Roth are prominent contributors. These early Elkin pieces contain another element, however, which at once undermines their continuity with that tradition and also predicts the kind of fiction he was subsequently to write, a fiction bearing greater similarities to the work of writers like Pynchon, Coover, Barthelme, and Apple than to the work of Malamud, Roth, Bellow, et al. That departure from the form and assumptions of the typical Jewish-American short story is clearest in "Among the Witnesses," which, although similar in many respects to Roth's novella, nonetheless diverges appreciably from it in its final rhetorical purposes. "Goodbye, Columbus" is ultimately a work of realism, one that declares its continuity with the Jewish-American literary tradition—and thus, by extension, with European realism, which underlies that tradition—through its "criticism of the contemporary world," its "serious treatment of everyday reality," and its pretense of objectivity, of actions recorded in unmediated and untendentious terms, to use Erich Auerbach's criteria of literary realism.[21] Although Elkin's story might appear to be as much a work of literary realism as is Roth's, "Among the Witnesses" is finally less concerned with how people interact in society (Henry James is Roth's mentor, not Elkin's) than with the metaphoric potential of their interactions. Both stories deal with alternative interpretations of what Jewishness means. Neil's relatives represent middle-class urban Jews, the Patimkins a more prosperous suburban model; Preminger's sense of Jewishness as a kind of cultural self-abandonment and heedlessness is played off against the hotel guests' sense of it as a bond linking them all as suffering, guilty humans. But Roth concentrates upon the external signs of the two cultural worlds—upon what Tom Wolfe calls "status life details"—and their impact on the love affair between Neil and Brenda, whereas Elkin focuses upon the story's duality as competing conceptions of reality, as contrasting interpretations of a given cultural situation. To put the difference oversimply: Roth's characters think in order to act, and we understand them through their actions; Elkin's characters engage in more distinctly symbolic or exemplary conflicts, the source of tension between them arising quite clearly from their opposed conceptions of the real, the resolution of their confrontation representing the emergence of (in Elkin's view) a more tenable perception of things.

What has always prevented Elkin from becoming the realist some of his critics would prefer him to be[22] is his tendency to take more interest in metaphoric structures and conflicts than in societal ones, his greater concern with how his characters conceptualize than with how they act. The difference is not very great in the early short story "Among the Witnesses," which traces, in terms a more conventional realist could readily accept, the protagonist's gradually developing realization that the idea he has been trying to live out—that of the self-indulgent bachelor on the make—is ludicrously inappropriate in a world where children drown in resort swimming pools and where everyone but him knows that vacations from casual human suffering, and from the guilt often attendant on that suffering, cannot be had. For Roth—and for a number of his colleagues—the center of interest in such a narrative would be the consequences of Preminger's thinking upon the lives of others; for Elkin, the emphasis must be placed on the pattern of thought itself, its foundation and implications. For Preminger to move from seeing Norma, one of the hotel's guests, as a woman "on the edge of age," a woman who, "having tried all the other ways, having gone alone to the dances in the gymnasium of the Hebrew School, having read and mastered the *Journal of the American Medical Association* for April so that she might hold intelligent conversation with the nephew of her mother's friend" (*C&K*, p. 74)—for Preminger to begin to see this woman not as a sociological type of the husband-seeking Jewess-as-loser but as a possible marriage partner is reversal and recognition enough for Elkin.

Despite possessing some of the characteristics and concerns of the Jewish-American novel, then, Elkin's fiction ultimately diverges from that tradition for a number of cultural and artistic reasons. Primary among these is Elkin's determination not to situate his work within that tradition. A necessary precondition of that choice, however, was a cultural shift through which American popular culture transformed what had previously been recognized as a distinctly Jewish idiom or style of speech into something approaching a national syntax of humor, the mode of Jewish comedy coming more and more to seem simply the mode of American comedy.[23] Elkin's characteristic style, particularly in its previously cited capacity for accommodating divergent and often incongruous realities and in its general tone of mordant comedy, owes much to that idiom; significantly, that style, with only slight shifts in syntactical emphasis, can be used with equal effectiveness in narrating both the adventures of the Jewish Leo Feldman and the goyish Dick Gibson.

The Americanization of that familiar Jewish idiom reflected broader social changes occurring in the relationship between mainstream American and Jewish-American cultures. One paradoxical result was that the mainstream's adoption, through the Jewish-American novel of the 1940s and '50s, of the Jew as a literary type representing human alienation facilitated the real-life Jew's assimilation into American social and cultural life, his alienation, in these terms at least, decreasing in the process. While the mutuality of influence discernible in these cultural shifts culminated, on the one hand, in the emergence of Jews as major figures in the American literary landscape, it could also be said to point toward the subsequent appearance of a number of American writers of Jewish descent whose heritage would play very little role in their fiction. Max Apple, E. L. Doctorow, Leonard Michaels, Ronald Sukenick, and Elkin are a few such writers, all of whom share, beyond a common heritage, an interest in literary form that allows them to subordinate social and psychological realism to the exploration of pattern, of paradigm and its relation to meaning. Clearly the most accomplished writer of this group, Elkin is also the one who has managed most successfully and most extensively to apply the traditional materials of the Jewish-American novel to the unconventional ends of this kind of fiction. While "Among the Witnesses" can be seen as a story that manipulates a set of Jewish cultural assumptions for structural and aesthetic purposes, Elkin's subsequent novel, *A Bad Man*, pushes well beyond this, setting up a conceptual dichotomy between a metaphorical Jewish perception of the world and a WASPishly Christian one, the two perspectives combining to constitute a novel that effectively mediates between the Jewish-American tradition at one extreme and the self-consciously metaphorical, deliberately epistemological fiction of writers such as Coover and Pynchon at the other.

Elkin is hardly the first novelist to make the clash between Jewish and Gentile cultures his central metaphoric concern in a work of fiction. Nathanael West's "The Dream Life of Balso Snell" presents an allegorized version of the Jew's attempted entrance into Western culture; Bellow's *The Victim* delineates the conflict; protagonists in the fiction of Malamud and Bruce Jay Friedman fantasize at comic length about being goys or gaining admission to the goyish world; a good deal of Norman Mailer's early work, fiction and nonfiction alike, was concerned with the tensions between and the interpenetrations of these two cultures. Elkin's treatment of the theme is exceptional, however, not only for its willingness to transform this cultural conflict into a complexly resonant contest between metaphors, between conceptualizations of reality. *A Bad Man* is exceptional as well for its readiness to sacrifice verisimilitude to the exploitation of metaphors and metaphorical possibilities that arise during the narrative's development. Few rhetorical impulses are more characteristic of Elkin than this dedication to riding a metaphor as far as it will take him, and no other technical device so tellingly and unequivocally separates his fiction from the predominant mimetic purposes and cultural criticism aspirations of the Jewish-American novel.[24] *A Bad Man* is Elkin's contribution to the Jewish-American novel tradition, then, but it simultaneously declares and enacts his aesthetic disengagement from that tradition.

The novel's title gives the reader the first indication of what Jewishness means here. To be Jewish, in the view of Fisher, the autocratic warden of the prison to which Leo Feldman has been committed for a year for "doing favors" for customers in the basement of his department store, is to be a "bad man," to be a man more concerned with the self than with the communal order and societal structures with which Fisher aligns himself. Self-proclaimed "Fisher of bad men," the warden represents goodness in all its forms and ramifications: self-denial, generosity, logicality, a belief that human existence is rational and controllable because it is *ordinary*—that is, predictable, sane, consecutive, reducible to simple explanations, consistent with normal expectations, and amenable to the imposition of moral schemes. Feldman is the "bad man" opposed to all this, one dedicated to self-aggrandizement and to the philosophical assumption that the individual's only possible role in a contingent, senseless universe is to keep himself alive through extending his sense of his own extraordinariness, an undertaking that often necessitates the victimization of fellow humans and the recognition that he is the only one in the world capable of perceiving and celebrating his own specialness. Fisher is reasonable, whereas Feldman insists upon his passions and instincts; Fisher advocates compliance and accommodation, while Feldman keeps a weather eye out for that which can be resisted; Fisher repeatedly insists that " 'life is ordinary' " (p. 101), whereas for Feldman "Something was always at stake, every moment you lived" (p. 115); Fisher feels very much at home in the unheroic, unaspiring bureaucratic world of modern mass society, whereas Feldman feels a stronger tie to "a world that might have been charted on an old map, the spiky spines of serpents rising like waves from wine-dark seas...a distant, Praetorianed land, unamiable and harsh" (p. 42). Of such contrasts are the visions of Elkin's exemplary WASP and Jew comprised.

Feldman's position, not unlike Push's, assumes his own irreconcilability, presupposes individual isolation and the absolute finality of human loneliness. It is these notions that Fisher wants most to root out of his prisoner. Feldman is too much his father's son to submit to the prison's regimen, however, too much the son of a Jewish peddler who worked the streets of southern Illinois for a living and who once sold his entire wagonload of merchandise to an enthralled audience of WASPs watching an ox-pulling contest at a county fair. Feldman recalls his father's obsession with the question, " 'What's to be done with the unsalable thing?' " when he is assigned to work in the prison canteen. Encouraged by Fisher to increase the canteen's profits, he complies by selling only merchandise that prisoners couldn't possibly need or want—overseas mail letters, shoe trees, suntan lotions, crayons, guava soda, gummed reinforcements for notebook paper and the like. Recognizing this to be the merchandising scheme of a bad man carried out in bad faith, as the perversity of a salesman who sells only for the pleasures of self-aggrandizement and the victimization of others, Fisher condemns Feldman to solitary confinement, convinced that there he will learn the illusion of selfhood, the lesson that there is no Feldman (no bad man) in a room alone. Solitary confinement affects Feldman exactly as Fisher had anticipated. Visiting Feldman in his cell after a week or so, Fisher subtly offers him his release if he will only revise the ending of a story he has told Fisher about his son so as to make it reflect fatherly love rather than "bad man" perversity. Feldman ultimately submits to the lie in order to escape imprisonment with himself.

Feldman's capitulation here not only anticipates the final scene of the novel, in which he must plead for his life using the similarly self-incriminating narrative of his friendship with and betrayal of Dedman for his defense, but it also suggests the ultimate basis of Feldman's vulnerability to the warden's systems and machinations. Guilt convinces Feldman that he belongs in prison despite the flimsiness of the evidence brought forth to convict him; guilt, too, allows him to accept Dr. Freedman's explanation of a shadow over his heart as a homonculus, the fossilized fetus of a twin which succumbed to "some early Feldmanic aggrandizement" (p. 7) and which becomes, while he is in solitary confinement, an imagined critic of his heart, designating it " 'a desert, some prehistoric potholed thing...a moon of a heart' " (p. 141). Feldman's guiltiness stems less from what he does than from what he is—a fact not lost upon Fisher, who zeroes in on this point of vulnerability in his prisoner and lets fly with the novel's most explicit articulation of the WASP/Jew antinomy. Upon his release from solitary confinement, Feldman is invited to a party in the warden's quarters; the gathering is intended as an object lesson for him in WASP civics, as his host patiently explains.

"Say what you will, Feldman...but urbanity is a Christian gift. Rome, London, Wittenberg, Geneva—*cities*, Feldman. The history of us Christians is bound up with the history of great cities. I mean no offense, of course, but yours is a desert sensibility, a past of pitched tents and camps.... I've stood beside sideboards and spent Christmas with friends. There's leather on my bookshelves, Feld-

A Desert Sensibility in the Virgin Land

man. I've been to Connecticut. I know how to sail. What are you in our culture? A mimic. A spade in a tux at a function in Harlem.

"I make this astonishing speech to you not out of malice. It's way of life against way of life with me, Feldman. I show you alternatives to wholesale and retail. I push past your poetics, your metaphors of merchandise, and scorn the emptiness of your *caveat emptor.* I, the least of Christians, do this." [pp. 156-57]

Fisher, clearly enough, has forms ("'Civilization *is* forms,'" he tells a prisoner assembly) on his side. The way of life he espouses and represents is constructed self-consciously and obsessively out of rules, laws, conventions, customs, and similar components of humanly created order. The prison, of course, is the symbolic projection of the warden's vision, a "place of vicious, plodding *sequiturs*" (p. 58), a world so complexly suffused with regulations and ordinances that even Fisher, its inaugurator, finds the full comprehension of its workings difficult. Its intricacy seems to him no drawback, since for him even order maintained purely for its own sake is positive, its implementation offering additional proof that the life of man is subject to human reason.[25] It is for their anti-order tendencies that he holds bad men in contempt, then, reserving for the Jewish bad man a particular loathing born of his conviction that these disruptors of the norm can have no understanding of the civilization they have dedicated themselves to subverting, their own "desert culture" and values of "wholesale and retail" having given them no terms with which they might be able to apprehend the grandeur, complexity, and decorum of the Western, Christian model. Taunting Feldman with the simplicity with which his crimes were detected and the orderliness with which his conviction for them was accomplished, Fisher carefully adumbrates for him for a final time the institutional hierarchy that he and his prison represent, insisting, "'We have the system. Virtue is system, honor is order. God is design, Grace is a covenant, a contract and codicils, what's down there in writing'" (p. 70).

Rather than exemplifying a single philosophical point, Fisher represents a complex of ideas connoting form, order, system, and design, abstractions reflecting the primarily intellectual terms in which he addresses and attacks his inmate adversary. He is not, however,

Reading Stanley Elkin

Feldman's sole antagonist. Complementing Fisher's largely philosophical objections to Feldman and his "bad manism" is the more passive but equally disturbing opposition of a land developer of Feldman's acquaintance, whose very existence represents what amounts to a rebuke to and repudiation of Feldman's own life. The land developer—we know him only as the father of Oliver B., a classmate of Feldman's son, Billy—is the ideal of American WASPishness, a father who knows the names of things and how they work, who knows how to casually and unself-consciously pass his knowledge on to young Oliver so that the boy can join him in the practical, reassuringly tangible world of American technical competence. Feldman comes to know the developer first through seeing Oliver's dazzlingly excellent schoolwork on display at a parents' night at the elementary school Billy attends. The schoolwork is so clearly superior to the illiterate scribblings and ramshackle crafts produced by his own son that Feldman actually presents himself to one of the other parents as Oliver B.'s father.

Their paths cross again some months later, when the developer takes Feldman to inspect land on the city's outskirts to see whether it is suitable for the branch store he is half-heartedly considering. Listening to his breezy, articulate pitch, Feldman is aware of how thoroughly the developer is his son's father—lucky with machines, knowledgeable about the ways of nature, capable of tolerance, good will, and a fierce optimism. Feldman finally looks "deep down into the man's eyes, past good wishes, deeper than good hope, past faith itself to the saucy bedrock of the developer's vision, where he thought he saw the basic mix—the roily vats of molassesy premise that worked the circuits of his phoenixy will and gave him his feel for reclaimed land, for swamp and ashpit and trashy field where rats lurked and mice skittered" (p. 235).

The geological and mechanistic metaphors used here to delineate the levels of the developer's vision distinctly resemble the hierarchical terms in which Fisher views the world, the circuits of the one paralleling the sequiturs of the other, the developer's tropism for land reclamation analogous to the warden's ability to turn bad men into good ones. The developer represents an extension of the Fisherian interpretation of reality, a translation of it into different terms.

A Desert Sensibility in the Virgin Land

His American optimism and progressivism, his handyman's competence and camper's self-sufficiency, his ability to transform wastelands into shopping malls are all qualities marking him as one for whom—as for Fisher—reality is everywhere tractable, manageable, ordinary. Stirred by the recognition that he is confronting an enemy, Feldman refuses to participate in the developer's dreams of frontier and settlement, his WASPish visions of expansion and progress: " 'I won't have it. . . . Fuck your virgin land.' " It is once again "way of life against way of life," Feldman continuing, " 'We're in the home-stretch of a race: your energy against my entropy. The universe is running down, Mr. Developer. It's bucking and filling. It's yawing and pitching and rolling and falling' " (pp. 235-36).

Against his adversary's expansionist mentality Feldman pits a personal entropy; against his WASP frontiersman ethic Feldman opposes a cultural metaphor of his own—dispersion. Feldman's strongest argument, his self-justification and credo, lies in the implications of a concept his father had stressed during their travels together: the Diaspora, or the scattering of Jews throughout the Old World after the Babylonian captivity. Upon their arrival in southern Illinois, Isidore Feldman had introduced himself and his son to their new Midwestern neighbors by explaining what a Jew is and what his history consists in, pointing out that " 'ours is a destiny of emergency. . . . You see me sitting here fulfilling God's will. I bring God's will to the Midwest. I don't lift a finger. I have dispersed. Soon the kid is older, *he* disperses. Scatter, He said. To the ends of the earth. Yes, Lord' " (pp. 35-36). Isidore Feldman ends his phase of the Diaspora in the Illinois cornfields, and although his son believes for a time that he has moved beyond it—that he has disposed of the Diaspora as his sense of having lived an "old timey life in a strange world" with his father diminishes, and he becomes a "naturalized citizen" of the normal American reality (p. 44)—the spirit of the Diaspora, with its risks and restlessness, its contingency and excitement, remains alive in him, prohibiting him from succumbing to the empty purposefulness of the developer's vision or submitting to the sterile systematics and puerile moralism to which Fisher's mind, and the prison that is its physical projection, reduce the complexities of human existence.

His longing for this discarded sense of Diaspora leads Feldman

Reading Stanley Elkin

to marry a woman so ill suited to him that their life together is as hellishly miserable as he had anticipated, a life lived as if among the "spiky and fanged monsters" on the map of the world that he and his father had once shared. This longing, too, accounts for his taking on his father's occupation, less out of nostalgia or a sense of family tradition than out of his recognition that selling could become "his way of bearing down on the world" (p. 66), his means of exploiting one of existence's few infinites: the endlessness of human desire. When the exploitation of that desire through the merchandising of ordinary products begins to pall for Feldman, he responds by offering his customers more exotic goods and services, indulgently reveling in the heightened sense of self he derives from his overcoming of the authorities and regulations that stand between those desirers who patronize his basement operations and the gratification of their dark wants and needs. His contempt for the laws that frustrate his customers extends beyond them to all forms of regulation and control, a fact reflected in his manic denunciation of

the timers of the stoplights, and those who license, and those who make the rules for the safety checks of airplanes.... Damn, too, the snoops who oversee the construction of bridges and insist on precautions before letting a single worker go into a mine or tunnel. Damn that measly conspiracy of the civilized that puts safety before profit and makes hazard illegal, and damn finally, then, those at the top who would extend longevity by requiring dullness....[p. 271]

Feldman's Diaspora spirit is a spirit of contentiousness and resistance, of opposition and struggle. It is, above all, a spirit that wants to keep things moving and to keep possibilities open in a world too full of Fishers-of-bad-men and land developers intent upon locking things up and closing things down, of men who would define, classify, and circumscribe, reducing everything to a basic ordinariness at once static and devoid of all potential. The novel's major tensions—between WASPish decorum and Jewish "bad man" willfulness, between competing perceptions of reality which assume it to be tractable, comprehensible, and ordinary versus threatening, senseless, and incommensurable—are thus presented, in symbolic shorthand, in the two central metaphors of *A Bad Man:* Fisher's rison and Feldman's Diaspora.

A Desert Sensibility in the Virgin Land

So pervasive is the Diaspora metaphor and so extensive its implications that the reader is not surprised to find it the fulcrum upon which the novel's resolution is poised. Just as Feldman's surrender to the appeal of the land developer in claiming Oliver as his own son must culminate in, or be balanced by, a reversal—Feldman's explicit rejection of the man and his vision—if resolution of that scene is to be achieved, so the scene in which Feldman capitulates to Fisher, finally admitting the lie the warden offers him into his account of his relationship with his son in order to gain his release from solitary confinement, can only be completed by a similar reversal.

In the novel's last pages Feldman is again offered the opportunity to free himself from confinement by telling a story about himself, and Fisher is again the ultimate judge of his performance. In this instance, however, the stakes are higher. Brought before an assembly of inmates in a specially isolated cell, Feldman is subjected to a ceremony of denunciation, his fellow prisoners rising one by one to charge him with acts of selfishness, betrayal, and immorality. The point of the ritual is to determine—or, rather, affirm—Feldman's guilt. If found innocent, he will be allowed to serve out the few remaining days of his sentence and be released; if judged guilty, a trained boxer will be brought in to hammer at his homunculed heart, killing him. Entering the proceedings in their third day, Fisher assumes the role of presiding magistrate, throwing out all of the evidence that has been amassed against Feldman so that the disposition of his case will be decided solely on the basis of his own account of his friendship with Dedman. In presenting his version of their relationship (one he himself sees as inexplicable) to the kangaroo court, Feldman makes little effort to rationalize or extenuate his actions, recalling them as if recognizing for the first time their real justification. Having mocked the friendship Dedman offered him by reducing their conversations to exchanges of adolescent clichés of buddyhood, having ridiculed it further by turning their comradely activities into images of the hijinks characteristic of "A Date with Judy" films, Feldman has crowned their bond by trapping the unwitting Dedman into a terrible marriage on the grounds that he who gets married has an all-American responsibility to see that his bachelor companion gets married, too. Even after Dedman takes on his termagant mate, Feldman finds himself incapable of surrendering

Reading Stanley Elkin

this travesty of friendship, realizing it to be " 'something I needed to keep me alive' " and confessing himself " 'hooked on [Dedman's] doom' " (p. 335), a doom he has hastened by offering him loans in an amount calculated to let him start in, but not succeed with, numerous businesses.

Feldman's monologue sends Fisher into a paroxysm of rage. Forgetting the executioner standing by in the gym, he sets the inmates upon Feldman, convinced that the Dedman episode has convicted him as a bad man. The narrative persuades Feldman, quite to the contrary, of his innocence. In the seconds before the prisoners attack he sees that Fisher's final, desperate efforts to push him into "this last, closed corner of their justice" (p. 336) has had the opposite effect of revealing to him his own freedom, convincing him that he is neither a good man nor bad man but a man who affirms his life. That affirmation is made, Feldman concludes, despite the existence of "wars, history, the deaths of the past and other people's poverties and losses. Their casualties and bad dreams I write off. I remember all the disasters that have happened and all the disappointments of the generations from time's beginning to its end, and still I am permitted to live." Having often come close to acquiescing to the Fisherian view of the world and that view's interpretation of his own ethic, he here conclusively rejects the guilt that the prison has dedicated itself to making him feel, invoking against it a cultural value and tradition of his own. Perhaps the warden's lapse of memory, he speculates as his attackers close in, "was God's sign that the Diaspora was still unfurnished, and that, until it was, until everything had happened, until Feldman had filled the world, all its desert places and each of its precipices, all its surfaces and everywhere under its seas, and along its beaches, he could not be punished or suffer the eternal lean years of death" (p. 336).

Isidore Feldman's son has determined to disperse further, then, committing himself, should he survive his punishment, to serving a God of possibility and openness, as opposed to the "God is design" whose worship Fisher has been attempting to impose upon him. For Feldman, as for Elkin's bailbondsman, Alexander Main, the crucial thing is to keep possibility open, to preserve in the world the potential for the existence of the mysterious, the special, the extreme.

A Desert Sensibility in the Virgin Land

Main banishes a bailjumper into freedom, the involuntary fugitive representing to him a mystery still to be solved, a trail still to be followed; Feldman rededicates himself to his ethic of self-extension and dispersion, the civilized world, upon which guilt had previously impaled his impulses, being transformed into the ground of his absolute freedom in the process. The release from the prison of civilization's forms which awaits Feldman just beyond the novel's final page can be seen alternatively as a release into a post-penetentiary life or as a release into a beating-inflicted death; in either case, that release can represent nothing more than a confirmation and enactment in literal terms of the psychological liberation he has already achieved. Convinced of his innocence, certain of the rightness of his stance, Feldman has not merely vowed to carry on the Diaspora which justifies him as it had justified his father, but has, in a characteristically "Feldmanic aggrandizement," himself become it, scattering, in his vision, "To the ends of the Earth."

A Bad Man, in its concern with the Diaspora and with the cultural significance of Jewishness, demands inclusion in the Jewish-American novel tradition, but it also diverges from that tradition at crucial junctures. These points of departure can perhaps be best appreciated through a comparison of Elkin's novel of an imprisoned Jew with another novel whose subject is the same and whose approach to the tradition is less heterodox. As Robert Alter and others have noticed, Bernard Malamud's favorite metaphor for Jewishness is imprisonment, and in a 1966 review Alter argued that The Fixer was Malamud's most successful treatment of that theme because "the Malamudian prison is here not merely an analogy, a moral and metaphysical state, but has real, clammy stone walls, excretory stenches, heavy-fisted jailers, dank unheated cells. Similarly, Malamud's symbolic Jew is much more believable here because the character's symbolic implications flow naturally from the literal fact of Jewishness which is, after all, the reason for his arrest."[26]

Leo Feldman is also jailed for being Jewish—for being a bad man—but the prison to which he is sentenced is one whose physical reality is only intermittently allowed to overbalance its metaphoric implications. The reader is constantly reminded that this penitentiary *means* more than it *is*. (While writing the novel, Elkin, seeking

background material, gained entrance to a Massachusetts penitentiary; characteristically, he came away impressed that "the prison of
my imagination was so much better than their real prison."[27]) In his
own review of *The Fixer* (written while he was composing *A Bad
Man*) Elkin expressed—in necessarily oblique terms—the basic difference between Malamud's novel of the imprisoned Jew and the
one on which he was himself working. As we have seen, Elkin argued
that *The Fixer* gravitated toward "mnemonic postures, long art's
deepest friezes," its energies being consistently directed toward
"bringing about some telling stasis."[28] *The Fixer*, with its substitution of such exemplary tableaux for metaphors, sought finally to
communicate serious truths about the Jew, Elkin argued, its purposes being successfully achieved through the presentation of a succession of unambiguously tendentious images and scenes. *A Bad
Man*, for its part, uses the American cultural conflict as a vehicle for
the establishment of an alternative metaphor to the Jewishness-as-
imprisonment analogue favored by Malamud and echoed in the fiction of a number of other Jewish-American writers. Elkin's
metaphor, of course, is Jewishness-as-Diaspora. On one level, then,
Elkin's novel can be read as a kind of corrective to *The Fixer*, as a
similarly realistic and credible novel that opposes the values of dispersion and diffusion to the forms and sequiturs both of Fisher's
prison and—by implication—of Malamud's central metaphor. But
then Elkin's metaphor is so clearly a literary metaphor, so obviously
a consolidation and reconciliation effected by word and image, so
conspicuously a conceit that resolves novels far better than it resolves cultural conflicts, that it is difficult to know how seriously to
take it as an expression of Elkin's sincere personal belief, how far to
credit it as his attempt to metaphorically access the Jew.

This equivocation, along with its attendant impulses toward extravagant language, fanciful metaphors, exaggeratedly symbolic
scenes and the like, most decisively marked Elkin's disaffection
from the Jewish-American novel tradition as exemplified by the
work of Malamud, Bellow, Roth, and others. In *A Bad Man* Elkin is
years away from writing those works (particularly the novellas collected in *Searches & Seizures*) that make language, metaphor, and
the protagonists' relationships to them central concerns; there are,

however, hints of that later fiction in this early novel, in its obvious delight in rhetoric, in its willingness to subordinate representation to metaphor, and in the fact that Feldman must resort to language in order to save himself (and does, apparently, save himself) through words. It was Elkin's determination to treat language and metaphor not merely as means to mimetic ends but as supple, highly subtle artistic instruments whose manipulation is valuable for its own sake. This determination dictated his parting company with the tradition which had nurtured much of his early fiction, the form and content of *A Bad Man* reflecting and dramatizing that act of disengagement.

The Diaspora metaphor so crucial to the resolution of *A Bad Man* informs the novel on two different levels and thus determines the book's character in two different ways. Diaspora has a cultural as well as a metaphorical meaning in this work, and if its cultural significance contributes to the novel's usual placement within the tradition of the Jewish-American novel, its metaphorical aspect parallels and anticipates the metaphorical complexes that gradually come to dictate the directions and the resolutions of both *The Dick Gibson Show* and *The Franchiser,* novels only intermittently reminiscent of that tradition.

Although Feldman tends increasingly to think of the Diaspora idea in positive, life-affirming terms, it nonetheless contains implications and becomes associated with concepts that are, in human terms, considerably more sobering and dispiriting. Not only does the Diaspora notion deny the possibility of any real human community; it is also associated, through metaphoric elision, with the fact that the universe is running down—" 'yawing and pitching and rolling and falling,' " as Feldman puts it in defending his entropy against the land developer's energy. To disperse is to be in tune with this universal decline, Feldman clearly believes; to conceptualize, construct, or concretize—as Fisher does—is to vainly oppose the gravity of things. The Diaspora metaphor becomes the novel's shorthand for this overwhelming sense of things breaking apart and of centers failing to hold, of the fragmentation and atomization at the heart of reality. If the consequent throwing off of the trappings, ideas, sequiturs, and institutions once closely associated with those centers feels initially liberating, it is to a bleaker, less human, and

Reading Stanley Elkin

more desolate realm that it liberates us. For Feldman, a man with "no feel for patterns" (p. 198) and "no taste for the available" (p. 220), release into formlessness and extremity can only seem a deliverance, but he is the sole protagonist of the three novels to so unequivocally align himself on the side of these anti-order, anti-ordinary forces. Whereas Fisher's representation of and commitment to the rationalized ordinary is obviously viewed critically by Elkin through *A Bad Man,* the attempts of Dick Gibson and Ben Flesh to secure for themselves a solid foothold in the ordinary are much more sympathetically treated, the shift representing at once Elkin's abandonment of a central theme of the Jewish-American literary tradition and his decision to redefine the conflicting antinomies of *A Bad Man* in order to depict the ordinary's corruption and betrayal by the very forces that Feldman celebrates and embodies. What opposes Gibson's and Flesh's attempts to ground themselves safely in the routine and the everyday is a perceptible undermining of the fabric of reality as they understand it, a disintegration of the complex of assumptions supporting their generally optimistic conceptions of things. Dick Gibson's determination to become the voice of the American ordinary, the very sound of security and reassurance, runs afoul of the unraveling of the social fabric upon which such an ambition depends. The American public he seeks to comfort is gradually becoming fragmented into a mass of lonely and troubled individuals with obsessions too personal and private to be allayed by the "steady-as-she-goes pep talk" of a radio personality. The country that Flesh's franchises have helped to build undergoes a similar process of atomization in *The Franchiser,* its protagonist remarking upon "America's molecules floating away from each other like a blown balloon, like heat rising, the mysterious physical laws gone public" (*TF,* p. 306). The combination of the nation's soaring energy needs and dwindling energy resources culminates in a "new dispensation" characterized by brownouts, decreased mobility, and a general sense of severed connection and electrical failure, a condition vividly dramatized through its metaphoric analogue—Flesh's multiple sclerosis, the progressive sensory deterioration of his demyelinating nervous system.

Placed against such massive social, physical, and existential dislocations, the ordinary seems a necessarily puny foe. But Elkin refuses in these novels to reduce the two protagonists to deluded proponents of an impossible position, choosing instead to present their advocacy of the ordinary as a commitment both comic and serious, simultaneously hopeless and heroic. Once it has been dissociated from the perspective of Warden Fisher, who sees in it nothing more than a means of rationalizing his subjection of others to his own capricious will, the ordinary comes to be an increasingly ambivalent concept in Elkin's fiction. Dick Gibson perceives it as the very medium of his self-affirmation and expansion; Ben Flesh finds it in the only possible refuge from the intolerably grim facts of his precipitously declining existence. Whereas *A Bad Man* treats the ordinary more unambiguously as that against which the solitary self must struggle in order to define itself, in both *The Dick Gibson Show* and *The Franchiser* it is presented instead as a necessarily contributory element in that self-definition, the ordinary and the self no longer merely opposing, but now interacting with, each other. In the tension between the ordinary and the extraordinary, between routine and extremity, lies the major dynamic of Elkin's two most completely successful novels, then, the attempts of Dick Gibson and Ben Flesh to patch the rents in the consciousness of the contemporary humanity with talk shows and HoJo's providing many of these books' most moving, comic, and resonant moments.

NOTES

1. Thomas Pynchon, *The Crying of Lot 49* (New York: J. B. Lippincott, 1966), p. 181.
2. Robert Coover, "The Cat in the Hat for President," *New American Review #4* (New York: New American Library, 1968), p. 12.
3. Robert Coover, *Pricksongs & Descants* (New York: E. P. Dutton, 1969), p. 70.
4. Stanley Elkin, *A Bad Man* (New York: Random House, 1967), p. 331. Subsequent quotations from this work will be followed by page numbers in parentheses in the text.
5. Donald Barthelme, a writer little less interested in the reality of the ordinary than is Elkin, has the narrator of his "Critique de

Reading Stanley Elkin

la Vie Quotidienne" describe the state in these terms: "Slumped there in your favorite chair with your nine drinks lined up on the side table in soldierly array, and your hand never far from them, and your other hand holding onto the plump belly of the overfed child, and perhaps rocking a bit, if the chair is a rocking chair as mine was in those days, then it is true that a tiny tendril of contempt—strike that, *content*—might curl up from the storehouse where the world's content is kept, and reach into your softened brain and take hold there, persuading you that this, at last, is the fruit of your labors, which you'd been wondering about in some such terms as 'Where is the fruit?' " (*Sixty Stories* [New York: G. P. Putnam's Sons, 1981], p. 184).

6. Elkin gives the name Feldman to four different protagonists: Meyer Feldman, the central figure of his first published story, "The Sound of Distant Thunder," Stephen Feldman of the early uncollected story, "The Party"; and the Feldmans of "In the Alley" and *A Bad Man*. Elkin makes no attempt to link these characters, using the name primarily for its punning suggestion of felled man and because, as he mentioned in an interview, it was his mother's maiden name (LeClair, "Elkin: The Art of Fiction," p. 56).

7. Elkin's dissertation description of the convict in Faulkner's "Old Man" precisely describes the situation of and defines his attitude toward the Feldman of "In the Alley." "In the convict we are confronted with an existential figure," Elkin wrote, "a doomed man who despite consciousness of his doom. . . resists. Such resistance, in Faulkner, is a warrant for salvation" (Elkin, "Religious Themes," pp. 167-68).

8. Stanley Elkin, *Searches & Seizures* (New York: Random House, 1973), p. 12. Subsequent quotations from this edition are cited in parentheses in the text.

9. Max F. Schulz, *Radical Sophistication: Studies in Contemporary American Jewish Novelists* (Athens: Ohio University Press, 1969), pp. viii, 25.

10. Saul Bellow, *Herzog* (New York: Viking Press, 1964), pp. 92-93.

11. Sanders, "Interview," p. 140.

12. Saul Bellow, introduction to *Great Jewish Short Stories*, ed. Saul Bellow (New York: Dell Books, 1963), p. vi.

13. Leslie Fiedler, "Saul Bellow," in *To the Gentiles* (New York: Stein & Day, 1972), p. 63.

A Desert Sensibility in the Virgin Land

14. Sanders, "Interview," pp. 140-41.

15. Bernt and Bernt, "Stanley Elkin on Fiction," p. 19.

16. Irving Howe, introduction to *Jewish-American Stories*, ed. Irving Howe (New York: New American Library, 1977), p. 15.

17. Sanders, "Interview," pp. 140-41.

18. Ibid., p. 133.

19. Stanley Elkin, *The Living End* (New York: E. P. Dutton, 1979), p. 54. Subsequent quotations from this edition appear in parentheses in the text.

20. Stanley Elkin, "The Sound of Distant Thunder," *Epoch* 8: 1 (Winter, 1957): 57. This, Elkin's first published story, is one of two stories written before but not included in the *Criers & Kibitzers, Kibitzers & Criers* collection. The other uncollected story is "Fifty Dollars," which appeared in the *Southwest Review* (Winter 1962).

21. Erich Auerbach, *Mimesis: The Representation of Reality in Western Literature*, trans. Willard R. Trask (Princeton: Princeton University Press, 1968), pp. 490, 491.

22. One such critic was the novelist John Gardner, who in *On Moral Fiction* ([New York: Basic Books, 1978], p. 110) charged Elkin with "preferring comic surprise to energetic discovery and looking for fictive energy not in character and action but in the power of the writer's performance or in poetic language."

23. Leslie Fiedler discusses some of the implications of the major role that Jews have played in the creation of American mass culture over the past half-century in "Some Jewish Pop Art Heroes," collected in *To the Gentiles*, pp. 133-34. Nat Hentoff's "Yiddish Survivals in the New Comedy" points up the part that Jewish comedians of the twentieth century have played in making Yiddish inflections and cadences an important vehicle of American humor. His essay is collected in *Jewish-American Literature: An Anthology*, ed. Abraham Chapman (New York: New American Library, 1974), pp. 690-94.

24. In a 1960 essay Philip Roth criticized in Herbert Gold a parallel tendency toward sacrificing world to wordplay, his comments suggesting in approximate form what might have been a Jewish-American novel tradition response to *A Bad Man*. Gold's overheated style, he argued, represented "a symptom of the writer's loss of the community—of what is *outside* himself—as subject" (Writing American Fiction," collected in Philip Roth, *Reading Myself and Others* [New York: Farrar, Straus and Giroux, 1975], p. 131).

25. In one of the earliest serious critical treatments of an Elkin

Reading Stanley Elkin

work, Raymond M. Olderman viewed Fisher as the Fisher-King of his prison wasteland, his illness proving incurable "because he fails to recognize his disease and therefore rules his land by locking it in its wasted condition" *(Beyond the Waste Land: The American Novel in the 1960s* [New Haven: Yale University Press, 1971], p. 62).

26. Robert Alter, "Bernard Malamud: Jewishness as Metaphor," collected in his *After the Tradition: Essays on Modern Jewish Writing* (New York: E. P. Dutton, 1971), p. 126. Frank Kermode had discussed the centrality of the prison metaphor in Malamud's work in a review/essay of 1962, in which he commented that "the physical prison is only an external symbol of the real thing, which is the Jewish capacity to suffer, to achieve a sort of dignity in suffering, as a substitute for success and freedom" ("Bernard Malamud," collected in Frank Kermode, *Continuities* [New York: Random House, 1968], p. 218).

27. Jeffrey L. Duncan, "A Conversation with Stanley Elkin and William H. Gass," *Iowa Review* 8: 1 (Winter 1976): 69.

28. Elkin, review of *The Fixer,* p. 388.

3

The Sound of
the American Ordinary

The cultural underpinning provided in *A Bad Man* by the Diaspora metaphor, with its evocation of the Jew's history and his assimilation into American culture, has its counterpart, in *The Dick Gibson Show* and *The Franchiser,* in the American cultural figure whose genius underlies the visions of both Dick Gibson and Ben Flesh. Although Elkin never specifically identifies this figure, Gibson's habit of referring to himself as "Poor Dick Gibson" and Ben Flesh's first name and initials both invite us to see behind their distinctly American optimistic materialism the spirit of the nation's most famous champion of the commercial, the civic, and the secular. It is not the historical Ben Franklin with all of his human complexities that these characters recall, of course; it is the literary creation, the deliberately fictionalized narrator of the *Autobiography* and *Poor Richard's Almanac,* for whom human existence is reducible to explicable patterns of behavior and pithy maxims. Beyond a number of character traits and philosophical assumptions that Dick Gibson and Ben Flesh share with Franklin (practicality, purposefulness, and endless energy; the conviction that technical competence alone is sufficient to render reality tractable), there are two far more compelling explanations for his allusive presence in these novels.

First, Franklin is both the proponent and the self-proclaimed proof of the American dream of limitless opportunity, the notion that, as he explains in the *Autobiography,* "one Man of tolerable Abilities may work great Changes, and accomplish Affairs among Mankind, if he first forms a good Plan, and cutting off all Amusements or other employments that would divert his Attention, makes the Execution of the same Plan his sole Study and Business."[1] This idea, which Dick Gibson refers to as "the self-made, from the ground up vision of the world" (p. 23), is one that both he and Flesh enthusiastically endorse, each attempting in his own way to act out a part of its truth. More important to both of them, however, would be Franklin's articulation and dramatization of a secular myth,[2] his demonstration that one need not test the boundaries of human civilization in order to transcend human limitation and expand the terms of human possibility; rather, one need only become a rarefied version—a symbol—of human possibility in order to raise himself above the mass of men. This is precisely what Dick Gibson and Ben Flesh attempt to do.

"Mythic" is not, of course, a word Franklin uses to describe his ascent from the "Poverty and Obscurity in which I was born and bred" to "a State of Affluence and some Degree of Reputation in the World,"[3] this sense of the word postdating his eighteenth century. And yet, his insistence that his progress through the world is exemplary ("I have been the more particular in this Description of my Journey," he explains in the *Autobiography*, "and shall be so of my first entry into that City [Philadelphia], that you may in your mind compare such unlikely Beginnings with the figure I have since made there"[4]), as well as his introduction into the work of a letter describing its first part as "a sort of Key to Life"[5] for men of affairs and ambition, qualify his "Life" as very much mythic in our modern sense of the word. Mircea Eliade's definition of myth, for instance, necessarily encompasses an exemplary "Life" like Franklin's in its assertion that the function of myth is to "reveal models and, in so doing, give a meaning to the World and to human life. . . . It is through myth that the ideas of *reality, value, transcendence,* slowly dawn. Through myth, the World can be apprehended as a fully articulated, intelligible and significant Cosmos."[6]

What distinguishes this Franklinian myth from those with which Eliade is typically concerned is its apparent lack of any sacred element—its omission of any sort of supernatural background against which human action can take on meaning. While Franklin has much to say about reality and value, he pays transcendence little

The Sound of the American Ordinary

heed, at points even repudiating the metaphysical when it opposes his establishment of his own vision of the world. Denying the possibility of man's entrance into higher realms of significance, Franklin posits an alternative scheme of values, a myth which, though lacking in metaphysical or cosmological explanations, nonetheless encompasses all other perquisites of archetypal narrative. The real—and only—mythic progress, Franklin suggests, is upward through the human world of affairs. The young man's rise in business is as stirring a primal episode to him as is the Easter story to a devout Christian. So convinced was Franklin by this myth that he composed a parable expressing it. The *Autobiography's* protagonist is as elemental as Oedipus, as one-dimensional as Job, and as adventurous as Odysseus. That this quester's adventure never leads him beyond the ordinary realms of eighteenth-century business and politics represents not an objection to his undertaking but an articulation of its basic premise: that, in a world without transcendence, the everyday stage is the only possible platform upon which mythic journeys may be carried out. Thus the *Autobiography* is a sacred story that denies the existence of sacred stories, a myth that repudiates the validity of mythic thought. It is also the vehicle through which Franklin translates himself into the image of the archetypal young-man-on-his-way-up, thus creating a place for himself in the American imagination as symbol and exemplar of that reified state, the figure and summation of our communally shared aspirations.

Dick Gibson, too, would make himself a symbol and an exemplar; he would have his name come to "define a condition" (*DGS*, p. 334), just as Louis Quatorze defines elegance or Benjamin Franklin defines American success. Instead of turning himself into a character in a written narrative, however, Dick chooses (or is chosen by) radio as his medium of transformation. His goal is to become a placeless, timeless voice—"Dick Gibson of Nowhere, of Thin Air and the United States of America Sky" (p. 11). He has no "Plan" to offer the world, but he does have two messages to deliver which are, in effect, one: "Dick Gibson" and "Please remain calm. Please stand by. Please be easy" (p. 8). These messages are the same because Dick wants his name to become synonymous with the American ordinary, a sense of extremity held off and the extraordinary

routinized, a sense of the normal and the everyday sustained and preserved. To become the sound of that sense of American well-being is
Dick's goal, for he hopes that, in becoming its aural embodiment, he
will personally be able to transcend it. As Franklin rose above the ordinary by becoming its champion, so Dick hopes to embody the normal and the everyday—hopes actually to transcend them, placing
himself beyond their realms by becoming their very symbol, turning
himself into the quotidian's champion, the mythic embodiment of
the anti-mythic view.

Dick's attempts to propel himself into myth resemble Franklin's
successful realization of that stature in a number of ways. Their passages differ significantly in two aspects, however, and in those differences lie the seeds of Dick's failed undertaking. First, Dick is highly
self-conscious about his quest, frequently expressing his desire to
live a mythic life and caring more, apparently, about the achievement of that condition than he does about the idea—the American
ordinary—whose embodiment might allow him to achieve it. The
greatest boon he has to offer humankind, to put it another way, is his
desire to be recognized as a larger-than-life mythic figure. Second,
and perhaps more important, the world he attempts to be mythic for
is a very different one from that which was willing to see Franklin's
parabled experience as "a sort of Key to Life." His own contemporaries, Dick finds, tend to splinter off into individual, isolate selves,
frustrating his attempts to rely upon them for communal affirmations of his representational efficaciousness. The source of his failure
to successfully emulate Franklin's mythic progress rests in his
double-edged message of "Dick Gibson" and "Please be easy," a
message at once inadequate as a response to and symptomatic of the
cultural problems he takes it upon himself to confront. That his
quest is a failure is less the point of the novel, however, than is
Elkin's success in creating through it a compelling myth of our
own—and Dick Gibson's—mythless condition.

What originally prompts Dick to think of his life in mythic
terms is the circumstance under which he is initiated into professional broadcasting, an incident resonant with suggestions of selec-
tion and fate. Working as an engineer and spot announcer for a
Butte, Montana, radio station, he is suddenly called upon to fill a

half-hour of airtime when the scheduled transcribed program proves defective. Not only does he deal efficiently with this emergency, words and phrases flowing easily and unself-consciously from his mouth as he assures the audience that all is well, but he also experiences the inspiration of his life as he signs off, his radio name-to-be—Dick Gibson—coming to him "from the air" (p. 7). Thus the air that he is filling with his voice provides him with a name, the name he will save for that period in his career when he approaches the radio self "he was meant to be," when he has proven himself "worthy of his voice"—the name, as he later thinks of it, that "consolidates in its three crisp syllables his chosen style, his identity, a saga, a mythic body of American dash" (p. 83).

This incident marks the beginning of Dick's quest to live the mythic life. Ironically, he only partly recognizes the extent to which his adventure recapitulates mythic paradigms. He is fully aware that he is emulating the Franklinian pattern of young-man-on-the-rise, of course: "The American Dream, he [thinks], the historic path of all younger sons, unheired and unprovided. The old time test of princes" (p. 13). He is less aware, however, of his quest's resemblance to the archetypal narrative of the adventure of the hero, the Ur-story of heroic passage that Joseph Campbell has called the "monomyth." In *The Hero with a Thousand Faces* Campbell distinguishes the three major stages of the hero myth, designating them the Departure, or Separation, in which the hero leaves the world of everyday reality to begin his adventure; the Initiation, in which he learns the mysteries of the unknown realm he has entered and undergoes his ordeal; and the Return, in which he reappears in the ordinary world bearing a boon for humankind.[7] That the three parts of *The Dick Gibson Show* can be demonstrated to correspond to these three stages in the hero's progress is not particularly surprising, given the level of generality upon which Campbell's Ur-story is constructed. More interesting, however, is that many of the monomyth's substages are equally apparent in the novel, suggesting that Elkin was using a mythic structure not unlike this one to undergird the adventure of his myth-aspiring hero. Established early on, then, is a tension between the archetypal backdrop of Dick's adventure and the non- or anti-mythic resolutions of the novel's major scenes. The protagonist himself contributes to this dynamic by peremptorily dismissing all imputations of transmundane significance to his experience, in order to preserve his assumption of the world's non-mythic ordinariness.

His initiation into broadcasting in Butte, for instance, is an experience so portentous that even he must submit to its insistent symbolism. If he doesn't think of this incident in such Campbellian terms as the "call to adventure" or "sign of vocation," he comes close, fully recognizing the role that accident and chance have played in his sudden elevation to radio personality and understanding that he has conceived not merely a name but an identity in his "Dick Gibson" inspiration, an ideal self equal to the rigors of a quest. That self can be developed only through a process of deliberate conditioning, he sees, and so he takes upon himself his apprenticeship, a self-imposed regimen of preparation and education designed ultimately to deliver him from being an anonymous aspirant to radio jobs and to transform him into that ideal self, Dick Gibson, "the generalized sound of American life" (p. 84).

Denying himself the appellation of Dick Gibson until his apprenticeship has been completed, he takes a job in Roper, Nebraska, under the alias Marshall Maine. This juncture of his quest—as his abandonment of the mythic name would suggest—corresponds to the "refusal of the call" substage in Campbell's scheme. Hired by the Credenza family, who own much of the state (including the area's only radio station) and utterly control its politics, Marshall acquiesces to his employers. Awed by their power and intimidated by their wealth, he comes finally to see them as parts of one numinous, omnipotent whole, a godhead he calls Credenza. So worshipful is his attitude toward this communal deity that he aspires not to be accepted merely as an employee but to be taken into the family itself, his hope being that their gratefulness for his excellent broadcasts will prompt them to elevate him to their level. When they not only decline to raise him to familial status but actually begin tuning out his broadcast homages to them, Marshall perceives their disaffection as his first major setback. What he understands less clearly is the incident's verification of the mythic truth that the hero can never advance merely through submission to or petition of the supernatural powers. The god—Credenza—will not intercede to raise the hero to

The Sound of the American Ordinary

his level; the hero must raise himself. What this episode dramatizes, in Campbell's "refusal of the call" terms, is the hero's "impotence to put off the infantile ego, with its sphere of emotional relationships and ideals," his "timorous soul, fearful of some punishment, failing to make the passage through the door and come to birth in the world without."[8] What it dramatizes to Marshall is, more simply, a defeat. Although he manages to plant the seeds of a later triumph in the final days of his KROP employment, he leaves Nebraska with an obscure sense of failed mission, feeling little closer to the ideal Dick Gibson than when he arrived in the state.

From Roper the discouraged radio man travels east, his disgrace having so undone him that he feels himself utterly isolated from the everyday world of American competence and success. "A greenhorn to ordinary life" (p. 51), he must be tutored by his fellow bus passengers in the commonplaces of routine living: how to read his ticket, whether to wear his coat on the bus, how to schedule his overnight stay in Chicago. Their helpfulness gradually reorients him in the ways of the ordinary world. Marshall notices but tries to deny the role that one of them has played in his retrieval: "The old man," he thinks, "was an old man, no high priest, but a stranger with a good wish no stronger than my own" (p. 51). Marshall's objections notwithstanding, the old man *is* something like a high priest reinitiating a supplicant into the everyday world, and he is the first of a number of figures whose purpose it to return Marshall to and confirm him in his adventure. The second of these figures (whom Campbell would designate "spiritual helpers"[9]) appears initially in the contrary guise of the temptress who lures the hero away from his journey by ensnaring him in somnolence and sensuality.

Miriam Desebour, a woman who sits next to him through the long night's bus ride, becomes his subsequent guide. Suddenly consumed by desire for one another, they heedlessly grope and fondle each other through the night, their lust's surprising onset seeming "like something in a charm: one smash of passion and poof went the world" (p. 53). The world remains poof for nearly a year as Marshall moves into Miriam's one-room apartment in the Morristown, New Jersey, convalescent home toward which she had been traveling to take up duties as a practical nurse. Their connubial arrangement in

Reading Stanley Elkin

the home is accepted by its directors only because Miriam presents Marshall as a permanent invalid who requires the constant nursing of his "wife," and although there is nothing physically wrong with him, he nonetheless assimilates the mien and attitude of his fellow patients, cultivating in himself their "fortitude and resignation—all the loser virtues, all the good sport resources" (p. 55). By treating him as a patient—feeding and bathing him, emptying his bedpan— Miriam encourages his lassitude and intensifies his dependency upon her, and only her voice prevents him from becoming catyleptic in her presence. While nursing her patients Miriam habitually talks, her ministrations accompanied by a steady stream of anecdotes, opinions, questions, reminiscences, and insights. Marshall initially accepts these as merely an extension of her professional ability to soothe, heal, and pacify her charges, as nothing more than "a compulsion to fill up the silence imposed on patients whose blood pressures and temperatures are being taken" (p. 58). But her voice's capacity to lull him and her other patients into a state of complacency and quiescence fascinates the "please be easy" radio man, keeping him alert and interested, and he responds to her demand that he leave her by agreeing to move on as soon as he as "broken the secret code of her voice" (p. 63). That that secret code has something to do with Marshall's chosen profession is made perhaps more explicit than necessary by his comment, " 'If I didn't know you I'd tune you in and listen to you on the radio' " (p. 63). But Elkin is attempting to establish what radio means in this novel by drawing together a number of motifs, and for this reason the convalescent home monologue is suddenly interrupted by a return to the frame narrative. The juxtaposition of these two scenes effectively dramatizes what radio must signify to Dick-Gibson-to-be.

We learn of Marshall's relationship with Miriam through a monologue that he—now billing himself as Dick "Pepsodent" Gibson, mythic man compromised by the commercial—delivers to an audience he is supposed to be warming up for a Bob Hope radio show some years later. Baffled by his warmup man's eccentric, highly self-conscious performance, Hope interrupts him, easily winning over the audience with a few quick one-liners as Dick retreats to the wings to watch. What he learns from the comedian—or what he can articulate

The Sound of the American Ordinary

having watched him—is that time is the battleground of radio and the enemy as well; that he who stands up in it, as Hope does, is a hero who has taken on the awesome task of making himself a medium of time's mastery, his voice, his jokes, and his pauses "scheduling it, slicing it into thirty- and sixty-minute slices" (p. 67). What Hope represents to him, then, is radio viewed in its heroic, time-conquering aspect—viewed, that is, from the perspective of the insider who knows its risks and understands the gravity of its task. Miriam's voice, on the other hand, bespeaks radio in its domestic, commonplace aspect, radio as it is heard by listeners, as a soporific and tranquilizer, reassurance's twenty-four-hour beacon. These two perspectives will ultimately constitute Dick's notion of what radio is, define for him its dramatic—perhaps even tragic—edge, and provide his justification for wanting to live his life in it. But to reach that state (his employment with Hope is still years off) Marshall has to extricate himself from the torpor of the convalescent home. The narrative now circles back upon that episode in order to bring it to a conclusion. He accomplishes his rejuvenation largely by forcing himself to attend to Miriam's spellbinding voice not as a listener (one soothed) but as a professional (one who would seek the source of her voice's soothingness and attempt to assimilate it into his own technique). This mystery reanimates him, waking him from his languor so completely that he begins challenging the patients' by now habitual characterization of him as an ineffectual, helpless cuckold, a reputation he gained through Miriam's rumored services to her other charges. His resurgence culminates in a number of victories scored in competitions held at the home's annual picnic. His sweep of the invalid decathlon symbolically delivers him from the ranks of the afflicted and the handicapped while turning him into something like a hero to his fellow patients, who see in his stunning recovery hope for their own improvement.

To fully liberate himself from the home's influence, however, he must solve the mystery of Miriam's voice, a feat he accomplishes when the two of them wander into a "dead room" in a nearby house. The chamber is acoustically constructed to be 99.98 percent free of reflected sound, thus making it "the quietest place in the world" (p. 70). Sensing that he is on the verge of a breakthrough (an earlier

Reading Stanley Elkin

published version actually has him declare, " 'I haven't been on the radio for months, but this is Dick Gibson' "[10] moments before his epiphany), he prompts Miriam to speak into this all-but-total silence, blurting out finally his solution to the mystery as the juxtaposition of her voice and the surrounding soundlessness reveal it to him. " 'You were naked,' " he explains, recalling her stories after their lovemaking sessions, " 'I'm a sucker for the first person singular' " (p. 72). Her voice is naked—" 'You spoke naked' " is the earlier version's more explicit line[11]—because it is pure, undisguised, unadulterated, a "first person singular" that fills the nonhuman silence (that of both temperature-taking pauses and of the dead room's nearly absolute stillness) with speech, with an unapologetic, unembarrassed affirmation of being.

Aware now of what Miriam's voice has unconsciously represented to Marshall, and having been given, through the flash forward to the Bob Hope show, advance notice of what the comedian will define and help him to articulate about the radio life, we are able to anticipate many of the conclusions he will reach once he arrives home in Pittsburgh to sort out his life. What had fascinated him about her voice had been its unself-consciousness, its capacity to sustain lengthy personal anecdotes and reminiscences without betraying the slightest hint of embarrassment. Throughout his nascent broadcasting career he has never *not* felt embarrassed, Marshall admits to himself; the announcements he has had to read, the interviews he has had to give, and the products he has had to sell all make him feel obscurely silly, abashed at his spokesman's role. "For the truth of the matter was," he realizes in inventorying his career to date, "that radio was silence as well as sound; the unrelenting premise was that the announcer's voice occurred in silence, in the heart of an attentive vacuum disposed to hear it.... *Nothing* was worthy of violating such silence; nothing yet in the history of the world has been worthy of it. That's why he was embarrassed" (p. 83). Miriam is not embarrassed to inject her life story into that silence, aware that its sound will comfort and reassure whomever she is treating. Nor does Bob Hope hesitate to fill it with jokes, thereby giving it a human dimension and a shape. Both of them understand, in their own spheres, the two fine points that Marshall has yet to master: first, the crucial

The Sound of the American Ordinary

thing is to turn one's voice into an instrument of self-expression and self-confirmation; second, that voice must be trained to do unceasingly what the veteran radio man does in an emergency, interposing himself between the crisis and the listener, thus "creating a sense of the real silence held off, engaged elsewhere" (p. 5). Translating these lessons into his own terms with his father's subsequent assistance, Marshall resolves that he must "become immodest." He must make a creed of the notion that to say Dick Gibson—even Dick "Pepsodent" Gibson—is infinitely better than saying nothing, in order that he be able to "dispassionately enter the silence" (p. 83) and tame it, shape it, humanize it for others. He is still years away from delivering the two-pronged message—"Dick Gibson" and "Please be easy"—that will become his trademark, but he has come to understand that that will have to be what he will say into the silence.

This conception of the dialectics of radio broadcasting presupposes the existence on the far side of the speaker of a clearly defined and endlessly predictable listening audience, glimpses of which we are given in the narration of Marshall's Credenza employment. It is the era of "Allen's Alley," "Manhatten Merry-Go-Round," "The National Barn Dance," and "Town Meeting of the Air," programs that figuratively denied geographical differences by turning the airwaves into a kind of pan-American home where the nation's listeners could come together to recognize their shared values and mutual ideals. Such programs perfectly express, in Marshall's view, the homogeneity of Americans, the "form, order" that underlie their territorial peculiarities and the "national sense of the institutional" (p. 25) that insures their coast-to-coast solidarity. The basic constituent unit of this sense, he is convinced, is the family, and he delights in the encyclopedia photographs of Dad, Mom, Brother, and Sis gathered around the set, certain that they are not only radio's ideal audience but also its real audience—four attractive people in prescribed relationships to one another, secure in both familiar and social roles, who have joined each other in their living room to listen, "together in time, united, serene" (p. 26). This image of the American family as audience originally inspired Marshall to make a career of radio, we are told, out of an obscure need to "join his voice to that important chorus, that lovely *a capella*" (p. 26). A similar assumption of a constancy, communality, and homogeneity out there in the land motivates all of his subsequent efforts in broadcasting, even in the face of growing evidence that such terms no longer accurately reflect his actual listenership.

It becomes clear during Marshall's stay in Pittsburgh that the encyclopedia image of the American family bears little resemblance to his own family. During his first half-hour there his mother plays the part of a "dowdy Irish washerwoman from the Sunday funnies" welcoming home her adventurous, profligate son, while his brother appears in a wheelchair, impatient with any profferings of assistance or pity and pathetically determined to discover whether Dick (their name for him) has made his fortune out in the big world while the family has been suffering their crippling reversals at home. His mother and brother both abandon their role-playing after a short time, becoming recognizable and reassuringly predictable for the remainder of Dick's visit. But his father has become even more mysterious than Dick had remembered, and he soon understands that the enigma of his father, like the mystery of Miriam's voice, is "in some way related to his testing, more grist for his ongoing apprenticeship" (p. 81). At the core of his father's enigma, too, is his propensity for role-playing, though his theatrics are distinguishable from his wife's and his son's by the fact that he never stops acting, making it impossible for Dick—his primary audience—to tell whether there is actually a man behind all the masks.

Their relationship, though not specifically resembling that of any other father-son pair in Elkin's fiction, is typical in its awkwardness and in the inability of each to approach the other without embarrassment or uncertainty.[12] That the father-son relationship is one to which Elkin has paid considerable attention is reflected by his discussion of it in William Faulkner's fiction in his 1961 Ph.D. dissertation. "The father is, or course, the Lifegiver, the ruler, a kind of God," he argued. "It is perfectly consistent with Faulkner's theology for the father to remain aloof, inaccessible.... it is precisely this sort of non-involvement on God's part that makes it possible for man to save himself.... In all of Faulkner's novels,...there is no full scale portrait of a warm, easy relationship between fathers and sons."[13] This final comment is as pertinent to Elkin's work as it is to

The Sound of the American Ordinary

Faulkner's, certainly, but more interesting in terms of *The Dick Gibson Show* is the notion that man is able to save himself as a consequence of God's non-involvement, for this—reduced to human, familial terms—describes accurately Dick's solution to the mystery of his father. Approaching him to discuss his apprenticeship and his prospects in life, Dick watches his father promptly adopt the guise of the indifferent dad, a character out of generation-gap comedies who cannot begin to understand or sympathize with his son's aspirations and ideals. Frustrated, Dick walks off to work it out for himself, concluding finally that the point of his father's theatrics is to teach him how easy it is to be unself-conscious and to instruct him in the rewards of becoming immodest. His father's continued distance offering no contradiction, he consequently resolves to "dispassionately enter the silence" by resuming his apprenticeship, possessed now of the knowledge his father has "taught" him.

In one sense, then, the meeting with the father is successful. Dick's interpretation of the meaning of his father's mysterious performances represents at once a confirmation and a reinforcement of the truth gleaned through his solution of the mystery of Miriam's voice. The two episodes have the combined effect of propelling him out of his stagnation, setting him off on his adventure again. The parallelism can, however, obscure the important point that, while Miriam can nicely serve Dick's journey as a "supernatural helper" figure, the father, in mythic terms, represents much more than this—or so both Elkin's description of the significance of the father and Campbell's explanation of the "atonement with the father" stage of the hero's journey would suggest. In these terms, Dick has received only an equivocal blessing from his father; he has succeeded in revealing the meaning of his father's impostures, but he has failed to disclose the face of the father that exists behind them all. The significance of the meeting with the father, as Campbell characterizes it, is that the son comes to understand through the father how the sickening and insane tragedies of this vast and ruthless cosmos are completely validated in the mystery of Being. The hero transcends life with its particular blind spot and for a moment rises to glimpse the source. He beholds the face of the father, understands—and the two are atoned.[14] Dick's father does try, in one of his inexplicable mono-

Reading Stanley Elkin

logues, to prove a bias in nature that leads it to tear the arms off toughminded blue-collar types, in preference to white-collar workers; but, outside this, the closest he comes to evoking the mystery of Being for his son is by becoming an embodiment of it, never once allowing Dick to see his true face and thus to understand.

Dick's failure to pass successfully through this stage has psychological ramifications as important on the narrative level as its mythical elements are to the novel's underlying themes. For, as Campbell points out in his introduction to *The Hero with a Thousand Faces,* the purpose of the societal rituals corresponding to each of these stages in the hero's journey is "to conduct people across the very difficult thresholds of transformation that demand a change in the patterns not only of conscious but also of unconscious life."[15] To unsuccessfully pass through one of these stages is to fail to develop fully in psychological terms, to become fixated at a certain psychic plateau. His failure to achieve atonement with his father leaves Dick as selfless a man as his father seems to be, one who must project a destiny for himself as a kind of substitute for personality. The foundation of that destiny is, of course, his apprenticeship, Dick's Franklinian attempt to make adherence to a prescribed plan of action endow him with characteristics. His longing for a destiny and a stable identity are abruptly gratified when he is drafted into the army during World War II. But his want of a stable identity remains a major concern in the two later parts of the novel, as it becomes increasingly clear to him that this characteristic of selflessness, although suiting him admirably to be the ordinary's broadcast embodiment, is a devastating lack when the social fabric to which he has dedicated himself as voice and representative (or as representative voice) unravels all around him.

The military not only imposes upon Dick a number of people to be, but it also provides him with the circumstances of his most ecstatic and triumphant moment. Before that occurs—or that occurs only because—Dick resolves to become a brute. Initially assigned to a combat unit, Marshall (his G.I. name is never revealed; we know only that he is not Dick Gibson) effects a transfer to Special Services for himself by doing an hour's audition for the division commander, parading before him all the broadcast roles and selves he has been learning to master. He brings to his new Armed Forces Radio assign-

The Sound of the American Ordinary

ment the memory of the brute mentality to which he had been introduced in his original unit, and, impressed that such men exist within
a nation of whose character types he had thought himself to have ex-
haustive knowledge, he secretly declares himself one of them. When
an air raid alert is signaled in the middle of one of his transcriptions
of "The Patriot's Songbook" on AFR, Marshall is ordered by his studio engineer, Lieutenant Collins, to finish the taping before retreating to a shelter. Terror prompts him to strike out at the oppressive
military hierarchy, attacking it by filling the transcription with anti-
army propaganda, obscene parodies of service anthems, and incitements of his "fellow animals" to desert. His engineer tapes it all for
use as evidence of the charge of treason he now plans to bring
against Marshall. The taping finished, Collins turns Marshall over to
the military police, the alleged seditionist secretly delighting in the
myriad selfhood potential implicit in the well-defined, familiar role
of prisoner.

Whereas every "please be easy" he has delivered into a microphone in the last years has failed to advance him toward mythic status, his explosion of fear, anger, and frustration on the transcription
proves much more successful. The tape is played for a "famous general" who, having heard about the incident, is considering making
an army-wide example of this sergeant and his broadcast treason, but
who changes his mind upon hearing who the offender is. Traveling
through Nebraska one winter night years earlier, the general, too exhausted to drive the icy roads, had tuned in KROP and was waked
up—rescued—by a voice identifying itself as Dick Gibson. Marshall
had used the name in the last days of his Credenza job, during a period when he had felt himself to be in a kind of post-fall (or post-
firing) "state of grace, of classic second chances." He had sensed
then that one listener could make the difference between "one conception of the place and another" (i.e., Roper as defeat vs. Roper as
significant state in his mythic progress), and he imagined that listener out there being guided by his voice, preserved "on the treach-
erous road as art preserves, as God does working in mysterious
ways" (p. 43). The famous general was that imagined listener, Marshall finds when he is brought before him. The mythic conception of
Roper, and of his entire life, is confirmed by this revelation.

Overtaken by emotion, Marshall weeps openly before the gen-

eral and his staff, knowing now "that it was over: his apprenticeship
was really finished, the last of all the bases in the myth had been
rounded, his was a special life, even a great life—a life, that is,
touched and changed by cliché, by corn and archetype and the old-
est principles of drama." As if out of some ritual necessity, he
launches into a silent recitation of a litany of the clichés appropriate
to the moment, evoking the name of the founding father of quests
such as his and conferring upon himself not only that name but his
own ideal name in the process: "Good work, Dick Gibson, he
thought. Poor Dick Gibson, he thought. You paid your dues and put
in your time and did what you had to. You struggled and fought and
contended and strove, and many's the time your back was against the
wall, but you never let up, you never said die, even when the night
was darkest and it seemed the dawn would hold back forever. You
showed them. You, Dick Gibson" (pp. 105-06). The Franklin allusion
aside, Marshall's characterization of himself as "Poor Dick Gibson"
reflects his conviction that the mystical event of the general's intercession has magically transformed him into his ideal self by confirming his "mythic turn," thus vindicating his years of self-imposed
suffering and trial. It also represents his approximation of the pity
the truly great must feel for themselves, the delightful sorrow that
comes from one's recognition that greatness necessarily separates
one from ordinary men and women. He dissolves this pleasantly mel-
ancholy reflection by assuring himself that the solitariness he will
suffer is not "niggling loneliness and apprentice's uncertainty" but
a loneliness that exists "inside power"; thus he opens himself to
"the exceptional life he has been vouchsafed to live," a magnificent
life, "but familiar too, unconventional, but riddled with conventions
of a different, higher order" (p. 107).

Having entered the army and symbolically crossed the "first
threshold" bounding off everyday reality from the "regions of the
unknown" or the "zone of magnified power,"[16] Marshall undergoes
a metamorphosis. His changes from normalcy's prime advocate into
a brute, and his broadcast on the brutes' behalf, are necessary steps
in his ultimate elevation through the intercession of his final "supernatural helper," the famous general. Restored to himself through
the general's account of his magical KROP broadcast, Marshall—

The Sound of the American Ordinary

now Dick—is confronted with his first cliché situation even before he can silently pledge, "I am ready for things to happen to me. Let the clichés come. I open myself to the great platitudes" (p. 108). Like all of Hollywood's reluctant war-heroes-to-be, he is given the choice of court-martial or a hazardous duty assignment. Good mythic man that he now believes himself to be, he opts for the latter. His task is to become the "voice of the war," as he had once been the sound of the ordinary, the "Patriot's Songbook" tape having made clear that his voice is a perfect barometer of prevailing conditions and can thus be used by the general and his staff to give them an accurate feel for the war's progress and emotional tenor. And so Dick, in the company of Lieutenant Collins, is dispatched to Mauritius to send back reports on a war that has not yet arrived there.

The closing episode of Part I, a tour de force of such richness and imaginative breadth as to be unequalled anywhere in Elkin's endlessly inventive creations, pits the competing conceptions of reality—the "life is ordinary" view and the mythic view—against each other in a kind of first-movement finale. Dick again insists upon the ordinariness and unmysteriousness of life, while his own actions continue to replicate archetypal paradigms too little like clichés for him to recognize them and embrace them as mythic experiences in his personalized, secularized, untranscendent sense of the word.

The precipitating event in the episode is the account, delivered by one Sansoni, a Japanese ornithologist, of the miraculous role a dodo played in Japan's past. Confronted with this narrative, which at once illustrates the efficacy of mythic experience and enacts that point through its effect on its listener, Dick nonetheless dismisses the story as a mere nationalistic fable, overlooking the extent to which the myth adumbrates a progress very much like the one to which he has committed himself in striving to have his name come to define a human condition. The psychological transformation undergone by Shobuta, the thirteenth-century Japanese emperor in the myth, leads him from tenderness to jealousy to invincibility; this final state is achieved when he bears his fallen dodo across a battlefield, the palpability of his grief sapping the rage of the combatants around him, his mournful figure epitomizing a human sorrow tran-

Reading Stanley Elkin

scending the incitements to battle and inspiring in their place a redemptive compassion. Thus does Shobuta render himself *rosichicho*
(invincible) and thus, too, does he prove himself worthy and exemplary of his name, which means "compassion." Dick undergoes a
similar process upon his induction into the army, initially feeling
cowed by the brutality he sees in his fellow soldiers, then becoming
himself a brute, and finally achieving a kind of invincibility when he
recapitulates the Shobuta myth, imitating the sacred story of the dodo's miraculous flight. His reenactment of the tale allows him to
stroll unhampered through the encirclement of Japanese troops, the
dodo he has killed and tossed in the air to simulate flight borne fu-
nereally in his arms, the myth having rendered him invincible.
" 'Oh my god, it's the miracle!' " Collins, Dick's army sidekick,
cries when the dodo rises from Dick's arms. But Dick assures the
high-command audience supposedly listening to his transmission
that it was only craft: " 'It's all in the wrists,' " he insists, invoking
the age-old American belief in the primacy of technique and execution over magic and myth.[17]

Dick's skepticism toward myth doesn't prevent him from being
transformed by his experience with the dodo; it does blind him to
the personal significance of his sacrifice of the dodo for himself and
his career aspirations. Pausing in his narrative to ponder the dodo's
lack of wings, Sansoni wonders if " 'we have all along paid too much
attention to its winglessness and not enough to its voicelessness. Perhaps voicelessness is a choice—the choice of silence. Perhaps winglessness is one. Perhaps there are birds that reject the air and choose
the earth. Perhaps even extinction is a choice of sorts' " (p. 126). The
man who aspires to be "Dick Gibson...of the United States of
America sky" should understand very well Sansoni's argument here,
for he has himself "chosen voicelessness" in the past, retiring into a
Morristown convalescent home, thereby rejecting "the air" (pun on
radio's sense of "the air" intended) and "choosing the earth." Failure, embarrassment, and self-consciousness had driven him into that
withdrawal—for the radio man, a "choice of extinction"—and he
has since dedicated himself to overcoming these inhibitions. The culmination of his experience with the dodo is symbolic of his successful completion of his undertaking.

The Sound of the American Ordinary

Sansoni's insistence upon the significance of the dodo's voice-lessness is not the only inducement to associate Dick's failings with the bird; the ambiguous syntax of a crucial sentence further invites the linking of the two. "Over the old ground we went, a trade route of the extinct," Dick explains, recalling his secreting of the dodo beneath his shirt as he wandered in the dark amidst Japanese troops seeking the prey, "and I thought of dinosaurs and mammoths and the sabre-toothed tiger, and here was I, Dick Gibson, with that other loser, the dodo" (p. 130). Although "that other loser" literally places the dodo in the ranks of the extinct beasts that Dick lists, the sentence's syntax conveys instead that Dick is one loser accompanied on this trek by another. This "crippled bird" becomes a kind of doppelgänger for Dick, a living projection of the scruples, fears, insecurities, and weaknesses that imprisoned him among the invalid and the handicapped and that his apprenticeship was supposed to eliminate from his character. The apprenticeship cannot end here, but in slitting the dodo's throat Dick has effectively destroyed its—his—disposition toward voicelessness and self-extinction, affirming and confirming, in the process, his own resolve to subsequently "dispassionately enter the silence" and fill it with words. This sacrificial rite proves Dick worthy, then, and his elevation is reflected in the circumstance to which he has ascended in Part II. Dick Gibson is transformed, on Connecticut radio station WHCN, into "The Dick Gibson Show."

In one regard Dick appears to have been as successful as his mythic predecessor, moving smartly from one level of psychological awareness to another; viewed from another perspective, however, the apotheosis achieved by Shobuta utterly eludes him. To understand why Dick's apotheosis is truncated, it is helpful to consider Daniel Hoffman's comments on the similar failures of American folk heroes to advance beyond a limited form of self-transformation through their adventures. "In the American folk hero," Hoffman argues, "the transformations are metamorphoses without being rebirths. The concentration of psychic energy necessary for spiritual commitment and spiritual change is not apparent in either the bourgeois get-ahead values of Ben Franklin or in the sly or boisterous go-ahead values of Sam Slick–Davy Crockett." Dick's metamorphosis, we no-

72

Reading Stanley Elkin

tice, resembles those undergone by these heroes in being "only outwardly comparable to the rebirths achieved by initiatory rites in cultures or institutions of sacred orientation. Their function, nonetheless, is a ritualistic one: not a *rite de passage* but a ritual of intensification, in which the powers of self are affirmed, reinforced, and glorified by each demonstration of their successful use."[18] What these figures—Franklin of the *Autobiography* and Dick Gibson included—experience is not rebirth but the confirmation of self through action, the enigma of identity solved through deed and task, the resulting self a construct formed out of the accumulation of all such acts. Dick's transformation in particular consists largely in a redefinition of the claims of the self, his resolution to "disspassionately enter the silence" being his answer to the "plan" through which the *Autobiography* Franklin sought to impose the pattern of himself upon reality. But such a plan, as Hoffman's argument suggests, can take the planner only so far: it can culminate in greater and greater affirmations and confirmations of the self, but it cannot affect any "spiritual change" or make possible the passage into any higher state of being. This would come as bad news to Dick Gibson, a man who believes that his life has already been transformed into one exceptional, mythic, and who spends the remainder of the novel waiting for that special dispensation to take effect upon him. Instead, he experiences only the succession of incidents, the "rituals of intensification," that allow him to know himself more and more thoroughly through actions but that fail to lead him toward the achievement of a stable, knowable self. His evolution into Dick Gibson continues, in other words, but is unaccompanied by the rebirth that would transform "Dick Gibson" into someone to be, rather than merely leaving it as a name to adopt and a voice to become.

A second, equally crucial difference between the mythic journeys of Shobuta and Dick involves the impact of their undertakings upon others. Shobuta's gesture of grief on the battlefield brings a civil war to a halt, saving lives and renewing the state while subsequently becoming a national symbol of the redemptive powers of human compassion. His deed is mythic because it can effect the transformation it dramatizes in those to whom it is related; its efficaciousness is further testified to by its ability to "unsergeant" Dick.

The Sound of the American Ordinary

On the other hand, Dick's apotheosis—insofar as it is one—is of the first-person singular, a transformation so personal and private as to affect only himself. His anti-mythic gesture of tossing up the dodo makes him *rosichicho,* but his invincibility is not potent enough to prevent the death of his sidekick, Collins, in the battle following the bird's "miraculous" flight. To embody the truth of human compassion is to accomplish miracles of rescue and redemption, a comparison of the two men's mythic journeys would suggest. But to emerge from sacred time with no message but technical efficiency and American know-how is, at best, only to save one's own skin.

The inadequacy of Dick's anti-myth, anti-magic stance is reemphasized through his reaction when he discovers the army's purpose in having him broadcast from Mauritius. They were merely trying out a new type of radio transmitter, he realizes, using his lengthy broadcasts as elaborate aural test patterns. Mauritius was chosen as the site of this test because there had been no military activity in the area; little that he could report would be useful to the enemy, even if they were able to intercept this new signal. Dick was never told what to report because the high command had never intended his transmissions to be meaningful. But even Dick understands that meaninglessness is neither easily achieved nor preserved, and he explains in his final report to the high command that, despite the fact that he and Collins were sent only to conduct a test, their arrival attracted attention. The Japanese command deployed troops to watch them and stumbled upon the dodo in the process; these troops were followed, in turn, by allied forces suspicious about the sudden military buildup. Through a complicated series of actions and reactions, a test of equipment culminates in a major engagement and thousands of lives are lost, prompting Dick to point out, in signing off for the last time, that he knows his messages were supposed to be meaningless but that " 'that's very hard, you know? Meaning is everywhere, even in Mauritius' " (p. 133). Dick's final transmission constitutes his grudging acceptance of the existence of a mode of significance he had earlier tried to deny. It has become necessary for him to acknowledge some kind of force in the world—call it meaning—which turns tests into slaughters and transforms meaningless messages into realities of frightful import. Mauritius, he is tacitly admitting, *is* extraordinary, its "terrible light" proving too bright to be dimmed by his attempts to syntactify it into normalcy. In this, the most distinctly Pynchonian moment in Elkin's fiction, Dick must acquiesce to the existence of a portentousness at the heart of the world for which he cannot account.

Typically enough, his acquiescence is not quite complete. Having, in his previous paragraph, accepted "Meaning" in Mauritius, Dick immediately launches into his debunking of the dodo miracle in the name of technique. The precipitation with which he does so throws into question once again whether his idea of "Meaning" is too limited and mundane to encompass the mysterious events in which he has participated. However little credence he may place in the myth of the redemptive dodo, in other words, it has played no small role in the eventuation of the battle of Mauritius. This myth was primarily responsible for the majority of Japanese soldiers having been brought to the island, to seek out and capture the bird in hopes that its magic would win them the war. Furthermore, reenactment of the myth allows Dick to stall those forces long enough for English troops to surround them in ambush, the resulting battle proving more of a decimation than an engagement. Dick may have tossed up the dodo in imitative parody of the myth, but to these Japanese forces this sacred story becomes something to die for. The implication is that those who fail to recognize the imperiling power of myth may actually become its victims—an idea that will be echoed in the obsessions of Dick's listeners on his call-in radio show. Against all evidence that in Mauritius, as everywhere, unforeseen circumstances develop and coincidental connections occur, Dick pits his "the world is ordinary, technique is enough" vision. Against the overwhelming certainty that a Japanese company has been obliterated as a direct result of their participation in a mythic reenactment of sacred events, he continues to oppose his belief that existence is explicable, circumscribable, safe—ordinary.

That there is no one listening to this broadcast—to its content, at any rate—suggests that Dick may not have advanced far beyond the days when he was turned off by the Credenzas. In any case, his progress through Part I has met with only mixed success. He has made the crucial commitment to "dispassionately enter the silence" but he still lacks anything to say save "Dick Gibson" and "Please be easy." He continues to aspire to the mythic life, yet he finds himself compelled to deny the truly mythic elements of his own experience. At this stage in the novel Dick remains a man without a self, one whose mythic aspirations too often disintegrate into the perpetration of empty roles and meaningless histrionics. The end of Part I foreshadows, in fact, what will happen to him again and again in the remainder of the novel. The military assignment he had thought to represent the first real test of his newly achieved mythic estate finally proves to be nothing more than an extended version of the hack radio man's stock litany, "Testing one-two-three."

With the opening of Part II the narrative surface of *The Dick Gibson Show* undergoes a significant shift. Whereas the reader had grown accustomed to a succession of movements forward and backward in time reminiscent of the swirling, looping, and overlapping temporal perspectives of *Light in August* or *The Wild Palms,* Part II quickly establishes a straightforward narrative movement. The density of texture achieved in Part I by that interweaving of temporal contexts is replaced in Part II by the diversity of voices telling their stories on the air. Dick's own role consists in introducing these guests and in his subsequent confrontation with one of them, the confrontation representing his ultimate ordeal and triumph. What is significant in this shift is not only that Dick's story has given way to the stories of others (he has never, after all, denied others' accessibility to the same ordinary world he champions), but also that even at this apparent pinnacle of his career he has already forfeited control of the radio world. The linearity of Part II reflects how severely his mythic aspirations have been compromised by mere chronicity, by the routine succession of minutes, hours, and days which opposes his own ideal conception of time as a palimpsest of epiphanic moments culminating in the realization of mythic destinies, in the revelation of humanly transcendent truths. (The novel's temporal scheme will undergo still further deflation in Part III: there, even the midnight-5 a.m. boundaries of Dick's all-night program, which provide the temporal structure of Part II, are gone, replaced by purely contingent successiveness, Dick proving ultimately as incapable of ordering the one-after-another events of his life as he is of ministering to the ran-

dom obsessions of the listeners who call in to his two-way talk show.)
Part II is, then, *The Dick Gibson Show* (one of them, at any rate), the
novel's middle term mediating between the complex surface and
mythic resonances of Part I and the utterly linear, one-dimensional
and ordinary character of the narrative of Part III.[19] Although Part
II dramatizes Dick's arrival and his most triumphant moment, fulfilling, to a degree, his Part I hopes and aspirations, it tempers them
with foreshadowings of the hollowness and disappointment in which
that triumph will culminate in Part III.

The most striking characteristic of Dick's program (and, given
the protagonist we have come to know in Part I, its most predictable
element) is its odd admixture of the ordinary and the mythic, the
everyday and the marvelous. The program's format is the familiar
one of the late-night celebrity talk show pioneered by radio person-
alities such as Long John Nebel, Barry Gray, and Jean Shepherd,
three of the broadcasters to whom Elkin has dedicated the novel.
For this evening's program Dick has invited four conventionally
controversial guests of divergent interests and opinions, as well as a
special guest about whom he knows less than he should. Each guest
is expected to speak from his or her own corner of the world: Dr.
Jack Patterson, professor of English at a local junior college, represents the humanities; Pepper Steep, a woman who owns and runs a
charm school, can talk manners, morals, and etiquette; Bernard
Perk, a Hartford pharmacist and fluoridation proponent, is the program's specialist in health and physical exercise; and Mel Son, a disc
jockey with extensive experience in running for city office, provides
a sociopolitical perspective. Together, these four ground the program in the everyday world, its activities, and debates, with Dick
serving merely as a noncontroversial "control" mediating their dis-
putes and insuring that each gets an equal say. Despite the thoroughly routinized and utterly premeditated character of the show,
Dick is, typically enough, able to think of it in distinctly mythic
terms. Going through the program's ground rules for the panel of
guests and for those they have brought to watch, Dick is responding
to his conviction that these visitors deserve insights for having come
to the studio, and he is "only sorry that the show was so much what
it seemed. Those who came to the house of magic," he thinks, "were

The Sound of the American Ordinary

entitled to secrets." The only real secrets here, as it turns out, lie in Dick's perception of his nightly broadcast and its meaning:

Besides, he loved the people who saw him work. The capsule-like character of the studio, the heavy drapes hung down over solid, windowless walls, and the long voyage to dawn created in him a special sense of intimacy, as though what they were about to do together was just a little dangerous. Even more than the people who watched him work he loved the people he worked with. They were comrades. For him it was as if place—all place—was ridiculous, a comedown, all studios makeshift, the material world existing only as obstacle, curiously unamiable, so that, remembered later, the night they worked together became some turned corner of the life. [p. 139]

The studio described here not only recalls the one in which Collins ordered Dick to transcribe an AFR broadcast during an air raid; the passage also suggests that, through "The Dick Gibson Show," Dick has risen to the attainment of his ideal conception of time. The program metamorphoses its five hours of air time from just another evening of pure successiveness into a nightly ritual of "turned corners of the life," time rendered significant through mythic transformation, with Dick blissfully seated at the controls of this sublime process. Through the program, too, he is able to throw off place and become what he has always hoped to be: "Dick Gibson of Nowhere, of Thin Air and the United States of America Sky" (p.11).

He is ready, then, to undergo the final stage of the hero's passage, the ultimate ordeal, or initiation, for which his previous life has been but a preparation. That ordeal appears embodied in the figure of his fifth, and special, guest of the evening, Edmond Behr-Bleibtreau.

Dick experiences his sense of arrival and fulfillment only inso far as he feel himself to be in control of his radio world, and Behr-Bleibtreau quickly undermines this sense of well-being by all but literally stealing the show out from under him, making this particular journey toward dawn more than "just a little dangerous." Professionally, Behr-Bleibtreau is psychologist who dabbles in psychic phenomena and UFO's, but his primary interest lies in psychokinesis, the notion of mind over matter. No sooner has the show gone on the air than Behr-Bleibtreau is using auto-suggestion to set the other guests bickering at each other and at him, and Dick's attempts to bring the discussion back to issues meet with little success.

The psychologist then proceeds to compel each panelist to relate a particularly personal and embarrassingly private experience to the radio audience while the remaining guests sit dumbly by, psychically checked against interrupting their fellows' self-exposures. Jack Patterson speaks not of literature and art but of his infatuation with a ten-year-old songstress who has the body of a child and the face of a woman; Pepper Steep ignores etiquette to recall a failed affair with a memory expert for whom the lure of show business proved stronger than her love; Bernie Perk forgets fluoridation, rhapsodizing instead about the humiliating ailments and astonishing physical characteristics that women bring into his store for his inspection; oblivious to political concerns, Mel Son threatens to commit suicide with the gun he has brought to the studio and discusses his adolescent resolution to be sexually touched but never to touch others, his goal being to become sexually self-sufficient. In one sense, these four narratives (which comprise nearly four-fifths of Part II's ninety-five pages) anticipate the monologues of callers-in to "Dick Gibson's Night Letters," a later program, in Part III, but they differ from them in being more complete, less fragmentary accounts with beginnings, middles, and ends, these panelists proving more on top of their obsessiveness than the telephone contingent, and thus more in control of their life narratives as well. What links their four monologues with each other and with those of Dick's future callers is the tendency of their stories to revolve around a missed connection, a frustrated relationship, an ungratifiable fixation—any type of failure to make contact with people, with things, with life. Their compulsion to confess culminates in no absolution or communion; each lapses into utter silence once his or her story is through.

In bringing all this to pass, Behr-Bleibtreau is attacking Dick's ideal vision of the world and of his show's responsibility to it on two different fronts. First, the psychologist prohibits the normal debate of public-interest issues from taking place, frustrating the program's nightly attempt to give voice to the various constituencies and, through facilitating communication between them, to extend and expand the American social fabric. Not content merely to *prevent* such

The Sound of the American Ordinary

public-spirited exchanges, Behr-Bleibtreau manages to *transform* the conversation into the precise opposite of constructive social dialogue. In Part I Dick speaks movingly of " 'the private life. That everybody has' " (p. 48), evoking the sad situations of those reduced to their individual circumstances, of people hopelessly locked into their own conditions and thus deprived of the comforts and support of the public realm. Accounts of this utterly private life are what Behr-Bleibtreau elicits from Dick's panel of guests, compelling them to reveal to the world the extent to which they are isolated selves bounded by private obsessions, needs, and longings. (" 'Everybody has his secrets,' " Bernie Perk disgustedly objects after hearing out the self-revelations of Patterson and Steep, " *But it isn't people's business*' " [p. 183], he adds, before launching into his own rapturous paean to the dimensions of the private parts of one of his customers.) Against Dick's ideal image of the American family gathered cosily around their radio set, sharing a program on a winter's evening, Behr-Bleibtreau opposes the spectacle of solitary people too deeply tucked into themselves to see out. Against Dick's projection of an American social fabric in which all can be united, Behr-Bleibtreau counters a procession of personal narratives that intersect at no point and that provide no ground upon which any sense of community could be founded. What Behr-Bleibtreau accomplishes, in short, is to turn Dick's program into a cacophony of the first-person singular, giving its host his first lesson in the implications of being a "sucker" for that voice in relation to his ideal communal vision.[20]

The other aspect of the two-pronged threat Behr-Bleibtreau poses to Dick's vision of things was accurately articulated by Joseph McElroy in his review of the novel; he described Dick's special guest as "a silence into which the regular unpaid panelists eagerly plunge."[21] Having drawn out their private confessions, Behr-Bleibtreau has silenced each guest. He becomes a kind of personification of the dead room of Part I, a silence that attempts to absorb all sound into itself. The guests rendered speechless, Behr-Bleibtreau turns his attention to Dick, a man well acquainted with the silence. Not only was it Dick's self-imposed task to "dispassionately enter the silence" in order to become a radio man, but he has more recently suffered the loss of fourteen years of his own taped programs by fire in his apartment, a loss which represents to him "the word disintegrate...the wisdom forgotten and the madness gone, and only the silence for punctuation" (p. 140). He has now watched Behr-Bleibtreau reduce his guests—the representatives not merely of the listening audience but also of all the panelists he has ever had, that motley crew he would "keep talking forever" (p. 142) if he could—to wordlessness, and he must consequently confront the silence alone, combatting the psychologist's efforts to steal his voice and quiet him forever. Whereas killing the dodo and, in effect, "silencing its silence" had been a symbolic act of self-affirmation, his battle with Behr-Bleibtreau represents his actual initiation into the role of hero, a second, more threateningly literal confrontation with the powers of silence the triumphant emergence from which will— presumably—establish once and for all his claim to mythic stature.

Aware that the flames have already consumed a portion of Dick's voice, Behr-Bleibtreau attempts to silence the rest by assuming the guise of Sordino, a demon from the fiery depths, in order to strangle him. He is on the verge of succeeding when Dick's chair slides out from under him, upsetting them both and giving Dick the opportunity to wrest Mel Son's gun from him. Dick turns upon his attacker with the weapon, beating at his Adam's apple with it as he had cut the dodo's throat at the close of Part I, finally allowing the psychologist to escape with his life. Behr-Bleibtreau's departure frees the guests from their trances, and they rise to go, leaving Dick to ad lib his way through the remaining hour of the show, "using his voice because he still has it, because it's still *his*—uniquely inflected, Gibson-timbred, a sum of private frequencies and personal resonances, as marked as his thumbs—because the show must go on and he must be on it" (p. 229). So he signs off on a note not unlike that upon which he closed down his Mauritius broadcasts, his earlier assurance tempered now by the fact that he "has had a close call" and knows it:

"Well, ladies and gentlemen," he says, "there is no astrology, there's no black magic and no white, no ESP, no UFO's. Mars is uninhabited. The dead are dead and buried. Meat won't kill you and Krebiozen won't cure you and we'll all be out of the picture before the

The Sound of the American Ordinary

forests disappear or the water dries up. Your handwriting doesn't indicate your character and there is no God. All there is...are the strange displacements of the ordinary." [p. 229]

What might have been a genuine rite of passage (to recall Daniel Hoffman's distinction) becomes just another "ritual of intensification" for Dick, and a severely qualified one at that. His triumph is vitiated by his own acknowledgment that he was able to prevail largely because he had nothing that Behr-Bleibtreau could have deprived him of. Unlike his guests, for whom compulsory confession culminated in wordlessness, "Poor Dick Gibson had nothing to confess...his own slate is clean, his character unmarked, his history uneventful" (p. 229). If, as Dick insists at one point in their struggle, "the voice is the sound of the soul" (p. 224), then it follows that he has nothing that this Mephistophelean figure can steal, for he is only a voice without content, the very sound of the soulless man. For all the mythic buildup of this journey toward the dawn of spiritual rebirth, Dick emerges from the night very much the Protean man (to use Robert Jay Lifton's term[22]) that he was when he signed on the air five hours earlier. His sense of himself—insofar as he has one—continues to derive from his image of the world into which he sends his voice. He has gotten in a final good word on behalf of the ordinary—that is, on the behalf of that imagined community of listeners with shared values and concerns—but he has had to give its displacements nearly equal time. This concession is attributable to the fear Behr-Bleibtreau has put into him (the magnitude of which is not clear until Part III), or to his intuition that the narratives to which he has just been listening bear precious little similarity to the socially affirmative, public-spirited visions he would have expected to hear. Two options are left to him by the end of Part II: he can choose to remain nothing more than "what I say on the radio" (p. 209), a man who has only "the show must go on" for principles (p. 222) and is "a character as some are amoral" (p. 208); or he can follow his guests' example, confirming identity through obsession, throwing off all sense of the public, the social, and the communal in order to gratify immediate impulses and indulge private visions. He is, as it turns out, too much a radio man to choose the latter and too much a mid-twentieth-century man to opt exclusively for the former.

Thus he spends Part III in a state of desperate irresolution, now attempting to embody and encourage an American public life, now retreating into private answers and personal obsessions. This means, of course, that his apprenticeship has not ended. Dick has failed to move from one state of being to another through this initiatory trial; he has no boon to bestow as he reenters the daylight world. The only message he brings back—the same old one of "Dick Gibson" and "Please be easy"—seems inadequate now, even to him.

"The agony of breaking through personal limitations," Campbell argues at the close of his discussion of "The Initiation" stage of the hero's adventure,

is the agony of spiritual growth. Art, literature, myth and cult, philosophy and ascetic disciplines are instruments to help the individual past his limiting horizons into spheres of ever-expanding realization. As he crosses threshold after threshold, conquering dragon after dragon, the stature of the divinity that he summons to his highest wish increases, until it subsumes the cosmos. Finally, the mind breaks the bounding sphere of the cosmos to a realization transcending all experiences of form—all symbolizations all divinities: a realization of the ineluctable void.[23]

Although Dick has had his initiation, has confronted his dragon and conquered him, he has experienced not "spiritual growth" but only the reinforcement of his commitment to those "limiting horizons" that allow him to perceive the world as normal and life as ordinary. For a moment in Part III he imagines that he has become invested with the power of a divinity, but the moment turns out to be just another epiphany of his isolation and loneliness. If he is led to a realization of "the ineluctable void," it is not the void that underlies all being but the less cosmically prodigious, more dispiriting one that is the air into which his listeners and callers in Part III will hurl their obsessions, questions, and fears. Whereas *The Hero with a Thousand Faces* served as guidebook for the patterns in Parts I and II of *The Dick Gibson Show*, its argument proves largely inapplicable to Part III, where patternlessness has become the norm and the point. This section demands instead the gloss of works of social psychology with titles such as "The Me Decade" and *The Culture of Narcissism*. The return stage of the hero's passage, represented by Part

The Sound of the American Ordinary

III, is less a reentry into the everyday world than a series of half-hearted attempts on Dick's part to repeat those past moments when he had been convinced that his mythic life was just beginning, these efforts counterbalanced by his equally indecisive motions toward repudiating the mythic life in favor of the private one.

The allure of private gratifications confronts Dick even as he is delivering his "displacements of the ordinary" monologue to close out Part II. The sight of Pepper Steep's sister, Carmella, asleep in the visitors' section of the studio arouses in him feelings of concern and protectiveness, and the couple's subsequent relationship becomes the major concern of the early pages of Part III. Although Dick has fallen in love with her, Carmella resolves to stay with him only until she meets someone "who is already something," someone who has defined himself in conventional denominational and professional terms, a man whose character answers her passion for the "normal and the ordinary and the public" (p. 240). (Dick fails to fill this bill because he is only the ordinary's broadcast embodiment and not himself an ordinary man.) Carmella and Marshall—he has abandoned Dick Gibson upon being asked to resign at WHCN following the Behr-Bleibtreau evening—travel to Pittsburgh for his mother's funeral and end up moving in with his brother, Arthur, whom Carmella comes gradually to recognize as Mr. Average himself, the Methodist of her dreams. Aware of Arthur's reluctance to take his mistress from him, Marshall rises one night during a furious rainstorm to experience an old feeling and to respond to it with a magnificent, myth-worthy gesture. He ascends to the solarium of his brother's house and watches the play of lightning and the rain beating against the glass:

It was as if he were flying in it. He thought of radio, of his physics-insulated voice driving across the fierce fall of rain; it seemed astonishing that it ever got through. Now, though he was silent, it was as if his previous immunities still operated, as if his electronically driven force pulled him along behind it, a kite's tail of flesh. He stood in the sky. He raised his arm and made a magic pass.

"This is Dick Gibson," he whispered, facing the thunder, "of all the networks, coast to coast." [pp. 248–49]

Having lapsed into silence for a time following the Behr-Bleibtreau incident, Marshall here reexperiences the old mythic conception of himself as a man possessed of special powers and immunities. He feels, too, the familiar compulsion to send his voice out into the night, in affirmation of his restored certainty that his destiny lies in the airwaves, that his voice's true home is in the sky. He comes to think of Carmella "as of some mortal woman he had loved," and he prepares to make his great, tragic gesture of renunciation. Arthur appears, and Marshall grandly offers Carmella to him, suggesting that they are well suited to each other, whereas he—although it breaks his heart—was meant for higher things and greater sacrifices. This Kierkegaardesque relinquishment of Carmella clearly constitutes one such act. The grandeur of his gesture is immediately deflated when a flash of lightning discloses Carmella, naked, standing behind Arthur, what Marshall was offering his brother in humility and self-denial having, quite clearly, already been given. Unable to leave Pittsburgh with a sense of having willed his fate and having chosen his departure (just as, in Part I, he had arrived there in answer to no call, and had left without the requisite paternal boon), Marshall leaves nonetheless. The public self he will resume as he returns to the air now seems less an ideal than one of love's rejects, an involuntary dropout from private life.

Necessarily turning his attentions back from private to public realms, Marshall resignedly resumes his radio apprenticeship, seeking the program format best suited to the promulgation of his community-fostering, extroversion-prompting assumptions. Marshall's new project is strongly influenced by the introduction of two advances in radio technology which considerably alter the medium's capabilities while also expanding its claim to have triumphed over time: the "instant on" feature that eliminates the frustrating pause listeners had to endure while waiting for the tubes in their sets to warm up, and the tape delay, a device that makes feasible two-way talk programs by providing a means of monitoring (and censoring) the conversations of callers before they go out over the air. (This device, as Irwin Schlueter, a radio technologist, points out in his lengthy paean to the innovation, has combined with the ordinary house telephone to make "every home in America its own potential broadcasting station, and every American his own potential star" [p.

The Sound of the American Ordinary

237], all of which must necessarily turn upside down Marshall's image of the ideal American family, who now gather not around the radio to be entertained, but around the phone to be entertainers.)
Aware of this advance and sensitive to the prevailing zeitgeist, Marshall decides that a two-way talk show is required, with a format in
which the listeners are given full opportunity to express themselves
in their own voices and their own words. Thus is born "Dick Gibson's Night Letters," his Miami Beach talk show, and thus does Marshall become, for the last time, Dick Gibson once again.

If Dick's mystic passage through the novel can be said to culminate in the conferral of any concrete boon, the format of his "Night
Letters" program, although not original with him, is necessarily it.
This format allows Dick to give the public its voice and to insure
that, during his hours on the air, there is continuous dialogue going
on in the world, irrefutable broadcast proof that the "real silence"
can be held off merely by the chatter of two people on the radio. He
believes that his "Night Letters" show can become a kind of forum
for the exchange of American wisdom as well as a demonstration of
the nation's homogeneity, a broadcast umbrella under which everyone of his communal persuasion is invited to huddle. The problem
with this format, as it turns out, is that few listeners share his vision,
and fewer still want to talk about anything other than themselves.

Whereas it had taken the auto-suggestion of Behr-Bleibtreau to
deflect the conversation on "The Dick Gibson Show" from customary civic concerns to the secret shames and private obsessions of his
guests, Dick's "Night Letters" audience requires no psychic
promptings. Their arguments, frets, reminiscenses, and general self-
disclosures, which comprise much of Part III, present Dick with
more "first person singular" than he could ever have wanted, and it
is only appropriate that one of his callers is Miriam Desebour, the
woman responsible for his discovery of his predilection for that
mode, the fruits of which he is now reaping.

His callers generally fall into two different groups. One is the
contingent of isolates and boundary-squatters, the self-obsessed too
deeply involved in "the private life. That everybody has" to even
imagine participating in the communal world that Dick is attempting to project. This group includes a woman fixated upon the mean-

Reading Stanley Elkin

inglessly horrible circumstances of her childhood ear-piercing; a boy orphaned at the age of ten who is trying to manage the vast financial holdings bequeathed to him by his deceased relatives; a young, enormously bright couple whose impressive cultural contributions have been brought to an abrupt halt by the arrival of their first child, born blind; a man whose obsession with moneymaking schemes turns into a kind of solipsism, the world existing for him only as validation or repudiation of his latest project; and Miriam Desebour, whose lengthy soporific monologue reflects not only her assumption that she will never be interrupted, but also her corollary indifference to the utter lack of relevance her soliloquies must have to anyone who would sit through them. Exasperated at last by these egotistical outpourings, Dick finally complains,

"What's happening to my program? What's the matter with everybody? Why are we all so obsessed? I tell you, I'm sick of obsession. I've eaten my ton and can't swallow another bite. Where are all my Mail Baggers, the ones who used to call with their good news and their recipes for Brunswick stew and their tips about speed traps between here and Chicago? How do your gardens grow, for Christ's sake? What's with the crabgrass? What'll it be this summer, the sea or the mountains? Have the kids heard from the colleges of their choice? *What's happening*?" [pp. 321-22]

What's happening, all too clearly, is that his listeners have been cultivating the garden of the self for too long to be worried about crabgrass in the external world; their inward preoccupations insure that neither a summer vacation nor a son's or daughter's advancement through institutional America will allay their anxieties or resolve their dilemmas. His callers are the Americans discussed at length in works of social psychology such as Richard Sennett's *The Fall of Public Man,* individuals "concerned with their single life histories and particular emotions as never before," who find this concern "a trap rather than a liberation"; they are people who attempt to realize "an intimate vision of society," those who refuse to acknowledge the necessary discontinuity between public and private life and consequently must reject social existence when it fails to provide them with the psychological rewards and personal gratifica-

The Sound of the American Ordinary

tions that their misguided view has demanded of it.[24] Too introspective to have tips, directions, or recipes to present to the outside world, they speak only to confirm their sense of existence by seeing it reflected in the eyes of others or by hearing it substantiated on the air.

Significantly, Dick aligns himself with the compulsive confessors and the helpless obsessives in this complaint, implicitly affirming the communal vision he has promulgated all along as the ideal and yet suggesting that he, like his callers, has failed to live up to it. He may have in mind an incident shortly antedating his Miami Beach employment. Tired, discouraged, and a little drunk, he had called into a radio program, unburdening himself in a lengthy account of his apprenticeship, failed love life, and increasing sense of hopelessness. He responded to the host's attempts to assure his sobbing caller that everything is all right with the testy reply, " 'No, it isn't. But if you want to know who I am...I'm Dick Gibson' " (p. 257). The ideal, public self represented by the magic name here coalesces with the private, suffering self, and although Dick has not given up on his mythic aspirations completely, he has used this public forum to acknowledge that what he had once referred to as "niggling loneliness and his apprentice's uncertainty" will necessarily exist within that mythic self once it has been realized. In these terms, then, it is something of an admission of defeat for him to legally change his name to Dick Gibson (as he does shortly after this phone call), for it compromises what Dick Gibson can become by dictating that he will never again *not* be Dick Gibson.

Still more compelling evidence of Dick's divergence from the ideal, public-spirited life he has championed is the fact that he has developed an obsession of his own. An anthropologist who calls "Night Letters" one evening asks Dick to put him on hold until after the show has ended, when he explains that his real study is not man but Dick's program, warning Dick that he must " 'be more careful...get his rest and try not to worry' " (p. 292). Alternately terrified and exhilarated, Dick is convinced that he heard Behr-Bleibtreau's giggle as the connection was broken; consequently, he interprets the call as the fulfillment of his heroic aspirations. The enemy, he believes, has reemerged to engage him in another struggle

Reading Stanley Elkin

and to reinfuse his flaccid life with mythic tensions. Inspired by this suspicion, Dick decides that the schemer from Cincinnati, the boy whose relatives have all been wiped out in accidents, and the patient from whose home Miriam calls him are all Behr-Bleibtreau using a disguised voice or a stand-in, and although he recognizes the accusations he throws at each of them as symptoms of an obsessiveness no less virulent than that of the pierced-earring lady's memories, he nonetheless remains vigilant, awaiting the confrontation he half-knows will never occur. He expects the ultimate collision with his adversary to take place at a picnic the radio station is holding for his "Night Letters" listeners, and immediately upon his arrival at the picnic's playground site he takes to the pitcher's mound, a raised vantage point that allows him to scan the crowd for Behr-Bleibtreau. Whereas an earlier picnic—the one at the Morristown convalescent home—culminated in Dick's liberation from his withdrawal into voicelessness and in the resurrection of his forsaken radio career, this one reaches no similar resolution; instead, the listeners who have driven hundreds of miles to meet their "Night Letters" host finally give up their efforts to lure him down from his perch. The picnickers abandon him to his preoccupation, circulating around him to meet other Mail Baggers and Listening Post members. Thus does the voice of communality become the very image of isolated, obsessed humanity, man trapped in the magic circle of the self while the external world moves on about him, unreal, unheeded and unheeding. Standing there in his solitude, Dick has become what he has always wanted to be: a symbol of his listeners. What he symbolizes, however, is not their oneness but their aloneness, not the truth that brings them together but the obsession that insulated them from each other, making them—in Sherwood Anderson's phrase—"grotesques," people whose attempts to embrace one truth as *the* truth have turned it, and their lives as well, into falsehoods.[25]

Behr-Bleibtreau never arrives at the picnic, of course, and Dick's subsequent attempt to recognize him behind a war-toys promotion advertised in children's comic books reflects the extent to which the psychologist has been transformed from specific individual into pure symbol in Dick's mind. Finally engaging the toymaker, the latest of his Behr-Bleibtreau avatars, through the mails, Dick

The Sound of the American Ordinary

finds him to be the center of nothing—no symbol, no representative, no embodiment, but just a dreary, pathetic, isolated symptom of a national illness that has placed visions of private gratification above all sense of what impact that vision, once realized, will have upon the world beyond the gratified self. To murder such a man, as Dick half-seriously considers doing, would be utterly pointless, for his share of the illness is too small, too insignificant, for its elimination to make the slightest difference. So Dick abandons the hope that Behr-Bleibtreau, whose reappearance would have "focused the great unfocused struggle of his life" (p. 323), will ever show up, save in his emanations, his adversary character so thoroughly diffused, dispersed into the American landscape, that it cannot be engaged but can only experienced as fragmentary revelations of the extent to which the nation's public life has been corrupted and destroyed by private visions, personal obsessions. In an important sense, then, Dick had been absolutely right in believing Behr-Bleibtreau to be behind a number of—if not all—the calls that came into his "Night Letters" show, for it is the psychologist's anti-communal, solipsism-inspiring vision that so many of these calls reflect. Not merely "a silence into which the panelists eagerly plunge," Behr-Bleibtreau is the circumstance of that silence as well, an embodiment of the modern psychic dynamism that leaves speechless those who have delivered themselves of their egotistical, self-obsessed life histories. The psychologist represents the enemy in a dual sense, consequently, not only embodying a contradiction to Dick's communal vision, but also becoming the very source of Dick's own fall from his commitment to that vision. Having always wanted to represent his listeners raised to a higher power, Dick ironically realizes this ambition through Behr-Bleibtreau, for while his listeners are obsessed with something, he, in his obsession with his adversary, is obsessed *with obsession*. His success in this undertaking, ironically, all but finally renders his mythic project a failure. The novel's most important symbol, Behr-Bleibtreau is introduced in Part II as the potent enemy who can be defeated only by the pure hero who has no self to steal; in Part III he is transmuted into obsession itself and the silence into which it leads, a force or spirit so pervasive and so protean that it strikes everywhere but can be attacked nowhere. Its ultimate effect is to un-

Reading Stanley Elkin

ravel the social fabric and reduce one and all to "the private life. That everybody has," and to the silence that surrounds it.[26]

The second group into which Dick's callers is divisible is that of the order compulsives, men and women no less obsessed than their fellow listeners but for whom the source of obsession is different. Their monologues consequently represent an objection to a different side of the Dick Gibson vision of things. One of these is a man desperately searching for a solution to the mystery of why people in all lines of work predictably and invariably tell each other jokes on their lunch hours; another sleeps on the couch in the waiting room of an emergency ward, secure in the knowledge that, whatever emergency should befall him from within or without, there is a specially designed implement or process available close at hand to cope with the situation; a third is the anthropologist, who presents Dick with an overload of insights linking apparently disparate objects and events, concluding that " 'Truth is everywhere, Dick; significance is as available as gravity' " (p. 291); finally, serving as a sort of spokesman for them all is an elderly caller whose discovery that telephone poles bear individual location tags—addresses, as he thinks of them—led him to the realization that, throughout the human world, " 'There's order. There's procedure. There's records on everything. There's system' " (p. 313). The monologues of these men could well be read as rebuttals to Dick's closing speech in Part II; his denial of the existence of various levels of significance and coherence that others have imputed to the universe has figuratively prompted this caller and his fellows to locate—or imagine—alternate systems of relation and connection in the human world to replace those denied them by secular, profane visions like Dick's. Meaning becomes for them an end in itself. The slightest glimmer of its presence in the world sends them off on Pynchonesque benders of significance-seeking, their hyperactive imaginations proving more than equal to the task of building massive structures of order and coherence upon the foundation of the slightest of nature's coincidences and convergences. To a man, each order compulsive delights in the tightly knit world that he has privately uncovered, and Dick's airwaves become the perfect medium through which they can reveal their discoveries to the world.

The Sound of the American Ordinary

If the private-life fixates are, at least in part, victims of an ethic like that projected by Dick's show, which unintentionally promotes and rewards the first-person singular, then the order compulsives are victims of that Gibsonian vision which would strip the world of all possibility of transcendence and all that smacks of metaphysics and the metahuman, rendering it safe, unthreatening, manipulable, and ordinary. The weakness implicit in Dick's vision is its failure to recognize the compensatory capacities of the human mind, which, once it is deprived of one form of sensemaking, will quickly engage another to take its place. The mental process involved here resembles that described by Erich Neumann in his essay "Creative Man and Transformation," where he discusses the effects of an excessive development of reason to the exclusion of the unconscious, or creative, mind: "If devaluation of the symbol-creating unconscious brings with it a severe split between the rational consciousness and the unconscious, the ego-consciousness, unbeknownst to itself, will be overcome by the powers it negates and seeks to exclude. Consciousness becomes fanatical and dogmatic; or in psychological terms, it is overpowered by unconscious contents and unconsciously remythicized."[27] The transformation of the world's terrors and mysteries—to return to terms more appropriate to Elkin's novel—into everyday realities can have only one effect: to oblige the disfranchised contents of the unconscious mind to attach themselves to ordinary, familiar surfaces, their customary objects having been rationalized out of association with them. In *The Dick Gibson Show* the confrontation between the sterilized surface of events and the unconscious mind's consequent need to remythicize it is presented through the narrative of a caller named Ingrid, whose "perfect pitch for machines" enables her to bridge the categories of Dick's callers, the private-life fixates and the order compulsives.

A divorcee with apparently conventional values and interests, Ingrid found herself shortly after her separation from her husband becoming obsessed with inventions, buying up all kinds of mechanical gadgets and delighting in watching them perform their trivial tasks in her home. The device with which she becomes particularly enthralled is an alarm in her new Buick intended to alert the driver when she has left the keys in the ignition or improperly closed a

Reading Stanley Elkin

door or failed to buckle a seatbelt. One evening she drives to a party that her ex-husband will also be attending (" 'We still know the same people,' " she tells Dick, and so it is " 'no big deal' " for them to meet this way) and inadvertently leaves the key in the ignition as she leaves the car; the alarm consequently sounds in the driveway as the party proceeds. Having had more to drink than usual at the party, she finally goes out to shut it off, but she feels inexplicably guilty upon doing so and decides instead to drive the car around the block to allow the device a chance to howl itself out. The lengths to which she goes to keep the sound from stopping become more and more improbable and manic, and by the end of her narrative the reader fully understands what she means when she explains that the siren " 'is what mourns. It's what says everything isn't okay. It's my gadget for grief' " (p. 298).[28] One of those for whom the domestication and routinization of reality has culminated in an incapacity for expressing real emotion, Ingrid must look outside herself for a medium to express her sorrow, a sorrow for her broken marriage and fatherless children, a sorrow for her tendency to drink too much and for the general sloppiness of her life, a sorrow incompatible with a world in which, by common consent, the most painful and harrowing of feelings can and must be dismissed as "no big deal." Denied the normal channels of emotional release by the contemporary ascendancy of routinizing visions like Dick's, the Ingrids of the world can do little else but fetishize their feelings, attaching them to objects to which they bear no apparent relation in order to express them at all, the unconscious mind through symbolic substitution circumventing the rationalistic obstacles that the Gibsonian view places in the way of that release. Feelings of grief and their expression may become culturally distasteful and socially discouraged, in other words, and normalcy may demand the suppression of real emotion, but the human mind's capacity to turn mechanical devices into "gadgets of grief" insures that such amelioristic visions can never be ultimately triumphant. On some level, the human mind must always reject this view, must always realize and affirm what Dick admitted over another announcer's air: that "everything isn't okay."

Having become no less obsessive than half of his listening audience, Dick is as order compulsive as are the callers in the other half.

The Sound of the American Ordinary

The significance or mode of meaning he seeks out is represented by the coherence into which—he is still trying to believe—his life is about to fall. He recalls the characteristics that he had thought life would have, among which is that " 'it would be as it is in myth' ":

I'd have this goal, you see, but I'd be thwarted at every turn. I've always been in radio. I thought maybe my sponsors would give me trouble, or my station manager. Or the network VP's. Or God, I admit it, the *public.* That somehow they'd see to it I couldn't get said what needed to be said. That I'd be kicked and I'd be canned, tied to the railroad tracks, tossed off cliffs, shot at, winged, busted, caught in traps, shipwrecked, man overboard and the river dragged. But that I'd always bounce back, you understand; I'd always bounce back and live in high places where the glory is and the tall corn grows. That my birthdays would be like third-act curtains in a play. [p. 270]

Dick's advocacy of the ordinary and insistence upon the mundane as the only reality victimizes him as thoroughly as it does his fellow order compulsives. His denial of metaphysical truth, extrahuman modes of meaning, and psychic necessity leave him only one source from which to draw the metaphors and *sequiturs* that could transform and magically organize his life: the national residuum of old movie clichés. He has a goal throughout his life, of course, but since his mythic aspirations pose no threat to anyone else, attempts at thwarting them have (save for the Behr-Bleibtreau incident) never transpired. Having never been certain what needed to be said (except his name and "Please be easy"), he has never experienced suppression or censorship. And, as for being thrown from cliffs or caught in traps, we have already seen how difficult it is to raise a flesh-and-blood enemy willing to inflict such injuries and indignities. The sequiturs, the befores and afters, have so far failed to materialize, leaving Dick with a life of unredeemed continuum.

There turn out to be no third-act curtains for Dick, no discernible transitions from one state of being to another, no demarcations or even temporary beginnings, middles, ends. There is only "an interminable apprenticeship he now saw could never end" (p. 331). The plottable, predictable, patterned life he has been anticipating, the life that would have confronted time on its own terms by dividing and defining it into humanly significant portions, never takes effect. His days are never transformed into epochs or periods; his hours never accrete, but only accrue. Behr-Bleibtreau is not the only evanescent, ever-dispersing, all-pervasive enemy that Dick unsuccessfully battles; time is the other. The failure of his life to turn mythic, to become characterized by recognizable corners and resolutions consonant with beginnings, reflects Dick's ultimate submission to this, his second substanceless adversary. The mythic life would have imposed upon the purely successive nature of time a human meaning, treating it much as radio does, taking it on "at its own game, scheduling it, slicing it into fifteen- and thirty- and sixty-minute slices" and thus making its beneficiary time's "single master" (p. 67). The mythic life's medium of defining and organizing time is not by temporal units or programming schedules, but through plots or—in Frank Kermode's phrase—"concord-fictions,"[29] the clichés and platitudes Dick welcomes when he senses that the famous general's intercession has confirmed and set into motion his mythic destiny. Instead of being marked by coincidences and intricate relational convergences, Dick's life never moves beyond a state of uninterrupted apprenticeship, of perpetual preparation, no deadlines, significant stages, temporal objectives or resolutions interfering with its headlong, meaningless flow. Nor is this the only sense in which Dick is undone by time in the novel.

What Dick had admired about Bob Hope was the heroism that enabled Hope to stand up in time, to take upon himself the task of filling time with his voice, precisely observing the segments into which time had been divided and emerging from his entrance into it without a word he had planned to say left unsaid. By Part III Dick has relinquished this ideal on his own program, of course, adjuring the heroism implicit in defining and articulating radio time in favor of a broadcast format in which the callers designate the segments and determine the flow of time that will characterize each show. Rather than filling the time allotted with precisely scheduled jokes and anecdotes, as Hope had, rather than making each show a demonstration of his own sense of perfect timing, Dick allows the random complaints and contextless monologues of his callers to become time's sound. His renunciation of the heroic role of articulator of time's content deprives him of all control over his radio world, turning him into just another passive listener to the world's woes, a Miss Lonelyhearts of the airwaves. What Behr-Bleibtreau could not take from him he allows his listeners—acting under a Behr-Bleibtreauian compulsion—to appropriate, the surrendering up of his voice necessarily entailing as well the renunciation of any claim he might ever have had to being the hero who stands up in time.

In this convergence of reversals lies the ultimate meaning of Dick Gibson's mythic quest. Convinced that the American public, once allowed its own voice, would echo the "important chorus" and "lovely *a capella*" he had imagined to be the sound of the ideal listening family, Dick turns his microphone over to them in good faith, only to be greeted by a cacophony of narcissism in no sense resembling his anticipated harmonics of solidarity. He is equally unprepared for the discovery that his Gibsonian ethic, working in concert with advances in radio technology, has contributed to the fragmentation and alienation that cacophony expresses, the tape-delay device having made "every American his own potential star," and thus having made him indifferent to the pronouncements of his fellow stars. Dick's routinizing vision has denuded the physical world of its sources of anxiety, and thus has obliged the anxiety ridden to internalize their fears, turning them into obsessions by turning them inward upon the self. His only messages, "Dick Gibson" and "Please be easy," turn out to be exactly the wrong ones, ultimately encouraging self-absorption and obsession rather than facilitating the development of the communal sense which has been his objective. And beyond these miscalculations and misguided alliances lie the twin enemies, Behr-Bleibtreau and time, both handily surviving Dick's efforts at invading their centerless cores and reversing their inexorable and insidious effects in the world. All of these elements coalesce in Dick's undoing. The man who would be mythic aligns himself, at the end of the novel, with those overmatched others, his listeners, all of them "blameless as himself, everyone doing his best but maddened at last, all, all zealous, all with explanations ready at hand and serving an ideal of truth or beauty or health or grace. Everyone—everyone. It did no good to change policy or fiddle with format. The world pressed in. It opened your windows" (p. 331). His attempts at promoting and embodying an American public-spiritedness and solidarity, at common-denominating a national sense of time, having come to nothing, Dick is left at the end of his mythic journey listening hopelessly to the "scrambled I Ams" of Miami Beach radio station WMIA, his quest having led him not into ascension, reification, or mythic stature, but only into " 'the private life. That everybody has. Being loose in the world. On your own. On mine, Dick Gibson's' " (p. 148).

NOTES

1. Benjamin Franklin, *The Autobiography of Benjamin Franklin,* ed. Leonard W. Labaree et al. (New Haven: Yale University Press, 1964), p. 163.

2. Thomas LeClair discusses Dick Gibson's attempt to live out the American myth of success in "The Obsessional Fiction of Stanley Elkin," p. 153.

3. Franklin, *Autobiography,* p. 43.

4. Ibid., p. 75.

5. Ibid., p. 137.

6. Mircea Eliade, *Myth and Reality,* trans. Willard R. Trask (New York: Harper Torchbooks, 1968), p. 145.

7. Joseph Campbell, *The Hero with a Thousand Faces* (New York: Meridian Books, 1956), pp. 30, 36 et passim.

8. Ibid., p. 32.

9. Ibid., p. 71.

10. *The Dutton Review No. 1* (New York: E. P. Dutton, 1970) published an early draft of a section of the novel corresponding to the first edition's pp. 44-72 two years before Random House released the book. Although there are few substantive changes, Elkin did make a number of rhetorical and stylistic revisions in the final text that shed light on his customary process of composition. In general, *The Dutton Review* version is more expansive and explicit.

11. Ibid., p. 214.

12. In addition to the Isidore-Leo Feldman passages in *A Bad Man,* three other Elkin works treat prominently the father-son relationship. In "Criers & Kibitzers, Kibitzers & Criers," Jake Greenspahn, embittered by the death of his son, is compelled to confront the truth of the young man's human frailty and to abandon his grief-

The Sound of the American Ordinary

induced idealization of him; in "On a Field, Rampant," Khardov's father inexplicably and perversely masquerades as the boy's servant, filling his head with illusions of regal patrimony; in "The Condominium," Marshall Preminger becomes acquainted with the tawdry circumstances of his father's death, learning for the first time through them who his father was.

13. Elkin, "Religious Themes," p. 45.

14. Campbell, *Hero,* p. 147.

15. Ibid., p. 10.

16. Ibid., pp. 77, 79.

17. For this point and many others in this treatment of *The Dick Gibson Show* I am indebted to Raymond M. Olderman's essay, "The Six Crises of Dick Gibson," *Iowa Review* 7:1 (Winter 1976): 134.

18. Daniel Hoffman, *Form and Fable in American Fiction* (New York: W. W. Norton, 1973), pp. 80, 81.

19. The brief radio log reproduced on the first page of Part II:

    "12:00 Midnight
    WGR   Witching Hours (Music and News)
    WHCN   The Dick Gibson Show (Talk)
    WLLD   The World Tmrw"

cleverly suggests the novel's three parts and their salient characteristics in microcosm. "The Dick Gibson Show" mediates between the vaguely haunted past with its myths and songs and stories and the sterile future of "The World Tmrw," the truncated, flat reality of the novel's Part III, the abbreviation of "tomorrow" reflecting the utilitarian lack of grandeur that will characterize the world of that future.

20. Because the central concern of this treatment of *The Dick Gibson Show* is Dick's mythic—or unmythic—progress through the novel, a lengthy consideration of each of his panelists' monologues would be inappropriate here. In general, these narratives reintroduce or reinforce themes presented in Part I, especially those dealing with the ordinary and its meaning. The memory expert, for instance, refuses to accept the glasses that would enable him to preserve his extraordinary gift for remembering all that he sees, and in so doing chooses a predictable and depressing form of vanity over that superhuman ability, the world gradually becoming for him "as much a blur as it is to the rest of us" (p. 181).

21. Joseph McElroy, review of *The Dick Gibson Show* by Stan-

Reading Stanley Elkin

ley Elkin, *New York Times Book Review*, 21 February 1971, pp. 7-8.

22. Robert Jay Lifton discusses the protean man, one whose values are unstable and whose life has about it a quality utterly improvised and contingent, in *Boundaries* (New York: Simon and Schuster, 1979), pp. 37-39.

23. Campbell, *Hero*, p. 190.

24. Richard Sennett, *The Fall of Public Man* (New York: Vintage Books 1978), pp. 5 et passim.

25. Sherwood Anderson, *Winesburg, Ohio: A Group of Tales of Ohio Small Town Life* (New York: B. W. Huebsch, 1919), p. 5. In his dissertation Elkin wondered if the debt Faulkner owed to Sherwood Anderson for the concept of "the grotesque" had been fully recognized. ("Religious Themes," pp. 51-52).

26. Behr-Bleibtreau is an exact embodiment of the point Northrop Frye makes in one of his lectures, in which he argues, "In a world where the tyrant-enemy can be recognized, even defined, and yet cannot be projected on anything or anybody, he remains part of ourselves, or more precisely of our own death-wish, a cancer that gradually disintegrates the sense of community" (*The Modern Century: The Whidden Lectures 1967* [London: Oxford University Press, 1967], p. 25).

27. Erich Neumann, "Creative Man and Transformation," in *Art and the Creative Unconscious*, trans. Ralph Manheim (Princeton: Princeton University Press, 1974), p. 171.

28. The radio technologist whose speech before an "Annals of Broadcasting" dinner opens Part III takes a different view of mourning and its relation to the world of electronics. In the old radio receivers, he argues, there is a delay when the set is turned on, " 'a period of mourning, and mourning—I don't care what religion you're talking about—means one thing and one thing only: abstinence. And abstinence, humanitarian considerations aside, is bad for business. Solid state does away with all this' " (p. 235).

29. Frank Kermode, *The Sense of an Ending* (London: Oxford University Press, 1968), p. 59.

4

Demyelinating America and the Stricken Burger King

The world, the world itself, the world was strange; recognizing another face was strange; being alive was wondrous strange. But the others had families, pictures in their wallets, letters to write. You had to go it alone to make it mean anything.[1]

These sentiments, presented in Elkin's characteristic mode of indirect interior monologue, could be those of either Dick Gibson or Ben Flesh. Both protagonists are intermittently seized with astonishment at the vast panorama of being, experiencing odd moments of "the lost sense of wonder suddenly revived" that Elkin found so prevalent in Faulkner's novels; both also end up "going it alone," extemporizing lives for themselves without benefit of the ordinary supports of wife and family. The source of these musings is, however, neither of them. It is James Boswell, protagonist of Elkin's first novel, who shares with his successor characters not only a tendency toward wonderment and terminal solitariness, but also a preoccupation with death, a preference for living on the periphery, an isolation from the cultural forms of family which help human beings define who they are, and a conviction that beneath his actions and accomplishments lies nothing more than a man who wants to act and accomplish—a man, that is, who does things because if he didn't he would have no one to be.

The similarities among Boswell, Dick Gibson, and Ben Flesh recall the parallel characteristics uniting Push, the Feldmans, and Alexander Main. The comparison of the two groupings suggests that for the first twenty years of his career Elkin had largely divided his

Reading Stanley Elkin

fictional world between irascible, self-willed men for whom the affirmation of the self and the infliction of it on others is the ultimate good, and men who must undertake elaborate ventures and enterprises in order to fill in the blank of themselves, in order to project into the exterior world a pattern compensating for the patternlessness of their own lives. The general shape of that first group of narratives was briefly sketched out in the first two chapters of this study. The shape of Elkin's alternative narrative, which underlies *Boswell, The Dick Gibson Show,* and *The Franchiser,* is equally distinct, consistent, and extrapolatable.

A protagonist, literally or figuratively orphaned and thus lacking the sense of self necessary to translate ambition into accomplishment, is helped by kindly benefactor who confers boons upon him, confirms his feeling that his is to be a special destiny, and assists him in finding the area of endeavor in which he will make a name for himself. (In *Boswell* the benefactor is Dr. Herlitz, a psychiatrist who charts people's life courses for them; in *The Dick Gibson Show* it is the famous general, and in *The Franchiser* it is Ben's godfather, Julius Finsberg.) The protagonist gradually arrives at decisions concerning his mentor's scheme, finding that the cause to which he has committed himself (Boswell's courting of celebrities, Dick's promulgation of his communal credo, Ben's attempt to make America look like America everywhere) has run afoul of complexity and that his project must be simplified. His enterprise also collides with inertial forces in American culture opposed to the organizing, synthesizing nature of his vision and his project, and his narrative moves toward a close as the antagonistic agencies become more hostile and reality becomes increasingly inimical to his purposes. Hoping to salvage something from his life's contest with these entropic agencies, he undertakes one more project which is to be a final commitment of energies, a last confrontation of would-be selfhood with the forces of complexity and disorder. For Boswell, the final project is The Club, an organization that will unite him with all the great men in America; for Dick Gibson, it is his "Night Letters" format, with its democratic assumptions and communal ideals; for Ben Flesh, it is a Travel Inn in Ringgold, Georgia, his largest, most elaborate franchise, to the success of which he has mortgaged all the others.

Demyelinating America and the Stricken Burger King

Underlying this basic narrative structure are two familiar literary paradigms, the one feeding inexorably into the other. Each novel contains a kernel of the Benjamin Franklin/Horatio Alger story of the young man making his way in the world, accruing talents and influence as he ascends through American society. This pattern gives way to an opposed divestment pattern reminiscent of that of *King Lear*, the protagonists gradually casting off "lendings" (commitments, assumptions) as the parameters of their hopes are reduced. Elkin had subjected another of his characters to this dynamic even more explicitly in the early story "I Look Out for Ed Wolfe," where the title character sells off all his worldly goods not so much to discover himself "unaccommodated man" as to learn exactly what his life is worth in dollars and cents. Although that story resolves itself in different terms, its basic dynamic of reduction, of things being stripped away, is the same as the movement that constitutes the final third of each of these three novels. Their peripheral interests and subsidiary concerns renounced and abandoned, Boswell, Dick Gibson, and Ben Flesh all settle into an absorption in one final project. But something goes wrong with that enterprise, and that something takes largely the same form for all three.

Each protagonist gradually comes to recognize that his project is ultimately serving the force he had developed it to counter. (Elkin may have had this point in mind when he responded to an interviewer's assertion that the protagonists of his novels have no opponents by saying, "Their opponent is what they want."[2]) The Club that Boswell has created to be a worldly repository for his massive ego, an organization of celebrities the founding of which is intended to lift him out of his intolerable anonymity, turns out to be a betrayer of the self, rather than its redeemer—which Boswell realizes as he watches the arrival of the great from the throng of spectators across the street from the site of The Club's first meeting. Choosing to stay with the mob rather than to take his rightful place as Club founder with the gathering luminaries, Boswell momentarily recants the life-long "gluttony of the ego" that had inspired him to create The Club. But then he feels the old pressure to distinguish himself, to stand out in the crowd, and so he counters their adoring gasps and envious sighs with his own special ejaculations: " 'Hey, hey, down

Reading Stanley Elkin

with The Club... *Down with The Club!*'" (p. 387). The resolution of *Boswell* is a tentative one, forged out of a temporary reconciliation between the demands of the rapacious self and the expectations of the world beyond it. It is an actual resolution nonetheless, and Boswell's qualified assimilation into the realm of others in the final scene earns the novel its subtitle, *A Modern Comedy. Boswell*, then, unlike *The Dick Gibson Show* or *The Franchiser*, ends on the tonic—or perhaps only the subtonic—chord of comedy, its concluding and resolving movement founded upon the realization of two paradoxical truths: that the self may be affirmed through the renunciation of its creations, and that one may gain the self through losing it in a mob of others.

That The Club can be turned upon and attacked, that it can be made so conveniently to incorporate into itself the terms of the conflict that Boswell has been so fruitlessly living out—these characteristics distinguish it most decisively from the otherwise similar enterprises to which Dick Gibson and Ben Flesh finally commit themselves. Like those other projects, The Club embodies the contradiction that the protagonist's adventures—his very existence—dramatizes. But the fact that it can be separated from the mind of its creator and the extent to which it can be externalized and objectified make it a less compelling symbol of the ability (if not the necessity) of our creations to trap us in the very bind that they were developed to free us from. The separability of project from projector makes the comic resolution of *Boswell* possible, whereas the inextricability of the "Night Letters" format from Dick Gibson or The Travel Inn from franchiser Ben Flesh dictates that these novels cannot resolve, but must simply end. Dick Gibson cannot turn against his "Night Letters" format because it represents the real culmination of his talents and vision; it is the too-perfect vehicle for everything he has ever wanted to do on the radio. He can only continue to fill the airwaves with his listeners' lamentations and complaints (he is still doing so three years beyond the temporal close of *The Dick Gibson Show*; we know, because Ben Flesh tunes him in on his radio[3]), hoping that somehow the "Night Letters" audience will ultimately come to heed his message (that they should think communally, and not narcissistically) rather than the message implicit in his two-way talk show medium (that, as the radio technologist contended, such programs make every American his or her own star).

Ben Flesh's not unGibsonian desire to homogenize America by proliferating identical franchises across its landscape runs afoul of a similar contradiction to such visions of the collectivized American soul: Flesh finds that, rather than manifesting a communal, other-directed spirit, his attempts at symmetrizing the American landscape represent instead his effort to project upon the external world the increasingly undifferentiating characteristics of his own diseased self. The point of *The Franchiser* is that, however much we try to live out the teamwork visions of American public life variously embodied in the business ethic, in Broadway shows, and in advertising appeals, we are necessarily betrayed by our bodies—bodies in which "the plague builds nests," bodies that ultimately demand our absolute attention, their malfunctions and decays imposing at the last a self-absorption which renders us as irrelevant to the outside world as it has become to us. How better to dramatize the split between our public faces and private griefs, between our communal good will and our existential bad faith, than to express them through a protagonist whose grand design is to uphold and expand institutional America by multiplying its commercial manifestations, but whose very efforts reflect the disease that is unraveling his nerves and destroying his ability to distinguish one object or sensation from another? How better to evoke the crazy futility of human action than to embody it in a man who counters the "gravity of stuff," the "dead weight of reality" with the franchiser's vision, the belief that we will be saved by one who will speak "some Esperanto of simple need, answering appetite with convenience foods" (p. 259)? And how better to suggest the intricacy, seriousness, and pervasiveness of America's energy crisis than to present Flesh's Travel Inn, his ultimate commitment, as a victim of the altered physics that crisis has imposed upon American geography, as the external world imitates, through power failures and similar disruptions, the ruined circuitry of Flesh's demyelinating nervous system?

In an important sense, then, just as Dick Gibson's passage recapitulates the outlines of Boswell's, it is echoed in the pattern of Ben

Reading Stanley Elkin

Flesh's experiences. Perhaps the most crucial point of convergence between their journeys is, however, to be found in the paradox explicated by Boswell toward the close of Elkin's first novel. Musing over the fact that he has lived a life innocent of complexity, untroubled by a "proliferation of passions," Boswell finds complexity progressively forcing itself upon him and is surprised to discover that "complexity was not so much a proliferation of passions as a diminishment of them, a chipping away at whatever passion one might call his own" (*B*, p. 361). The conclusions of these novels delineate this paradox, then, as each protagonist gradually learns that the jettisoning of goals and commitments results not in greater feelings of simplicity and freedom, but in a life of progressively greater uncertainty, complexity, and impotence. It is to the expression of this truth that the final thirds of these three novels are dedicated.

The element that most significantly distinguishes these novels from one another is not plot, theme, or character; what is truly distinct about each is the system of metaphors it develops and exploits. This fact helps to explain why the occupations of his protagonists are such a major consideration in Elkin's work, these vocations providing the novels' primary stores of metaphor, while also shaping and defining characters who otherwise tend toward the amorphous. The dominant weakness in *Boswell*, it might be argued, is its protagonist's want of stable employment; the fact that he has only inconstant projects and vaguely defined enthusiasms leaves him an excessively protean character and leaves the novel without a central context of metaphors from which to draw. This difficulty is avoided in Elkin's subsequent novels, in which each protagonist is thoroughly identified with and defined by a specific profession. Since what happens to these professional men (and we can add bailbondsman Main to the list here) is largely the same, the different jobs they hold allow Elkin to approach the basic thematic, narrative pattern of their experiences through divergent systems of metaphor and analogy.[4]

The Franchiser is a highly successful novel largely because of its ability to translate its episodic plot structure into coherent form through the skillful manipulation of metaphor and through a thematic synthesizing of details. These two strategies (which to Elkin are very much the same operation) constitute what he has called "crossover," a crucial element in any mode of figurative expression and a central structural assumption underlying Elkin's own aesthetic. "In primitive form," Elkin explained, crossover is "often little more than an echo, or allusion, and is borrowed from one thing and imposed upon another for what might be almost homeopathic reasons, growing a sort of interest, as money grows interest." The effect of crossover is always "new wine in old bottles, some recycled but incremental and compounded sense of the world, the lifting of one occasion to enhance another."[5] The resonance of his (if not everyone's) fiction results mainly, in Elkin's view, from the imbuing of one situation with ideas and images from another one—the ascription of a poetics to bullying, for instance, or the depiction of a professional wrestler as the angel of death in *Boswell,* or the confrontation of a department store owner with the reality of prison life. From the simplest pun (the tapes of old programs designated "Dick Gibson's burned logs") to the most elaborate structural conceit (Brewster Ashenden in a fairy tale being set the unfairy-talelike task of gratifying a bear in heat), from the most elemental similes (sport coats worn by salesmen described as having "checks like optical illusions, designs like aerial photography of Kansas wheat fields") to the most audacious plot premise (the thousand years of "blue-collar blood" produced in the George Mills lineage), Elkin's fiction is founded upon crossover, "the lifting of one occasion to enhance another," which represents both how it works and what it does. Technical development in his fiction has meant, consequently, a moving away from plot-centered narratives[6] and a greater reliance upon crossover as a structural and thematic principle. *The Franchiser* is the first novel in which Elkin largely dispensed with chronological narrative and allowed a system of metaphors playing off one another to dictate the work's direction and shape, and if the general theme—that of the individual self's confrontation with the truth of its own isolation[7]—remains familiar, the form through which it was expressed was new. The scope of the novel allows for a wealth of invention and linguistic play, but the juxtapositions of metaphors and images—again, crossover—makes it, in Elkin's words, "a more tightly structured book than anything I have written before." Al-

Reading Stanley Elkin

though there are "stories in it that apparently have nothing to do with what is going on in the book," he added, "I know what they are doing there."[8] They are establishing and extending the system of metaphors that comprises this "tightly structured book."

The two occupations from which most metaphors in *The Franchiser* are derived are business and show business, and it is one of the novel's primary objectives to dramatize the continuity between the values these occupations assume and the perspectives upon reality that they imply. Ben Flesh is able to buy franchises only because his godfather, Julius Finsberg, who made his fortune in the theatrical costuming business, bequeaths him the ability to borrow money at the prime interest rate. Were it not for a specific proscription in Finsberg's will, Flesh probably would have reinvested his profits in the source from which Finsberg's wealth issued—Broadway shows. Flesh elaborates upon the connection between his business life and the life of the Broadway stage for the benefit of guests whom he has gathered to mark the closing of his Fred Astaire Dance Studio in Chicago. The room in which they are dancing, he informs them, once housed the Finsberg & Flesh theatrical costuming company before the partners moved it to New York and Finsberg bought Flesh's father out; the Broadway show tunes to which they dance are the same ones that made Finsberg a rich man, which, in turn, enabled him to leave Flesh the bequest. All of which means, Flesh concludes, that " 'We dance to the prime rate of interest itself. We compound it' " (p. 62).

Instead of becoming a theatrical angel, then, Flesh became an owner of franchises. This, by his own admission, makes him "like a producer with several shows running on Broadway at the same time. My businesses take me from place to place. My home is these United States' " (p. 34). It explains, too, his propensity for referring to the story of his inheritance as a "How I Got to Play the Palace" narrative (p. 37) and for summing up the closing out of an unsuccessful operation with the phrase " 'We ain't taking it to Broadway' " (p. 70). That franchising is a form of theatrical costuming is made even more explicit late in the novel, when the narrator explains Flesh's relative indifference to profits and success in terms of his overriding interest, "the backstage Finsberg propinquity to staged life, his need to costume his country, to give it its visual props, its mansard roofs and golden arches and false belfries, all its ubiquitous, familiar neon signatures and logos, all its *things*, all its *crap*, the true American graffiti, that perfect queer calligraphy of American signature, what gave it its meaning and made it fun'' (p. 270).

What Dick Gibson attempts to do with time—Americanizing it, transforming its relentless progress into the reassuring sound of ordinariness itself—Flesh wants to do with space. His efforts are undertaken to the tune and in the spirit of Broadway melodies, projecting a positive, communal vision of the world. That vision is most conspicuously embodied by what Flesh refers to as "that strange fairy tale crew," the eighteen identical twins and triplets produced by Finsberg and his Broadway showgirl wife. In addition to the fact that they all bear the names of Broadway luminaries (Moss, Lorenz, Gertrude, Oscar, Cole, and Jerome), they also, in their apparent duplication of each other—their "choruslike being"—are a living repudiation of the tragic. Their very existence suggests that there is always another to take up the failed challenge, and their interchangeability dictates that a certain inconsequence necessarily rules their lives. Significantly, theirs is the inspiration behind Flesh's franchising career. Having noticed that every Howard Johnson's restaurant is identical to every other, just as they are identical to each other, they encouraged him to invest in it and in similarly reduplicative franchises. The parallel between Finsbergs and franchises reinforces the association of both with musical comedy; all of them are protected against unhappy endings, defeats, and reversals by the fact that there are legions involved, that no individual will ever have to carry on alone, since there will always be other Kentucky Fried Chickens, other Finsbergs, other onstage characters to insure that a comedic resolution, the communal affirmation, is achieved. The interrelationship between the worlds of business, show business, and Finsbergs is effectively epitomized by the mistletoe that adorns the back door of the bus in which the adolescent Finsberg clan travels; the state flower of Oklahoma pays tribute to the musical comedy that made their father a wealthy man. When, in his excitement over the suggestion that he use his prime rate to build new Howard Johnson's restaurants, Flesh kisses Lotte Finsberg beneath the mistletoe image, he is embarking upon two careers simultaneously: the buying of franchises, and the romancing of recyclable, eight-times-renewable lovers who will allow him more than his share of happy endings.

The Finsbergs manage to maintain their collectivized and spritely "we're all in it together" front into early adulthood, despite the "dark diathenics" that will ultimately undermine each one's health and dissolve their solidarity. When this healthy minded resolve falters in any one of them, threatening to give way to purely personal anxieties, Flesh provides an object lesson intended to restore the falterer to the wholesome, communal view. On the pretext of showing her a Robo-Wash that he is considering buying in Queens, Flesh has Kitty (a lifelong bedwetter) accompany him through the dousing and soaping process, attempting to prove that the terrible nightmares that cause her to lose control of her bladder can be reproduced by a mechanism as ordinary as a public carwash, and to convince her that her nocturnal phantoms are as innocent as this harmless machine. Her nightmares are not so simply neutralized, and Kitty remains a bedwetter, her life irrevocably poisoned by the personal.

In the early pages, however, the Finsbergs are associated with solidarity and unity, with Flesh's organized and organizing vision; only later do they come to mirror the physical decline that afflicts him and that characterizes the power-depleted America through which he drives in carrying out his "grand rounds." The predissolution character of Flesh and the Finsbergs is most clearly summarized by Roger Foster, a Colonel Sanders impostor whom Flesh meets in 1956 and brings to the Finsbergs' Riverdale home for a visit. Likening their home to Brigadoon, Foster compares the twins and triplets to himself, arguing that they are all doppelgängers. He doubles for Colonel Sanders; they double for each other. Flesh, on the other hand, is a " 'doppelgängster,' " Foster insists, his borrowed businesses qualifying as doubles of each other, mercantile masquerades. " 'What *you* do,' " Foster concludes, " 'is a U. S. A. nightclub performance. You do John Wayne and Ed Sullivan. You do Cagney and Bogart. Liberace you do. Sinatra, Vaughan Monroe. Tell me something. Which is the *real* Howard Johnson's? Which is the real Holiday Inn or chicken from the Colonel?' " (p. 92). Foster's characterization establishes by analogy another aspect of the franchiser's personality: his suspicion that he is a man without a consistent self, his Dick Gibsonian sense that at the core of Ben Flesh is no one at all. The doppelgänger progression Foster delineates here, then, moves from himself, a man who masquerades as a real some-one else, to the Finsbergs, reflections of each other and thus (like Howard Johnson's restaurants or Kentucky Fried Chicken franchises) imitations lacking a central, "real" image to imitate, to Flesh, the reflection of a man in a mirror before which no one is standing, or the outline of a man rendered visible only by connecting the dots on the nation's face representing the franchises that he owns.

Flesh had begun thinking of himself in these terms as a young man. Years before receiving his inheritance he recognized that "because he had no good thing of his own" it would be best for him "to place himself in the service of those who had" (p. 46), and thus he was delighted to learn from the Finsbergs that he could buy the names of men with good things of their own and trade through them. He explains this to Kitty late in the novel, characterizing, in the process, the Elkinian selfless man as definitively as Push articulates the creed of the Elkinian self-full man in "A Poetics for Bullies." " 'Some people, me, for example, are born without goals,' " he dolefully confesses, " 'There are a handful of us without obsession. . . . I live without obsession, without drive, a personal insanity, even, why, that's terrible. The loneliest thing imaginable. Yet I've had to live this way, live this—sane life, deprived of all the warrants of personality. To team up with the available. Living this franchised life under the logos of others' " (p. 282). Rather than a personality, Flesh has a career, his franchise itinerary—"what he has in lieu of a life"—directing his steps, America becoming the stage upon which his play is acted out, his lines provided by Robo-Wash and Radio Shack, firms that, for a price, give him their corporate masks to wear.

Flesh's proliferation of these corporate facades throughout the American landscape represents an imposition of uniformity upon space, a calculated attempt by one man to transform the coun-

Reading Stanley Elkin

try's face, to re-create it in the image of his own undifferentiating vision. A "man of franchise," Flesh is a self-proclaimed "true
democrat who would make Bar Harbor, Maine, look like Chicago,
who would quell distinction, obliterate difference, who would
common-denominate until Americans recognize that it was America
everywhere" (p. 164). Later Elkin deliberately weaves together many
of his metaphoric strands into a single, synthetic paragraph, having
his narrator identify Flesh as

the man who made America look like America, who made America
famous...the man who knows that there wasn't a television in the
thousands of motel rooms in which he'd slept which wouldn't show
him in the course of a single evening at least two sponsored minutes
of the homogenized, coast-to-coast America he'd helped design, costuming the state, getting Kansas up like Pennsylvania, Georgia like
New York. Why, he *was* a Finsberg! A Julius and his own father Flesh
too, loose and at large in his beautiful musical comedy America!
[p. 262]

The basic technique of *The Franchiser* becomes apparent, then.
Rather than meting out his themes over the course of a linear plot
sequence, Elkin here presents a number of diverse and ostensibly
unrelated scenes, each gradually subsumed within a larger palimpsest of metaphors that justifies and reconciles them, the juxtapositions and overlappings of temporal planes emphasizing (as they
often do in Faulkner) parallel instances and metaphoric analogues
rather than plot sequence. Consequently, it becomes increasingly
difficult to isolate any one theme, so thoroughly has each, through
metaphoric elision, come to contain or imply the others.

Elkin's intentional manipulation of these themes in *The Franchiser* is not undertaken solely for the pleasure of watching things
transform themselves into other things through language (though in
his fiction, as in that of his friend and colleague William Gass, there
is some of this). Rather, in synthesizing these ideas Elkin intends to
demonstrate their real-world associations, the extent to which they
actually coalesce to constitute a peculiarly American, distinctly midcentury perception of things. In his delight with "the bouncy anthems of our firms, tears in *my* eyes in the face of all this blessed,

Demyelinating America and the Stricken Burger King

smarmy hope, even if I know, as I do know, what I know" (p. 75),[9] Flesh represents an exaggerated exemplar of this frame of mind, his every thought and action evoking a way of thinking that has, in the last two decades, given way to more pessimistic, less expansive conceptions of the workings of things. Flesh's midcentury American perspective is patched together out of a number of sources and assumptions, among them hopes for the future that came with peace, the burgeoning birthrate that attested to the avidity of those hopes, the prospect of tremendous economic growth with its promise of prosperity for all, and the corollary faith that American business methods conscientiously applied could remedy many of humankind's ills. Underlying and reinforcing all these expectations were musical comedies, their medium and message harmonizing with while helping to create the ethic in which the larger society had, in war as in peace, placed its trust: the idea that "we can do it together." Implicit in this vision is the same assumption that underlies much of musical comedy: the conviction that human experience transcends individual differences, the idea that we all recognize in ourselves the same basic impulses, joys, and sorrows, whatever the regional accents through which we articulate them. Beneath this assumption lies another, one crucial to the visions and projects of both Ben Flesh and Dick Gibson: the belief that Americans have so thoroughly dealt with the primary needs of clothing, shelter, and food that the only objective left is to expand the comforts that culture offers—to prove that existence is not a battle for survival, but a matter of settling down into the ordinary, of finding the real truth about ultimate things in the spirited anthems of Broadway. Flesh represents in extreme form all those who, despite "knowing what they knew," were secretly stirred by musical declarations like "Everything's Coming Up Roses" and "We know we belong to the land, and the land we belong to is grand"; who found themselves giving private assent to the notion that "There's No Business Like Show Business," or who found some gut-level conviction of human solidarity and possibility captured in the rousing choruses of "Seventy-six Trombones" or "A Real Fine Clambake."

Nor is Flesh reticent about affirming his exemplification of this sentimental, optimistic mode of thought. His representativeness sim-

Reading Stanley Elkin

ply reinforces the idea that he is less a man in his own right than a reflection of other men. Recalling the numerous, varied, largely inconsequential experiences that have befallen him, he asserts at one point that " 'they've got me programmed for an Everyman!' " (p. 111), and he subsequently tells Patty Finsberg, " 'I'm the culture! Ben Flesh the Avon Lady, Ben the Burger King' " (p. 193). Embodying the culture as he does, Flesh must experience a personal decline analogous to the one he sees afflicting America and intruding upon his vision in the 1960s into the '70s. For him, that decline is called multiple sclerosis.[10] The commencement of his decline is signaled by an incident in 1960, when, at the inauguration of his Kentucky Fried Chicken franchise, he suddenly finds himself blind in one eye. The condition turns out to be temporary, and not until ten years later is he told that the retrobular optic neuritis was an unmistakable symptom of the onset of multiple sclerosis. Within the year the disease is no longer in remission; symptoms begin to appear, and on a visit to his Rapid City, South Dakota, Mr. Softee franchise Flesh checks in to a hospital, only to have that diagnosis confirmed. His is a sensory strain of the illness, the doctor there explains; it will not inconvenience him severely unless it turns into the more serious (and necessarily fatal) motor form of multiple sclerosis, the symptoms of which are speech impairment, muscular dysfunction, the experience of an inexplicable euphoria, and ultimate paralysis. Flesh is sent off to continue his "grand rounds" with the reassurance that, even though he may suffer practically all tactile contact as "a shiver of electric plague" and may be constantly aware of the "ruined, demyelinating nerves sputtering like live wires in his fingertips" (pp. 133-34), he " 'really isn't in such bad shape.' " He drives back into the nation's heartland, finding the failure of his own internal circuitry mirrored in the towns and cities he approaches, a massive heat wave, combined with early '70s power shortages, having caused brownouts throughout the region. He spends the next week attempting to escape the regional short circuit, storing up gallon cans of gas and quarts of oil in a desperate search for an oasis of light, energy, power.[11] Flesh makes explicit the link between his own internal disintegration and the external world's failure when he tells the Finsbergs, " 'There isn't enough energy to drive my body. How can there be enough to run Akron?' " (p. 258).

Demyelinating America and the Stricken Burger King

The disease takes on a more private and immediate significance for Flesh shortly after he arrives in the energy oasis of Colorado Springs. Joined there by Patty, the Finsberg triplet nicknamed
"the Insight Lady" for her ability to decipher cultural symbols se-
miotically, Flesh and his latest mistress take off explications of social
realities. He wins the competition by launching into a demonstration
that ours is a tactile, preliterate culture, its bottles and boxes differ-
entiated by size and shape so that we can visually distinguish their
contents. For one whose own tactile relationship to the world is
growing more limited and less precise, this insight could hardly be
reassuring, even if the threat it poses to him is more symbolic than
real. Symbolic extensions of the disease's significance continue to
accrue over the course of the novel. Flesh's precisely depicted disin-
tegrating contact with the world enacts the pattern of gradual loss
reminiscent of the *King Lear* dynamic considered earlier, and anticipates Joan Didion's use of the same illness as symbol in "The White
Album,"[12] her essay dealing with the end of the 1960s.

The pivotal irony of *The Franchiser*, then, consists in the fact
that the man who has set himself the task of spatially uniting and homogenizing his country is himself suffering from a distintegrative
malady. The blurring of his neural distinctions is analogous to the
effect of his franchiser's mentality on the nation's geography. Flesh
has to face a truth not unlike that confronted by Dick Gibson: the
disturbing recognition that his ideals, once put into practice, somehow manage consistently to betray their own ends. Wanting nothing
more than to extend a sense of American communality and shopping
mall well-being, Flesh must finally see that he has only imposed
upon the land a spatial analogue of the disease that is destroying
him—that is, he subsequently concludes, "perhaps merely the physical configuration of his personality" (p. 308).

This central recognition reaches its dramatic climax when Flesh
is flying to New York in response to a summons from the Finsbergs.
He watches out the window as America flows by below him, taking
characteristic delight in this vantage point which, in its presentation
of the nation as one homogenized, continuous place, confirms his
own intuitive sense of its reality. His complacent meditations are interrupted, however, by the insistent intrusion of an alien thought. He
feels the country's "ultimate homogenity, a homogeneity squared,

Reading Stanley Elkin

the final monolithism of his country, the last and loftiest franchise, the air, the sky, all distinctions, whichever remained intact, whichever he had been unable to demolish in his capacity as franchiser, as absent, as blasted away as the tactile capacities of his poor motherfuck fingers and his lousy son of a bitch hands,'' (p. 245). Flesh proves no more capable of altering strategy or revising tactics than is Dick Gibson when it occurs to him that his efforts are extending the dominion of the very forces he sought to oppose. Both men simply push on, continuing to do what they have been doing in the hope that the results of their exertions will somehow reverse themselves. Aware now that America is too large for him to save, its atomization too advanced for his commercial song and dance to succeed in effecting its restoration, Flesh determines to redeem that ideal microcosm of the culture—the Finsberg twins and triplets. They need saving because, like everything else in the nation, they have begun to drift apart, their ''50's and 60's tract house mode'' submitting to the ravages of change, of difference in distinguishability.

In a dream Flesh sees himself as an archaeologist at the Finsberg digs, one intent upon ''restoring their old mass individualism, only with difficulty putting them together, a painstaking labor'' (p. 273). He wakes resolved to rise to its challenge, even though he suspects that it is a task beyond the capabilities of his blasted hands and demyelinating nerves, and he decides that he may be able to accomplish the necessary restoration by shaping his franchises in a more coherent, less arbitrary way. Instead of planting a franchise wherever there is a vacancy, he will arrange them ''in such a way as to coincide with a traveller's cicadian rhythms, his scientifically averaged-out need to pee, eat, rest, distract himself with souvenirs.'' The consequent success of these franchises, he reasons, will regain for him both the respect of the Finsberg boys and the love of the Finsberg girls; that respect and love will—he hopes—''somehow force them back into their odd single magical manifestations'' (p. 273). The Finsbergs, in short, represent Flesh's last hope of proving that it will be ''a franchiser who'll save us.... Speaking some Esperanto of simple need, answering appetite with convenience foods'' (p. 258). His attempts at turning himself into a serious, sober, profit-minded businessman run afoul not only of his habitual indifference to the financial success of his operations but also of a freak, unpredictable business climate. " 'The economy is spooked,' " he tells the Finsbergs during his Riverdale visit in 1974, " 'There's a curse on free enterprise' " (p. 255). His judgments are borne out by the fact that his elaborate and carefully considered reordering of his franchise portfolio causes him increasingly severe financial losses.

American business and the commercial vision it implies represent stability and certainty in the early pages of the novel. Flesh finds this so comforting and encouraging that he makes them the medium of his hopeful vision, through which he creates in life the "musical comedy democracy" that lives in his heart. Midway through the novel, however, they have come to partake of and contribute to the complex of ideas involved with deterioration, dispersion, and death. Flesh's dream of restoring the Finsbergs through business savvy comes to nothing not only because of the sudden instability of economic sphere, but also because the Finsbergs begin dying off before he is able to reunite them, the survivors consistently announcing their brothers' and sisters' deaths with the phrase "_____ bought it," so thoroughly by now has business become associated with death and dissolution. The business frame of mind, which Flesh has always valued for its opposition to and repudiation of any grave, somber, or hopeless perception of life, ultimately contains within itself these realities, veiled beneath an insistently comedic vision. If the business mentality and the world it creates and projects are fundamentally comedic, they are so because they are playing to endlessly renewable contingents of fourteen-to-twenty-year-olds, cross-sections of middle-aged males earning in excess of $20,000 annually, masses of housewives of a particular educational level. From the businessman's perspective these contingents might well be thought of as choral groups intoning their communal willingness to be sold Stridex pads, or a Betamax, or Palmolive dishwashing liquid; however, each individual within the group is a person with a private need, an isolate being characterized by some unfulfilled desire. The distinction between these perspectives is crucial and irresolvable, and Flesh makes much of it toward the end of the novel, when he realizes how thoroughly the business ethic has failed to bring about the world he has envisioned. He speaks for himself

Reading Stanley Elkin

and for other businessmen when he admits that, in the end, "he was no businessman but only another consumer," a man "who came to sell, almost always, what he had already first used, tried, bought himself. . .and all of it testimonial to nothing finally but his needs, to need itself" (p. 255). The comedic vision of American business cannot ultimately transform the individual's needs and their fulfillment into something more public, more communal, for at bottom all there is—the songs and commercials with their promises of oneness and solidarity through the products' gratification of desires notwithstanding—is Ben Flesh, the isolate Everyman-as-consumer, alone and inseparable from his needs. Neither need nor desire can constitute a communal nexus, for however they and their gratification are metaphorized into images of good-natured congregation (into "The Pepsi Generation," for instance, or into the assertion that "America is turning 7-Up"), they remain a source of human isolation, not of human solidarity. In the novel's terms, this realization means that Flesh has begun to experience, and to recognize that he has begun to experience, the increasing complexity of his life as a "diminishment of passions," as a gradual falling away from and loss of belief in the things that tied him to others.

Flesh's gradual transformation from outer-directed public man to inner-directed private self, from salesman exploiting human needs to consumer engulfed by them, is echoed by the parallel, though more extreme, passage of a number of Finsbergs from life into death. None of the eight who dies succumbs to the ordinary diseases statistically charted by the AMA; they die, instead, of absolutely individual defects. Kitty is poisoned by the salts in her urine in which she slept every night; Jerome defecates his colon in response to doctors' attempts to cure his chronic constipation; Noel infects his cradle cap by scratching it nervously upon learning of the other deaths; Moss slams into a truck sided with an alloy his eyes have never been able to perceive. The others are similarly struck down by grotesque consequences of their "dark diathenics," their fatal illnesses, as Flesh thinks, "like signature, like customized curse" (p. 307). The survivors are rendered dumbstruck by this chain of terrible deaths and appeal to Flesh for explanation, chorally lamenting that

"We don't," Lorenz said
"understand," said Ethel.
"We were always," Sigmund-Rudolph said,
"musical comedy sort of"
"people," said Patty, Laverne and Maxene. [p. 287]

Flesh can offer them little consolation, nor can he tell them how their Broadwayesque lives can result in something so grim as actual death. But he has considered the meaning of the passing of these godcousins, and he has decided in very un-franchiserlike terms what it is. He watches the survivors at the multiple graveside, realizing that they weep for themselves as much as for their lamented brothers and sisters:

Each mourning for each and for his own doom. As he was moved by his multiple sclerosis, his own flawed scaffolding of nerves. Everyone carried his mortality like a birthmark and was a good host to his death. You could not catch anything, and were from the beginning already caught. As if Lorenz or Cole, Patty, Mary or himself carried from birth the very diseases they would die of. Everything was congenital, handsomeness to suicide. [p. 290]

The Broadway vision cannot work if we are all, in some ultimate sense, our physical fates, that physical nature finally necessitating our withdrawal from the rousing American choral ensemble so that we might have the privacy in which to nurture our deaths. That affirmation cannot, Flesh has realized, offer any solace to one such as himself, a man whose choral identity is gradually being self-circumscribed by disease, a franchiser whose reports to the surviving Finsbergs become progressively less concerned with the businesses he is buying and operating and progressively more concerned with the symptoms of his internal deterioration. The franchiser is very much a man of flesh, then, one poorly suited to live in the realm of the ideal, even if that ideal is only one of American commercial optimism. His hands and nerves are an ever-present reminder that the physical is the ground of all being, and that the ground of his being is in the process of collapsing beneath him.

And yet Flesh never entirely abandons his commercial, communal, comedic understanding of things, partly because it has become so much a part of him that to reject it would be to throw off his only self. Consequently, he insists that the Finsberg dead be buried in like coffins, as if in parodic fulfillment of his former dream of restoring them to identicality. Flesh also wants the period of mourning in Riverdale to be filled with melodies from the shows that Julius Finsberg costumed, not the "you-can't-lick-us indomitable stuff" songs, but the chorus numbers, the entire cast tunes,

all the cowboys and their girls singing "Oklahoma!," the veterans singing "Call Me Mister," the elf and townspeople singing "On That Great Come and Get It Day," the fishermen and their families doing "June Is Bustin' Out All Over." It was, that is, the community numbers that reinforced them, the songs that obliterated differences, among men and women, among principals and walk-ons. Not the love songs, not even the hopeful, optimistic songs of the leads who, down and out, in the depths of their luck, suddenly blurt their crazy confidence. Again and again it was the townsfolk working as a chorus, three dozen voices singing as one, that got to them, appealing to some principle of twin- and tripletship in them, decimated as their ranks now were. The odd bravery of numbers and commonality, a sort of patriotism to one's kind. And Ben, more unlike them than ever, now he looked so old and felt so rotten, as cheered and charmed as any of the Finsbergs could have been. [p. 290]

This passage represents the novel's most detailed evocation of the Finsberg/Flesh Broadway vision and the values and hopes underlying it. If it reflects, too, the flimsiness of the vision's hope and the absurdity of its democratic ideals, it also catches some of the exhilaration and joy implicit in that vision—for Flesh, at any rate. It is no exaggeration to say that *The Franchiser* succeeds as a novel only insofar as it convinces its reader of the absolute continuity between the ideas expressed in this paragraph and Ben Flesh's desire to give the nation "its visual props...all its *things*, all its *crap*, the true American graffiti, that perfect queer calligraphy of American signature, what gave it its meaning and made it fun" (p. 270).

Flesh's vision is by no means to be dismissed as the sentimentalism of a seriously ill man or as the delusion of one who has taken the promises of American merchantry too literally, though both of these do figure in his character. He is better understood as an exaggerated representation of how a generation of Americans comprehended the world and their lives in it; his self-proclaimed decline into age and irrelevance reflects their parallel, if less precipitous, experience of the passing of the world they knew and their sense of their unsuitability to the one which has taken its place. The obsolescence of his ways of thinking first becomes obvious to Flesh when he visits Kansas City's Crown Center, a shopping mall predicated upon business assumptions very different from those under which he has operated his own concerns. Crown Center is something like a museum of mid-twentieth-century realities, an exposition of plants, trees, waterfalls, airplanes, streets—all those commonplaces of contemporary life that are expected to disappear with the further deterioration of the environment and the eventual exhaustion of the nation's energy resources. Even more troubling, from Flesh's perspective, is the preponderance of specialty shops (he is, after all, an obliterator of differences and queller of distinctions), shops that sell nothing but dollhouse furniture or candles or personalized hand stamps. These boutiques bear not the names of familiar national companies but names suggesting homey, cottage-industry sincerity and coyness—an art gallery named Ethnics, a bakery named The Bake Shop, a furniture store named Habitat. That such shops violate Flesh's franchiser ethic—his belief in the ultimate validity of identical franchise units reflecting one nationally familiar corporate source, situated such that random vehicular traffic will find them convenient and accessible—is obvious. Consequently, he flees the Center, making his way out "by means of necessary detours" much as he had fled the Midwest power outages seeking "a hole in the heatwave" (p. 164), intuitively aware that both Crown Center and energy depletions are confronting him with an exactly defined reality that has nothing to do with mansard roofs, fun, musical comedy, or—because he won't live to see it become the norm—him. It is partly in response to his premonitory aversion to Crown Center that an inebriated Flesh, eating dinner at a nostalgia restaurant with some fellow franchisers, begins to mock the restaurant and abuse its staff, sensing that the present is being systematically diminished from both directions. Restaurants like this one banish it in celebration of yesteryear; shopping malls like Crown Center usher in the fu-

Reading Stanley Elkin

ture before its time. What he is able to lash out against when drunk he must submit to in silence when sober, acquiescing to the knowledge that those who created Crown Center are "way ahead of him, way ahead of the franchiser with his Robo-Washes and convenience food joints. . . . Why, he was decadent, a piece of history, the yesterday kid himself, Father Time, Ol' Man River—his America, the America of the interstates, of the sixties and middle seventies, as obsolete and charming and picturesque as an old neighborhood" (p. 166).

The world that Crown Center and the brownouts foreshadow is all but upon him; Flesh admits this to himself even as he is building his Travel Inn, the franchise that is to represent the real culmination of his career. What he fears most about that world is not that he will be a cripple in it, or that it will "oldtimer him," imposing upon him the familiar mannerisms of outrage and astonishment that are the elderly's habitual responses to manifestations of the world to come. These prospects alarm him less than does the utter alienness of this world to anything he has ever thought, felt, or hoped. The man who wants to unite the nation under one commercial banner can only be appalled to find the "new dispensation" actually increasing the distances between places, altering the scale of things, "space compounding itself like the introduction of a new dimension." For the man who holds to the musical-comedy perception of things, with its assumption of ultimate inconsequence, human interchangeability, reversibility, and the promise of second and third chances, the "new dispensation" can represent nothing other than a horror; its omnipresence, inevitability, and imperviousness to the dreams of human beings utterly doom all his hopes. Whereas Flesh is attracted by consolidation, plenitude, and organization, the new dispensation is characterized by disunion, deficiency, and chaos. Flesh learns quickly to appreciate the power of this adversary, naming it "the expanding universe here, America's molecules drifting away from each other like a blown balloon, like heat rising, the mysterious physical laws gone public" (p. 306).

The "expanding universe" concept accounts for a number of occurrences in the novel, this new dispensation progressively overcoming the explanatory vision of Ben Flesh throughout the book's

Demyelinating America and the Stricken Burger King

final scenes. The deterioration of the Finsbergs' "tract house mode of being," their simultaneous decline into difference and death, is one manifestation of the emergence of this new human physics of drifting molecules, Flesh at one point explicitly referring to their dissolution as "an expanding universe theory of Finsbergs" (p. 273). This metaphoric extension of the significance of the Finsbergs' decline heightens not only the absurdity but also the crazy heroism of Flesh's endeavors to hold them together in the face of opposed scientific necessity.

It is no coincidence, then, that the event that culminates Flesh's various failures to rescue and reunite the Finsbergs is brought about by a circumstance clearly paralleling the expanding-universe notion. Having planned the location of his Travel Inn with great deliberation, in hopes of translating its success into a restoration of the Finsbergs to themselves and to him, Flesh discovers that the national fifty-five-mile-per-hour speed limit enacted between the time of the motel's planning and its completion has significantly altered the distances upon which his concept of the "gas/food/lodging synapses" of the American traveler is predicated. This new law transforms Ringgold, Georgia, Flesh's prime Travel Inn site, from a perfect midway point on the southern route from numerous northeastern population centers to the recently opened Disney World into a "sort of place" halfway between the post-law natural rest stops imposed— or created—by energy-drained America. The dislocation, which lands tourists in Chattanooga or Atlanta for the night, instead of in Ringgold, is infinitesimal in relation to the magnitude of the universe's expansion, but it is more than enough to insure that what has been intended as the crowning achievement of Flesh's franchising career will prove a losing proposition, its chances for success as dispersed now as "America's molecules drifting away from each other like a blown balloon" (p. 306).

Even before it opens, the Travel Inn proves to be a failure at what Flesh had most wanted it to accomplish, and all that is left for him is to experience the culminating repudiation of his franchiser vision on the first night of business. Once the few guests who have stumbled upon the new establishment are in their rooms, Flesh inadvertently overhears the moans of a couple copulating in the room next to his; he then tours the hallways to discover that all of his guests are involved in sexual activity of one kind or another. ("'What's this? what's this?'" he mutters as he moves from door to door, echoing Angelo's astonishment at the arousal of his own passion by Isabella in *Measure for Measure*, the two men having been previously and similarly reluctant to recognize sexuality as a central issue in human life.) Exhilarated and yet disturbed by this discovery, Flesh hurries to the lobby to report his news to other Travel Inns over the Inn-Dex, the chain's intercommunications system. Much to his disappointment, other Travel Inns respond that their rooms also resound with the exotic squeal and coital cry; one operator confirms Flesh's hypothesis, concluding that "YOU PUT YOUR FINGER ON IT, RINGGOLD, THE WORLD IS A VERY SEXY PLACE" (p. 329). Before long the franchise headquarters in Richmond knocks Flesh and his respondents off the Travel Inn airwaves, but by this time he has a new insight concerning the adhesive that binds the American nation. He had hoped the other Travel Inn operators would report that their guests were doing what Flesh had encouraged the couple next door to do as he ushered them to their room: take a swim, eat dinner in the restaurant, stop by the bar for a nightcap when the combo is playing, watch a little color TV, drift off to sleep in the motel's comfortable double beds. Instead they love, masturbate, commit incest, and do anything else they can think of to achieve physical gratification. Their indulgence in the sensual is so national and so unvarying as to compel Flesh to concede that this, like all nights, is "love night," and that "Not even the time differential made any difference, finally, Ringgold's nighttime, California's evening, love's mood obliterating time and space and all zones erogenous" (p. 329).

"Obliterating time and space" in the name of some unifying concept has ever been one of Flesh's fondest objectives, but for personal as well as philosophical reasons "love's mood" is not the agent he had hoped would accomplish the task, sexual appetite never having been the "universalized appetite" his life had been dedicated to appeasing. In personal terms, "love's mood" is no longer more than an inconstant reality for Flesh. His paresthetic fingers have "deadened others as well as himself," turning "whole populations into wood and stone" and giving them the "dead, neu-

Demyelinating America and the Stricken Burger King

tral texture of plastic" (p. 227). From a philosophical—or franchiser—perspective, "love's mood" is inadequate as a consolidating force because it brings two people together at best, and at worst it sets numerous others at odds with each other. Rather than providing a basis upon which the solidarity of mankind can be established and human suffering and loneliness diluted, sexuality as an ultimate value celebrates the individual's need for self-gratification, affirming the other only as a means to that end. It is no more capable, finally, of leading toward the realization of the communal ideal than is the commercial ethic. Both ultimately presuppose the irreducible self and its incommunicable and ungratifiable needs as the one absolute in existence.

As a cultural adhesive and bulwark against national dispersion, sexuality is an even less adequate agent than many of the comical possibilities that Flesh proposes—Burt Reynolds movies (the "PG's and R's of our collectivized souls and Esperanto'd judgment" [p. 232]), community sings from musical comedies, or a chain of indistinguishable franchises. What disturbs Flesh is that he has misunderstood everything from the beginning. Now he realizes that " 'love is sweeping the country and lyrics are the ground of being, singing the literature of the ordinary, and romance is as real as heartburn. Because guys score and stare at the woman next to them and trace their fingers gently over their sweethearts' eyebrow breaking like a wave' " (p. 330). He understands that, in spite of illness and death, the urge to love endures, and this nearly solitary passion (which he has known only in the most perfunctory ways) underlies reality, defines and shapes it more thoroughly than his paltry commercial candidates for deep-structure irreducibility ever could.

His communal vision necessarily pared down now to the unit of couples (" 'Everyone everywhere is evidence, datum,' " he tells his nightclerk, " 'We're the proof. Everyone at the Super Bowl is a fact of fuck' " [p. 328]), Flesh has still to experience the further reduction of that given by half before he confronts his own position in the world, though he perhaps mercifully misinterprets the significance of what he sees. Waking at 3:30 a.m. from a brief nap in the motel lobby following his "love night" communiques, Flesh glances up at an elaborately lit display board bearing a map of the United States with symbols designating the other Travel Inns. Rising to study this display more closely, he decides that its real significance lies in its confirmation of his franchiser's vision, in its demonstration of the fact that the interstates have made it necessary for there to be mileage signs for Washington, D.C., in the Bronx, for St. Louis to post signs directing through traffic to Des Moines and Tulsa. Encouraged by this apparent contradiction of the nation's endlessly disquieting tendency to disperse and expand, Flesh further considers the map and concludes that its superimposed circles joining cities within the same radius of each other suggest "loops of relationship" beyond anything he has previously perceived. "He is equidistant," we are told in the novel's indirect interior monologue narrative,

from the Atlantic Ocean and the Gulf of Mexico and Pine Bluff, Arkansas, and Centralia, Illinois, he could as easily be in Columbus, Ohio, as in Petersburg, Virginia. New Orleans rings him, Covington, Kentucky, does. He is surrounded by place, by tiers of geography like bands of amphitheater. He is the center. If he were to leave now, striking out in any direction, northwest to Nashville, south to Panama City, Florida, it would make no difference. He would stand before maps like this one in the older Travel Inns. Anywhere he went he would be the center.

Only the most obtuse reader will need the sentence that follows this passage and makes explicit the circumstance it dramatizes: "It was the start of his ecstasy attack" (p. 333).

Flesh's franchiser vision and his disabling disease, which have been metaphoric counterparts throughout the novel, at this point elide into one another, becoming literally indistinguishable. The euphoria that signals the onset of a later, more serious stage of his illness is now upon him, and he responds to it by seeking an external source for the sudden happiness he feels, locating it in the map of Travel Inns. What this map dramatizes, he imagines, is the ultimate success of his life's venture, the realization of his attempt to pull all of American place within one orbit and to achieve a visual consolidation of space, to prove that America is America everywhere. Having now seen the "loops of relationship" that had eluded his perception before, Flesh finally understands that his plan has worked, that he is

Demyelinating America and the Stricken Burger King

now justified in saying, "He could as easily be in Columbus, Ohio, as in Petersburg, Virginia," for the American commercial exterior that he has sought to impose upon the land has, he imagines, eliminated all differences between these places, and has thus succeeded in obliterating the human subjection to the necessity and inescapability of spatial limitation.

What Flesh imagines this map to signify is not, however, all that the reader takes it to represent. Rather than the gathering-in of spaces that Flesh sees as the map's object lesson, the reader cannot help but notice the similarities in Flesh's perception to the *expanding universe* notion, with its assumptions of the equality of distances increased between any two points, and the scale of all distances simultaneously increasing. Still more significantly, Flesh's perception refutes the very vision he believes it to confirm; his communal assumptions surrender in it to the ultimate paring-down implicit in the realization that "He is the center," and that "Anywhere he went he would be the center." This insight is, of course, a euphoria-induced delusion. But it describes quite precisely the extent to which circumstance and illness have reduced Flesh to an isolate individual, his own personal, portable center because he no longer has anyone but himself to care about. The Finsbergs have disinherited him because their depleted ranks make it impossible for them to hold his paper in difficult times, and they are themselves gradually retreating into death; in addition, he has mortgaged most of his other franchises to the success of his Travel Inn, and consequently his "grand rounds" are attenuated, reduced. He is left, then, with a reduced itinerary, a body that confuses him into happiness when circumstances dictate nothing other than sorrow, and an absurd sense (in some inverted way true), that he is the center, coupled with an inability to recognize how thoroughly this insight contradicts his ideal communal vision.

By the penultimate chapter Flesh has reached a point not unlike that reached by the protagonists of Elkin's other novels. We last see Boswell hurling imprecations at the celebrities arriving for the opening of the Club he has created as a monument to his own ego, his renunciation of the old self's medium of apotheosis representing an affirmation of the achievement of a new, equally voracious, self.

Reading Stanley Elkin

In the process of being beaten—perhaps to death—by Fisher and the inmates the warden commands, Feldman experiences the revelation that he is not a "bad man" but one who loves his life and whose expansion through the empty spaces of the world is just beginning. For Dick Gibson and Ben Flesh, on the other hand, the revelation of the ultimacy and primacy of the self is ambivalent in a different sense, one experienced, insofar as it is consciously registered, as a repudiation of the ideal vision of communality and shared human purpose. Not only does his "Night Letters" show fail to locate or create for itself an audience of other-directed, public-spirited Americans, but it actually encourages inwardness and self-absorption in Gibson's listeners as well as in himself, all of them finally submitting to "mindless obsession" and life's "Dow-Jones concern with itself" (p. 331). Still more ambivalent, and doubly poignant, is Flesh's Travel Inn map revelation, which he interprets as the confirmation of his franchiser vision but which is actually its ultimate refutation, a mere prefigurement of the solitude that is to be his as he sets off again on his "grand rounds."

The novel ends where it began, with Flesh gassing up at a service station in Birmingham, Alabama, in the late summer of 1975. What had been puzzling in the opening pages is clear now: Flesh's uncertainty as to whether he is in Birmingham, Alabama, or Birmingham, Michigan, reflects his euphoric sense of the common-denominating vision realized, as does the first chapter's closing sentence, "It's a beautiful day in the United States of America" (p. 5). Clear, too, now is his gameshow-host chumminess with the station attendant, his unrestrained delight in the commonplace features of this ordinary city, and his certainty that another driver having his car serviced here is his good friend; all of these eccentricities are attributable to his disease-induced ecstasy. The novel's final chapter, which functions more as an epilogue than as an extension of the plot, serves primarily to confirm two of Flesh's earlier established apprehensions. While the attendant services the car of a Minnesotan at another pump, Flesh regales its driver with an account of his stay in the Rapid City hospital, recalling for him an RAF lieutenant suffering from lassa fever (a rare and fatal tropical disease) with whom Flesh shared a ward. In the account of their hospital stay presented earlier in the novel we learn that their exchange of fears, complaints about the unbearable heat, and comparison of symptoms results in friendship; when Flesh is released from the hospital, he refuses to walk around the screen behind which Tanner is lying to say goodbye, afraid that he will find him dead and that this incident will become nothing more than a story that Flesh can tell in his old man's impaired speech, Tanner's extinction reduced to a neatly ironical anecdote. So he leaves the hospital, uncertain whether Tanner lived or died, and thinks little about him until he tells his "friend" from Minnesota about him at the Birmingham gas station. Flesh obviously has forgotten his resolve never to debase the friendship by reducing it to an ironic story to be told in his old age; he not only relates the story but also adds a climax that never happened, describing himself going behind the screen and finding Tanner dead. His speech seems not to be noticeably impaired as he recalls the incident, but it is clear from his frequent injection of "gosh" and "golly" how thoroughly his illness has "oldtimered" him, imposed upon him the "stagy mannerisms" of old age and rendered him vulnerable to the kind of self-indulgent and sentimental raconteurism to which in better days he had sworn never to descend.

He is little more aware of this incident as a trespass upon a previously adopted resolve than he is conscious of the significance of an action that this recollection prompts him immediately to undertake. Reminded of a boy who had started his car for him as he was leaving the hospital, Flesh recalls that his offer of payment had been refused when the boy insisted that Flesh's reassurance that his father, hospitalized by a stroke, would make a full recovery was payment enough. Flesh remembers the boy's father's name—Richard Mullen—and uses the station phone to put in a call to him in Rapid City to learn how he has fared. Mullen's wife answers the phone and immediately collapses the comedic scenario that Flesh had created for Mullen's son and nurtured himself, explaining that her husband had died in the hospital during that summer of 1971. What puzzles Flesh is that the woman is still reduced to tears by a stranger's mention of her husband's name four years after his death, Flesh's musical comedy assumptions having poorly prepared him to understand the irreconcilability of such a loss, his unmoored life having given him sadly little experience in appreciating such devotion.

Flesh's recollection of his friendship and parting with Tanner dramatizes the extent to which his multiple sclerosis has altered and debilitated him, how much it has betrayed him into cheap sentimentality and an old man's garrulousness; his recollection of his untruthfulness with Richard Mullen's son tends to reinvoke that act of selfishness and reinforce it through the heedless phone call, with its underlying assumption that everything always works out in the end. The difference between the fabrication and the phone call, however, is this: Flesh knows he is lying to the boy when he affirms that Mullen is improving, aware that he has talked to no doctors about the man's condition, and he worries about this thoughtless deception as he drives through the Midwest brownouts, convinced that his concern about the matter proves that he has not entered the euphoric stage of the disease that the doctor has recently described to him. By the end of the novel, when he is making the call to Rapid City, the euphoria is upon him, as indicated by his impulsiveness and sentimental presumption in attempting to contact a man he has never met and whose health he takes for granted. The epilogue, then, depicts a Ben Flesh markedly less responsible for the things he says, does, and thinks, and the painfully ambiguous feelings stirred in the reader by this chapter are a consequence of an awareness of the terrible disparity between what Flesh now feels and what the actual circumstances of his situation are, a disparity for which the entire novel has been gradually preparing the reader.

"The problem solved by the sentence in chapter one has *got* to be solved by a more elaborate sentence in chapter two," Elkin has said in an interview, "and by a still more elaborate sentence in chapter three."[13] The more elaborate sentences closing out *The Franchiser* so effectively, persuasively, and movingly articulate Flesh's franchiser vision that they almost compel the reader to forget that the vision is now largely euphoric, the joy primarily chemical. These sentences, in short, are not unlike those through which the vision has previously been expressed, and yet they are more immediate, more convincing, more precisely evocative of the "America of the interstates" in which he had placed so much hope and whose passing is reflected in his own decline. The final few pages of the novel are not, consequently, mere rehearsals of what Flesh has been saying all along; they represent, instead, rhetorical heightenings of his mes-

Demyelinating America and the Stricken Burger King

sage calculated to bring it into equilibrium with the increasing desperation of his circumstances and to emphasize the unresolved tension between the chemical necessity of his perception and its content—between his inability to keep from thinking what he thinks, and what he thinks—upon which the novel closes.

On his way to the Birmingham motel where he will spend the night, Flesh takes inventory of his life, toting up the debits and credits and deciding that it has been a good life, an exciting life, one full of extraordinary experiences (his parents killed in an auto accident, his inheritance of the prime rate, his "very big league" disease) as well as extraordinary people (his godfather, the twins and triplets). Continuing to count his blessings, he celebrates the "musical comedy in his blood. What a heritage! Songs. Standards. Hits. Top of the charts. Whistled. Hummed. Carried on the common American breath. . . . Melodies as familiar as appetite and as pressed upon others as their habits." And, in the final, culminating and synthesizing vision, he is part of it all,

Ben Flesh himself like a note on sheet music, the clefs of his neon logos in the American sky. All the businesses he'd had. The road companies of Colonel Sanders, Baskin-Robbins, Howard Johnson's, Travel Inn, *all* his franchises! Why, he belonged everywhere, anywhere. In California like the sound of juice, Florida like the color of sunlight, Washington and Montana like the brisk smell of thin height, and Missouri like the neutral decent feel of the law of averages. [p. 342]

That this moment represents an apotheosis for Flesh, even if a deluded one, is certain. Gone now is the notion that his franchising is only a configuration of his disease; it has been replaced by the fantasy that he is not merely the center but the consolidator of the nation, the one who holds it together and makes one place out of all its different places.[14] Having become all that he ever wanted to be, all that remains for Flesh is to experience the recognition of a final synthesis between himself, business, and Broadway.

At the motel he decides to order dinner from room service, sit before his window at dusk and "watch out for his signs as they came on in nighttime Birmingham, all the blink-bulb neon and electric extravaganzas that stood out sharp against the sky and proved that every night Broadway opens everywhere" (p. 343). Flesh imagines, clearly enough, that he has succeeded in spreading his Broadway/business religion throughout the nation, countering its expanding-universe tendencies with the values of coherence and consolidation and creating the American "musical comedy democracy" that has always been his ideal. The fusion is, of course, only a metaphoric one, Flesh's similes as much the product of pathology as of poetry; yet for him this resolution is joyful, his happiness chemical but real nonetheless. He knows that the Finsbergs are dying, that his Travel Inn is a disaster, and that he will soon be strapped to a wheelchair, but his euphoria breaks through all of this, allowing him to rededicate himself to his vision, to celebrate its realization, and to sing a Finsbergian hymn of praise to the miracle of existence, one no longer distinguishable from the sentimental choral affirmations that bring down the curtains on so many Broadway musical comedies.

The Franchiser dramatizes the passing not so much of a generation as of a generation's particular mode of thought, the ultimate synthesis of its elements embodied in the figure of Ben Flesh, franchiser. Flesh represents simultaneously the culmination of that way of thinking and its dissolution, its replacement by a grimmer, less anthropocentric and humanistic way of perceiving the universe. At the very moment when Flesh is celebrating the fusion of these elements into a single truth, into an idea of simplicity and purity, his body—his flesh—is enacting the dispersing, dissolving process that will defeat that vision and destroy the visionary. For the moment, however, the franchiser vision and the opposed, disintegrative vision meet and balance each other in a poignant equilibrium, their suspension allowing Elkin to accomplish with the epilogue exactly what he had planned to do: to write a novel with "one of the saddest endings in American literature."[15]

NOTES

1. Elkin, *Boswell,* p. 285.
2. Bargen, "Interview," p. 240.

Demyelinating America and the Stricken Burger King

3. Elkin probably owes the inspiration for carrying characters from one work to another to Faulkner, although he employs the trick far less extensively. In addition to Ben Flesh tuning in Dick Gibson in *The Franchiser,* the anthropologist Morty Perlmutter appears in *Boswell* and "Perlmutter at the East Pole"; Richard Preminger in "The Guest" has married Norma, whom he dates in "Among the Witnesses"; minor characters such as Nate Lace, Mopiani, and Harold Flesh appear fleetingly in a number of different works. Curiously, Elkin reuses surnames without ever suggesting any links between the characters. His three Feldmans are one example; his two Premingers (Richard and Marshall, of "The Condominium") and two Fleshes (Ben and Harold) are two more.

4. Doris Bargen emphasizes the centrality of occupations in Elkin's fiction in her entry on Elkin in *American Novelists Since World War II, Dictionary of Literary Biography,* vol. 2, ed. Jeffrey Helterman and Richard Lyman (Detroit: Gale Research, 1978), pp. 131-36, and throughout *The Fiction of Stanley Elkin.*

5. Stanley Elkin, "Performance and Reality," *Grand Street* 2:4 (Summer 1983): 110-11.

6. Elkin's relative indifference to the plot element of fiction is reflected in a comment to Scott Sanders: "I admire a writer like Iris Murdoch, whose novels are superbly plotted. I admire a writer like William Trevor, whose novels are masterpieces of plot. An attention to writing ought not to exclude an attention to plot. In my case it does" (Sanders, "Interview" p. 143).

7. In their *Iowa Review* dialogue Elkin and William Gass agree that, as Gass puts it, "Good books isolate you; they show how individual and unique and different—and the responsibility of that—experience is." Elkin adds, "Right. If my books have a theme, it is the theme of self, the self and its diseases, and the diseases as health" (Duncan, "Conversation with Elkin and Gass," p. 56).

8. Bernt and Bernt, "Stanley Elkin on Fiction," p. 25.

9. In his lyrical foreword to the paperback edition of *The Franchiser* ([Boston: Nonpareil Books, 1980], pp. vi-xv), William Gass plays variations on this line as a means of characterizing Elkin's characteristic attitude toward the grubby urban landscape he habitually depicts. Although Elkin "knows motels, as habitable space, are like the shaven cunt of a packaged whore, still he hums his hymns," Gass wrote, "although he knows how many streets are foul-smelling, dangerous, as full of *E. coli* as the lower intestine, he warbles away,"

and so on, the passage also echoing Flesh's end-of-novel amazement that, despite all the infectious diseases to which men and women are vulnerable, " '*still* they smooch!' "

10. It is exceedingly unlikely that Elkin would ever have thought of using multiple sclerosis as a cultural symbol had he not himself been afflicted with the disease, but the awareness of its autobiographical roots, rather than diminishing our sense of his achievement in *The Franchiser,* tends instead to make our admiration for his ability to transform a physical reality into a complex symbol that much greater. Dostoevski managed, T. S. Eliot once argued, to treat the hysteria and epilepsy from which he suffered in such a way that the afflictions "cease to be the defects of an individual and become—as fundamental weaknesses can, given the ability to face and study it—the entrance into a genuine and personal universe" ("London Letter," *The Dial* 19 [September 1922]: 301). Much the same could be said of Elkin's treatment of his disease in *The Franchiser.*

11. The ultimate futility of Flesh's search for uncompromised sources of energy is effectively foreshadowed by his exultant discovery of a blazing light emanating from Columbus, Nebraska. The light turns out to be the eternal flame of a monument honoring the town's war dead.

12. Didion compares the shift in attitudes and expectations that she (and, she implies, many others) experienced in the late 1960s to the disease's effect of rerouting the normal neural circuitry of the body so that the old impulses remain constant but become expressed through the wrong nerves. Values, by implication, become similarly confused for Didion and for her culture, because in light of the disease "all connections were equally meaningless and equally senseless" ("The White Album," in *The White Album* [New York: Simon and Schuster, 1979], p. 45).

13. Duncan, "Conversation with Elkin and Gass," p. 59.

14. Flesh's image of himself spanning from coast to coast here is reminiscent of similar self-expansions imaginatively experienced by other Elkin protagonists. Boswell has a dream that dramatizes his desire to be more than one single man: "I wanted to be everyone in this room and all the people in the streets outside the Club and all the people everywhere who had ever lived. What did it mean to be just Boswell, to have only Boswell's experience?" (p. 336). Compare, too, Feldman's vision of himself "filling the world, all its desert

Demyelinating America and the Stricken Burger King

spaces and each of its precipices, all its surfaces and everywhere under its seas" (*ABM,* p. 336) as the Fisher-led inmates close in upon him at the novel's end.

15. Elkin made this comment in a class of mine at the University of Southern California in November 1978. He told Doris Bargen, similarly, that he was attempting in *The Franchiser* to write "the saddest possible of happy endings" (Bargen, "Interview," p. 223).

5

The Flashy Grammar of Body Contact and a Condo's Siren Song

When an accomplished novelist is writing at the peak of his literary and imaginative abilities, it often happens that the protagonist of his novel gradually emerges as an embodiment or dramatization of some central, distinctive element of his style. It follows that, as Tony Tanner has argued in *City of Words*,[1] the character's struggle with circumstance on the plot level exists in analogous relation to the attempt of the style to master its chosen material on the work's formal plane. The most familiar and self-evident example of this circumstance in modern literature may be found throughout Hemingway's more successful fiction, where characters such as Nick Adams (in third-person narratives), Robert Jordan, or Harry Morgan come to dramatically represent (and even to defend against competing visions of reality) the style that has created them, so thoroughly have they come to embody that style, and so thoroughly has it come to imply them. We see the same process at work, as Richard Poirier has demonstrated,[2] in first-person narratives such as *Huckleberry Finn* or *The Catcher in the Rye*, where the protagonists' struggles to free themselves from social conventions include strong stylistic components that have themselves come to represent something like nationally recognized idioms of rebellion and renunciation. In such works form is not merely mirroring content, then; style is being given a dramatic analogue on the level of plot.

The Elkin novel in which this convergence of style and story is most conspicuously achieved is *The Franchiser*, that novel most successfully effecting a confluence of crucial elements of prose style with the perceptions and ideals of the protagonist.[3] Ben Flesh, as we have seen, is "a man of franchise, a true democrat," one who would "quell distinction, obliterate difference, who would common-denominate until Americans recognize that it was America everywhere" (p. 164). He is the perfect protagonist, then, for a writer whose favorite rhetorical device is the simile and whose style is elastic and inclusive enough to incorporate disparate, normally incongruous gatherings of reference, metaphor, allusion, and subject into its heedless forward rush. What his style expresses at its most basic level—and this is a central lesson of Elkin's Washington University writing workshops[4]—is that things look like other things, *are* like other things. In order to demonstrate this truth his style will often transform nouns into verbs ("Esperanto'd judgment," "Kopechne'd"), exploit the implications of a concept to translate it into a metaphor (good health being described as having one's "proteins in the Swiss banks of being," a shopping center where political candidates once gathered to debate presented as "a Gettysburg of the rhetorical"), turn phrases into elaborate adjectives (the "gas/food/ lodging synapses of the American public," "out-on-a-limb toe balances," " 'What a *live wire,* go-to-hell-god-damn-it town!' ") or into portmanteau'd verbs ("on-the-job trained in hamburgerology"). His style will manipulate familiar slogans or song lyrics into joking descriptions of objects or situations (Flesh responds to new-model cars with their concealed headlights and windshield wipers by wondering, "Where have all the headlights gone?" and asking, "What, it ain't gonna rain no more, no more?"); it will present a yoking of terms from discontinuous subject realms as a form of description (urban renewal depicted as "Real Estate's chemotherapy," the characteristic epicenity of one of the Finsbergs expressed as "all the citrics of plangent faggotry"); or it will offer catalogues proving that apparently dissimilar things are, from another perspective, closely related to one another (Flesh's listing of examples that prove the extent to which we live in remission—sleep, childhood, weekends and holidays, honeymoons, and so on). These characteristics by no means exhaust the distinctive quirks of Elkin's style; they don't begin to account for the almost Joycean plethora of rhetorical forms with which his work is studded, for instance. They do, taken in the aggre-

Reading Stanley Elkin

gate, suggest how thoroughly Elkin's style tends toward the inclusive, the undifferentiating—toward, in short, the anti-hierarchical.

Although not actually resembling the styles of Pynchon or Coover, Elkin's style is similar to theirs in its parallel tendency toward the denial of incongruity and of levels of significance, and in its deliberate attempt to demonstrate linguistically the indivisibility of existence by enveloping within its single frame all of the apparently disparate material it can assimilate. These writers' styles are, to put the matter another way, in- if not anti-decorous, inherently opposed to arbitrary and groundless divisions of human experience into seemly compartments or mentally useful categories. By their very all-inclusiveness of tones, dictions, and syntaxes, these styles deny hierarchical conceptions of reality and repudiate all those distinctions (high and low, cultured and vulgar, upper and lower, major and minor) upon which such conceptions necessarily rest; their styles implicitly affirm the basic impartibility of human experience by demonstrating that existence cannot be honestly comprehended in any terms other than holistic ones. For each of these writers the antinomies and incongruities of existence have their being on one and the same plane; they are not cordoned off from each other in value-laden compartments, but are inextricably mixed and mingled in human experience. That being the case, these writers' styles must mix and mingle them as heedlessly and indecorously as life itself does. A striking capacity of Pynchon's characteristic style, for instance, is its ability to move smoothly from a technical discussion of rocket telemetry to amusing recountings of old movie plots to meditations upon the relation between sex and death to the presentation of burlesque skits, the style of *Gravity's Rainbow* all but defying the reader to raise the objection of incongruity, for it has made of incongruity a kind of consonance and coherence. The third-person narrative voice that Coover uses in *The Public Burning* similarly refuses to distinguish or delineate between the serious and the trivial, between terror and cartoon, between culture and crap, its esemplasticity allowing for the narrative's successful introduction of a comic folk hero into an otherwise verisimilar and meticulously researched depiction of early 1950s Washington, D.C.

Although Elkin's style is seldom called upon to accommodate

The Flashy Grammar of Body Contact

subjects as disparate as those that Pynchon's and Coover's must habitually assimilate, his work resembles theirs in the extent to which its very existence repudiates hierarchical perceptions of reality and in its style's tacit assumption that life is unileveled and indivisible. Ben Flesh addresses himself to this point when he rises at a Radio Shack convention to salute a new technological advance in sound reproduction. " 'We live in a century of mood,' " he tells his fellow franchisers, " 'and until this afternoon only headphones gave the illusion of "separation." There is no separation. There are no concert halls in life. Nor do we see in 3-D. The chairs do not stand out. Only in stereopticons are the apples closer than the pears' " (*TF*, p. 174). With the exception of what we have been calling the selfhood theme, no notion so thoroughly permeates Elkin's fiction as does this idea of the wholeness, the simultaneity and impartibility of existence, a fact completely consonant with its representing one of the primary assumptive underpinnings of his style. Hierarchy—system, chain of command—is what Fisher represents in *A Bad Man*, for instance, and his description of God ("God is design, Grace is a covenant") accurately describes the Creator in *The Living End* Who has ordered the cosmos into Earth, Heaven and Hell, and Who Himself is revealed to be a distinctly human, remarkably unotherly deity in the course of the triptych. Jake Greenspahn has to relinquish his belief in his dead son's saintliness and recognize that he was not above life but in it in "Criers & Kibitzers, Kibitzers & Criers." Richard Preminger of "Among the Witnesses" is compelled to give up his bachelor's distinction between women one marries and women one toys with at resorts (or, to put it differently, he learns that there are no resorts from life). Bertie of "The Guest" delights in the prospect of showing the newly married Premingers that a clown can be a thief, that a schlemiel can inspire astonishment and fear. Underlying the whole collection of stories is the recognition that life is full of "criers, ignorant of hope," and "*kibitzers*, ignorant of despair": "each with his pitiful piece broken from the whole of life, confidently extending only half of what there was to give" (*C&K*, p. 35). Dick Gibson is thinking in the same spirit when he meditates upon his listeners (housewife, anthropology professor, cave man, rich kid, mobster) and the extent to which they (and he) share the same afflic-

Reading Stanley Elkin

tion, "everyone blameless as himself, everyone doing his best but maddened at last, all, all zealous, all with explanations ready at hand and serving an ideal of truth or beauty or health or grace. Everyone—everyone. It did no good to change policy or fiddle with format. The world pressed in. It opened your windows" (*DGS,* p. 331). That existence cannot be categorized or compartmentalized, segmented or arranged into hierarchical planes is hardly an idea original with Elkin, but it is nonetheless a central theme in his work, unmistakably present in both the content and the form of his fiction.

Insofar as the basis for such philosophical presupposition in an author's work can be explained, the leveling tendencies of Elkin's style and content might be attributed to the idea expressed in the first line of his first novel, *Boswell:* "Everybody dies, everybody." Elkin's preoccupation with death, which he has quite openly discussed in interviews,[5] invokes at once the existentialist writers for whom he had admitted a youthful enthusiasm, but it is suggestive, too, of medieval conceptions of death as the great equalizer, the ultimate leveler of the arbitrary ranks, roles, and status of humanity. Boswell is not, as a number of commentators have noticed, the only Elkin character who is obsessed with his own mortality.[6] Feldman of "In the Alley" sacrifices all comfort and dignity to insure himself a heroic death, one experienced in extremity, while his namesake in *A Bad Man* thinks constantly about the "eternal lean years of death" that await him. Dick Gibson wants his show to counter all morbid thoughts, seeing it as "a sign in the night that there was no death" (*DGS,* p. 206), and Flesh responds to the passing of the Finsbergs by evolving his view that "everyone carried his mortality like a birthmark and was a good host to his death" (*TF,* p. 290). Whether the certainty of mortality can be said to underlie the leveling tendencies within the form and content of Elkin's work is debatable, but death constantly appears associated with equalizing, undifferentiating tendencies in the world, and these combine to constitute a complex of ideas opposed by a contrary formal and philosophical strain in his stories and novels.

To recognize the common-denominating aspect of Elkin's style is, in other words, to recognize only half of that style's predominant effect—to represent it only as crier and not as kibitzer. It is to ignore as well the element of his style that has been most enthusiastically celebrated by his fans and most roundly condemned by his detractors. Elkin's style is nothing if not elaborately and self-consciously poetic in its concern with the sound of the English language and in its dedication to vitality and evocativeness; it is tirelessly committed to visualization and novelty, precise and all-but-exhaustive descriptions of objects tumbling breathlessly upon outbursts of puns, neologisms, comic solecisms and barbarisms, apostrophes and similar rhetorical pyrotechnics. John Gardner's description of "Elkin at his best," though itself somewhat overwrought, accurately gauges this aspect of Elkin's characteristic conjunction of form and content: "It's raw energy that Elkin loves—in prose and in characters. He's Ahab smashing through the mask with jokes, an eternal child whose answer to oppressive reason is to outperform it, to outshout it."[7] Elkin has himself made similar comments about the centrality of energy—often rhetorical energy—as a value in his work,[8] and it is not difficult to connect this aspect of the prose with the thematic strain in his fiction that counters its leveling, normalizing tendencies—the affirmation of the isolate individual or, as Elkin summarized the theme in an interview, the notion that "The SELF takes precedence." It is not surprising to discover that the primary conflict we have located in Elkin's fiction (which might be variously described as a confrontation between uniformity and individualism, communality and self, the ordinary and the particular or the personal) reduplicates itself in antinomies discernible on the formal level, but it is a point worth examining because of its special importance in the novellas of *Searches & Seizures,* works that dramatize the tension between these contraries in remarkably explicit terms.

The protagonists of "The Bailbondsman," "The Making of Ashenden," and "The Condominium" have two important characteristics in common. They are all (as Elkin's prefatory note points out) men extraordinarily aware of their own mortality, men whose actions arise in large part out of that very recognition; but they are also extremely sensitive to the language through which they present themselves to the world, constantly considering how the language works, what it means, and what it commits them to. These three novellas, then, represent three different versions of the confrontation

Reading Stanley Elkin

between the contraries that underlie Elkin's style, that constitute its paradox and give it its sense of tension—the antitheses of the awareness of death and the ability of language to hold death off, to pit form, structure and meaning against their ultimate dissolution. Or, to put the opposition in different terms, these novellas dramatize the self's confrontation with the fact of its own extinction, and its attempt to at once deny and reconcile itself to this fate through the self-assertions of language. This basic antithesis is not expressed in such Manichean terms in the novellas, of course: the language can be put to the service of death, of dissolution and the extinction of the self, and the assertion of self can, conversely, leave the self-asserter with no choice but self-destruction. The basic antinomy, manipulated or qualified as it might be, remains crucial to the understanding of these novellas, however, as language offers the only medium through which the self can be reconciled (and then only tentatively, temporarily) to the imminence of its own extinction. The paradox of and tension in Elkin's prose is attributable to its denial of distinction and difference on the one hand, and its simultaneous claims to distinctiveness on its own terms on the other. The style becomes an argument against death and the dissolution of structures and forms, even as it demonstrates that everything succumbs to, is leveled and rendered uniform by, these forces in the end.

Of the three protagonists in *Searches & Seizures*, the one least concerned with death and least consistently self-conscious about his use of language is Brewster Ashenden, the central character of the collection's second work, "The Making of Ashenden." The relative unimportance of these themes, compared to their centrality in the other two works, is perhaps attributable to the fact that only after he finished "The Making of Ashenden" did the idea of a sequence of novellas occur to Elkin.[9] The simplicity and directness with which these themes are addressed in this novella tends to make them more distinct and immediately graspable than in the other two works, where they are more firmly embedded in metaphors and analogies.

Brewster Ashenden doesn't initially think very much about death, but he knows very well what language is and what it is for. Language for him is simply an index of one's social standing and a barometer of one's taste. Ashenden's social standing is very high and his taste refined to an extreme, for he is the scion of a wealthy family, a well-educated and highly civilized young man who is welcome in the most exclusive jet-set homes on all continents. His breeding and good taste are, of course, reflected in his language, which permits nary a "damn," "hell," or "pain-in-the-ass" (his prissy hedge is "pain in the you-know-what") to intrude, and which insists upon the euphemization and sublimation of any term or subject that might be judged unpleasant, physical, or crude. He teasingly tells his dying mother, for instance, that she is a "naughty slugabed" for failing to leave her deathbed and join him in a round of golf, his only explanation for such deliberate fatuousness being that "a code is a code" (p. 136).

It takes very few pages of Ashenden's hyperbolically civilized patter to convince the reader that he is no mere adherent of a code but an utterly encoded being, one for whom taste is a fit substitute for experience and whose every action, verbal and otherwise, is mediated by the best guides to etiquette and social deportment. Having no need to earn a living, Ashenden dedicates his days to the obligatory aristocratic ritual of self-seeking, ultimately finding himself in the person of Jane Loes Lipton, a wealthy socialite so perfectly suited to him that each can anticipate precisely what the other is going to say before he or she says it. She is the "perfection" that has eluded him in his lifelong journey from one estate to another, the embodiment of the "magnetic, Platonic pole, idealism and Beauty's true North" (p. 133) for which he has searched. Her only drawback (which is, within the aristocratic romance tradition in which Ashenden and the story are operating, a definite advantage and seductive virtue) consists in the fact that she is dying, a case of *lupus erythematosus* causing her body to produce antibodies against itself, making her progressively allergic to her own chemistry. To marry her would be to inflict himself with the same necessarily fatal illness. Inspired by the poetry of this romantic doom, Ashenden presses his suit, only to be rejected as unworthy of her hand because he is not a virgin, while she is. She sets him a task: to purify himself or lose her forever, her challenge uniting her with all the fairytale princesses who demand similar (if less earthy) tests of their suitors' ardor and fidelity. Ashenden resorts to mere rhetorical trickery to uncorrupt himself, deciding

Reading Stanley Elkin

that he has attained to a "self-loathing" so extreme that "it *is* purity" (p. 167). Too excited to sleep away the hours before he can bestow his newly chastened self upon Jane, he wanders out into the game preserve that surrounds the estate where he and she are staying to pass the time until dawn.

He is not, as it turns out, fated to escape with a simple self-confrontation, the mere joining of self with its feminine mirror image. Instead, his initiation suddenly becomes a much more menacing confrontation of self and other, the other being, in this instance, a bear in heat. Nor is this a task that he can finesse with language, as he had the initial one, for the bear has a language of its own:

Again it made its strange movement, and this time barked its moan, a command, a grammar of high complication, of difficult irregular case and gender and tense, a classic aberrant syntax. Which was exactly as Ashenden took it, like a student of language who for the first time finds himself hearing in real and ordinary life a unique textbook usage. God, he thought, I understand bear! [p. 178]

Whereas Jane has demanded that he uncorrupt himself if he wants to become one with her in death, the bear is telling him that he must sully himself in sexual contact with her if he hopes to live. Even Ashenden's attempts to reduce the situation to allegory and thus dismiss it ("What this means, he thought, is that my life has been too crammed with civilization. . . . I have been too proud of my humanism, perhaps, and all along not paid enough attention to the base" [pp. 179-80]) cannot save him from the necessity of satisfying the beast. He subsequently discovers that he desires the bear, but by this point his ardor has cooled and he has to whip himself back up by regaling her with conventional endearments, offering seductive smalltalk and predictable verbal inducements (" 'I love you. I don't think I can live without you. I want you to marry me' " [p. 184]), exciting himself into tumescence with the cheap sentiments of ordinary courtship.

His experience with the bear changes not only his language—" 'We are all sodomites,' " he tells himself in mid-coitus, " 'all ped-

The Flashy Grammar of Body Contact

erasts, all dikes and queens and mother fuckers' '' (p. 185)—but also alters his plans, convincing him to renounce the aristocratically romantic death he had resolved to share with Jane in favor of travel to places "further and wilder than he had ever been" (p. 187). What he is repudiating here is not merely death but a solipsistic kind of self-extinction, a death engendered by the self's mating with its mirror image and one characterized, appropriately enough, by a chemical pathology in which the victim's system poisons itself. His coital adventure with the bear has also accomplished the very purpose Jane set him in his task—it has revirginized him through a purification by soiling. He is pure not in the sense that she demanded, of course, but pure in the sense that his sodomy has redeemed him from a life thoroughly insulated by formalities and dictated by codes. In choosing the language of sensuality and anti-social impulse over the lure of romantic self-annihilation, Ashenden frees himself into possibility, tempering his taste with the awareness of the bestial in himself and expanding his notions of heritage to include among the air, earth, water, and fire one additional element—honey.

If it is through activating the language of bear[10] within himself that Ashenden manages to escape the prison of forms and formalities in which he has lived, it is though a similar process that Elkin's language leads his reader in the novella. The excessively refined, fastidious prose with which Ashenden narrates the first two-thirds of the novella gives way to a third-person narrative in the bear fuck scene, where Ashenden's particularity is replaced by evocative precision, his delicacy abandoned in favor of the immediacy of dramatization.[11] The scene is one of the most ambitious, exuberant, and (as numerous reviewers were quick to point out) moving moments in Elkin's fiction, a triumph of language so striking that it fairly overwhelms the protagonist whose experience it describes. The novella not only depicts the situation of one whose expanding lexicon emancipates him from a sterile life, then—it also dramatizes this process by giving the reader a word experience as extreme, as affecting, and as imaginatively liberating as the one that is, in both senses of the phrase, the "Making of Ashenden."

The most lighthearted of the *Searches & Seizures* novellas, "The Making of Ashenden" is also the one most consistently and

Reading Stanley Elkin

comically permeated by the mediating presence of other voices, other books—fairytales and Henry James novels conspicuous among them. "The Condominium," which follows it, is the darkest of the three, largely because it permits, neither the reconciliatory movements nor the peripeteia that allow "The Bailbondsman" and "The Making of Ashenden" to conclude in redemption and the rediscovery of possibility, however qualified. It is also, consistently enough, the novella in which language is revealed to have no redemptive value, no power to pit against the inevitability of death. Language, instead, comes to play a contributing role in the protagonist's suicide. "The Condominium" makes no more final statement than the other novellas, of course, and if its placement at the volume's end gives it a kind of emphasis, its real authority is grounded less in its location than in the unremitting bleakness of its depiction of human existence.

Whereas both "The Bailbondsman" and—in a different sense—"The Making of Ashenden" close upon paroxysms of language that free their protagonists into possibility once again, "The Condominium" opens with a lengthy passage neither capable of redeeming nor reflective of redemption for its writer. The narrative suggests more than anything else the psychological and emotional problems facing Marshall Preminger, a professional lecturer inspired to discourse upon the human instinct toward home-building, toward the ownership of shelter, on the occasion of his inheritance of his father's Chicago condominium. " 'A place to live, to be' " is his theme, his lecture's central question being " 'Out of what frightful trauma of exclusion arose this need, what base expulsion from what cave during which incredible spell of rotten weather?' " (p. 191). He never completely answers this question—or, to put it more precisely, he never becomes conscious that he is answering it—because he doesn't complete the lecture, putting it aside when responsibilities attached to his new property demand his time. What the fragment of the lecture does address itself to is the evolution of a New Jersey summer resort at which his parents had once rented, then owned, a bungalow when he was a boy. In his account he traces the decreasing importance of the open air in the lives of those who inhabit the resort every summer; the canoes, tennis courts, and baseball diamond

The Flashy Grammar of Body Contact

fall into disrepair through lack of use, as if the residents " 'had no interest in the out-of-doors at all, had repudiated it, as if life were meant to be lived inside and the games they once played as bachelor boys and bachelor girls—"The Good Sports," "The Merry Maidens"—were over, literally, the scores frozen, more final than Olympic records' '' (p. 193). What Preminger is unintentionally prefiguring here is his own fate as a thirty-seven-year-old virgin who has never played the games that "bachelor boys and bachelor girls" play, and who will be driven more and more emphatically inside— not only inside the condominium that he has involuntarily inherited, but further inside still, into the absolute solitude of the lonely, irreducible self. His suicide, then, becomes a partial answer to the question, " 'Out of what frightful trauma of exclusion arose this need, what base expulsion from what cave during what incredible spell of rotten weather?' '' But that answer is necessarily a limited and partial one, and the actual source of the specific trauma remains to be revealed.

Preminger's lecture not only addresses itself to the problem that will prove fatally insoluble for him, it also dramatizes it. As he traces the year-by-year growth of the resort and its bungalows, he becomes less capable of cleaving to those issues that make his oration interesting to others, "solipsism" (as Dick Gibson would put it) "drowning out inquiry" (*DGS,* p. 322) over the course of his remarks. At various points in writing the lecture he wanders off into nostalgic reminiscence of his own childhood, becomes so excited about the accuracy of his insights that he must stop and cool down for a day or two before continuing, and generally proves that ordered discourse, the subjugation of self to subject, is no longer within his power. But he begins work on this lecture well after his father dies and he takes possession of the condominium, and only after we understand what his father's death means to him can we begin to see what the apartment and all that comes with it will come to signify.

Preminger is summoned to Chicago by an acquaintance of his father's, and he arrives for the funeral only to suffer two immediate surprises. First, he sees that his coffined father has grown long hair, sideburns, and a mustache since Preminger had last seen him; second, he learns that the estate he had anticipated consists of the condominium and a backlog of unpaid maintenance assessments. The financial disposition of the unit is such that Preminger cannot sell it without forfeiting a third of his father's investment, and thus he resolves to move into the condominium, having his belongings forwarded from Missoula, Montana, because, as he admits to himself, "a life like his could be lived in Montana or Chicago. It made no difference" (p. 221). In an important sense Preminger is not so much transferring his life as exchanging it for another's: "He was in his father's skin now," we are told, "plunging into Pop's deepest furniture, but all along the attraction had been that it was someone else's, that he'd been granted the dearest opportunity of his life—to quit it, a suicide who lived to tell the tale. (But to whom?) Wrapping himself in another's life as a child rolls himself in blankets or crawls beneath beds to alter geography" (p. 224).

The urge of the son to escape his own life and symbolically or literally enter the life of the father is a familiar one, and we are not surprised to find distinct allusions to the archetypal version of this situation appearing shortly following this passage. A neighbor named Evelyn Riker comes to Preminger's door, asking to be let in so that she might explain her relationship with his father, and Preminger is immediately reminded of the women who began coming to his parents' home after the rise of his father's fortunes, women whose appearance he "associated with the TV, and the new gadgets and the other merchandise. Perhaps his own low-level sexuality had to do with his being broke, the hard-on [which he experiences when Mrs. Riker embraces him in grief]...with his being in his father's house again. Which made him an Oedipus of the domestic for whom jealous of his father's place meant just that: *place*" (p. 227). This tacit disclaimer notwithstanding, the two senses of place (as home and as sexual access to the wife/mother figure) prove difficult for Preminger to differentiate; his search for the man whose life he is taking over culminates in the discovery of tawdry details of that man's sexual life. That sexual life is then revealed to have its roots in the upward mobility and achievement of financial security with which Preminger earlier associated it.

Mrs. Riker divulges, in her explanation, that she and the elder Preminger were only friends, residents of the same building who would occasionally talk together at the pool. As they became better acquainted, she would write him letters articulating her views on literature and politics, agreeing in return to keep a key to his condominium so that he might fantasize about her using it one evening. The two responded to each other, she insists, purely as "outlets," their relationship never exceeding the limits of pen pal from one side and object of fantasy from the other. He approves her version of their relationship, surrenders her letters that his father had saved, and accepts her promise that she will return his key as soon as she locates it. Satisfied with this exchange, Preminger rededicates himself to the new life he has moved into, convinced that he can finally elude the "tourist condition" of his old life and rid himself of the "unsavory quality of displaced person" that he has up to now given off (p. 233).

All that initially prevents him from fitting in with the "ordinary life, H.O. scale" of the condominium (p. 234) is his temper, his tendency to lash out against regulations. He admonishes himself, "If I don't stop violating the dress codes I'm a dead man. Where do I get my fury? he wondered. What nutty notions of my character have come on me? What is it with me? What do I think I am—where three roads meet?" (p. 240). This second allusion to the Oedipus story pushes the reference's significance beyond the previously established analogue and aligns the father (the victim of the son's rage at the spot where the three roads meet) with the condominium whose regulations Preminger lashes out against. The aptness of this parallel becomes increasingly clear as it becomes more obvious to Preminger how thoroughly his father had internalized the condominium's ethic and become indistinguishable from the world that it implies.

Preminger proves as capable of turning his anger in upon himself as he is of projecting it outward upon the world, and this trait more than any other dooms his efforts to live a normal life among normal people in the condominium. When a group of chairmen of the complex's association committees visits Preminger to acquaint him with their functions and activities, he is deeply moved. He is impressed, too, by their united front, their reasonable speeches, their "low-court style like foreign language converted in dreams" (p. 249). They express the hope that he will become active in committee work, and he seizes the occasion to answer (" 'I think I can give you assurances now,' " he grandly begins) in the identical civic tone. But only a sentence or two into his remarks his gratitude for their concern quickly shades into self-deprecation, and before long he is discomfiting them all by explaining his lamentable circumstances and bemoaning his fate, much as he does in the autobiographical intrusions in his lecture: " 'My life is a little like being in a foreign country,' " he tells them. " 'There's a displaced person in me. I feel—listen—I feel...*Jewish*. I mean even here, among Jews, where everybody's Jewish, I feel Jewish.' " (p. 250). (The association's spokesman responds to Preminger's confession by pointedly citing a few of the association's regulations, emphasizing particularly that its members must approve all new residents:" '...no chinks, no PR's, no spades,' " he insists, as if he has just found one of these living on the premises in disguise.) To be the one alienated man in a community of the supposedly alienated is Preminger's fate. His loneliness and concomitant certainty that that loneliness is his just desert convince him that his fellow residents must "have his number"—one.

His isolation is temporarily interrupted by his appointment as lifeguard at the condominium swimming pool when a fall hot spell necessitates its being kept open past Labor Day. The role gives him the comforts of a prescribed code of behavior and involvement with those who use the pool. He is encouraged, too, by a letter from Mrs. Riker in which she discusses aspects of "our permissive society," a Philip Roth novel, Mike Nichols's films, and the heat wave, concluding with a postscript noting that she has not yet located his key, but that she will return it to him as soon as she can "lay her hands on it," which she anticipates will be soon. He responds enthusiastically, convinced that she is cryptically promising him that she will soon use the key, sending her a lengthy telegram inviting her to bring the key whenever she finds it. Gradually the hopes he had placed in his pool duties and in Mrs. Riker prove groundless, and he is forced back into himself, bearing a devastating knowledge as the only result of his foray into the world of others.

The pool proves a disappointment because his role allows him only peripheral involvement in the community that gathers there. The bathers and sunners are content to have him listen in on their conversations dealing with the buying of their condos, the gas mileage of their automobiles, their cleaning women, and other concerns of the settled in and secure, those whose apartments give them a platform from which to speak contentedly of life's trivia. Preminger, of course, has achieved no such foothold, his ownership of a condominium notwithstanding. When he is directly addressed by any of the poolside kibitzers, it is usually as a representative of the younger generation whose values aren't their own and whose sympathies they find abhorrent. Normally defensive about the position in which they have placed him, Preminger finally embraces it while attacking those who have imposed it on him. On the pool's closing day he criticizes them for voting Sunday rules into effect for weekdays, thus denying use of the facilities to sons, daughters, and grandchildren, and for never discussing or exchanging pictures of those whom their Sunday rules have excluded. His own father, he angrily insists, could not have lived this condominium life with its implicit denial that the residents had ever had families; he must have proudly displayed pictures of Marshall around this very swimming pool, Preminger is certain, and surely he talked avidly of his son's success on the lecture circuit. But Preminger suddenly recognizes that his father would have concurred in the rules change and talked little of his son, so thoroughly had he bought into the condominium ethos. " 'Shit,' " he complains through his revelation, " 'He never said a word. Like the rest of you. You should see the place. A swinger. He had hair like a pop star' " (p. 294).

Underlying Preminger's petulant outburst is his conviction that the bonds of posterity have been utterly eliminated in the condominium, that the elderly have abandoned completely their parental and grandparental concerns, seeking instead only the gratification of their own private needs and desires. This sour insight into the significance of his father's Danish modern furniture and altered styles of dress and hair is the first of two revelations so devastating to Preminger's sense of the fitness of things that, if they don't actually unhinge his mind (he tells the poolside contingent that he is experiencing a nervous breakdown), they do deprive him of any reason to go on living.

The final revelation takes the form of a second letter from Mrs.

Reading Stanley Elkin

Riker. He finds it under his door upon returning from his emotional outburst at the pool. This letter is not unlike its predecessor in its discursiveness, disingenuous humility, and banal cordiality; her narration of a trivial argument she once had with her former husband is presented in the same stiffly informal, platitude-ridden prose in which she had commented on the work of Roth and Nichols.[12] Nor is that style altered significantly when she shifts from this anecdote to the discussion of the circumstances of Preminger's father's death, a death she not only witnessed but actually caused.

She had decided to return the key, she explains in the letter, and she used it to let herself in when no one answered her knock. She found the senior Preminger, dressed only in briefs, lying on his bed looking seriously ill, and she decided to stay with him despite her awareness that he had misinterpreted the impulse behind her visit. She called a doctor and agreed to lie in bed with the sick man until he arrived, believing that this would calm him. Fearing that the erection resulting from his seizure was exacerbating his discomfort, she "reluctantly" submitted to his entreaties, undressed, and copulated with him. The exertion of coitus killed him. She cleaned away all traces of their intercourse and departed, leaving the dead man to be found by the doctor she had summoned. Her explanation complete, she asks Preminger not to answer her letter, and she promises in a postscript to get his key back to him.

Nervous breakdown notwithstanding, Preminger understands this letter quite fully; he realizes completely, too, with a rising sense of horror, the conflicting impulses of attraction and repulsion that her narrative has inspired in him. What he comprehends only intuitively is the fathomless banality of the document he has just read, its outrageously unintentional dramatization of the extent to which its writer has rationalized into ordinariness her unquestionable complicity in his father's death. Her bland recounting of the event reflects absolutely no hint of awareness of what impact such revelations would have on the victim's son. That her letter is an exercise in unimaginable self-delusion is established by her continued reluctance to surrender the key, with its implicit unwillingness to abandon the hope that the game she played with the father can also be (and is being) carried on with his son. Preminger, however, is concerned with the letter less as a revelation of the bland vileness of Mrs. Riker than as a vehicle of self-confrontation, his reaction to its contents—his hope that the accomplice in his father's death will use the key now, his awareness that this hope reduces him to the same desperate circumstance in which his stricken, tumescent father hopelessly and terribly waited out his final minutes listening for the sound of the key in the lock—manifesting the abject helplessness of his own situation. Her second letter, then, closes off a series of revelations that began with his surprise at his father's modish wardrobe, hairstyle, and apartment, that continue in his realization that the man was not the familiar dad whose life revolved around his pride in his son but a late-middle-aged bachelor desperate to get laid, and that culminate in the disclosure that his reckless and frantic priapism, in concert with a self-deluded, obliging neighbor, resulted in his death.

Preminger also understands the relationship between his father and his father's final home, seeing that the condominium in which they have consecutively lived represents a retreat into private worlds of fantasy and self-gratification. With this recognition comes the related revelation that the condominium can never be a foundation upon which to build the ordinary life to which Preminger has aspired, for, despite the complex's surface communality, its poolside neighborliness and appearance of social interaction, it is ultimately a place of withdrawal into the self, a place that allows its residents to turn away from the concerns of the world and to trivialize themselves so thoroughly that they will no longer be obliged to notice their lives slipping away. Less clearly connected in Preminger's mind is his sense that sexuality is somehow related to financial success, to the rise of one's economic fortunes, with his father's death in the home that signifies the achievement of retirement security; involved here, too, of course, is the fact that his father died in the arms of a woman whom Preminger had associated with those women who appeared at the Premingers' home during his father's working life. It is safe to say that he intuits these connections, however, and understands through them that he must push beyond his father's retreat into a condominium death by withdrawing so thoroughly from the world that he himself becomes his home. He eliminates all purchase in space by leaping from his apartment's twelfth-floor balcony, intent upon destroying the self's last refuge—the body. As he falls, he tries to deliver his habitation speech, but the wind stops the words on his lips. His one final go at articulating the world into some kind of coherence is jammed back down his throat, the lecture halted by his ultimate commitment to silence and death. His suicide, clearly enough, represents a kind of response to his lecture's crucial question, then, but the only trauma it points to is his own, the only "spell of rotten weather" the one that led him toward the discovery of his own hopelessness. For Preminger, anthropological questions—all questions—must become autobiographical, and it is against this final turning inward, or in complicity with it, that he hurls himself to his death.

In "The Condominium" the language that prevails is Mrs. Riker's epistolary prose, a prose blithely unconscious of and indifferent to its own effects, a prose chatty yet artificial and consummately bland, a deadly language that destroys extremity by trivializing it. Hers is, without question, the banally seductive siren song of the condominium, and Preminger must succumb to it because his own sense of self is too crippled to counter that voice's tendencies toward trivialization and sameness with its own force of articulation, differentiation, and self-expression. Of the three protagonists of *Searches & Seizures,* then, Preminger the lecturer strikes the poorest bargain between style and substance, proves least able to reconcile the inevitable human conflict between self and other, word and world. Alexander Main, a man of primitive impulses, learns the necessity and value of sublimating that impulsiveness into a style, of formalizing it into a constructive verbal means of bearing down on the world, it having become clear to him that such compromises with the world's terms are unavoidable if that world is to be counted upon to restore his "sense of his possibilities." Brewster Ashenden, by self-proclamation "one of the three or four dozen truly civilized men in the world" (p. 149), learns to mediate the emptiness of style-for-its-own-sake with a bit of carnality and impulse, the bear having awakened in him the awareness of his forgotten grammar of animality. Only Preminger fails to reconcile the opposing strains, retreating further into the self as the world rejects him and the sibyl of the condo seduces him, perhaps unknowingly, toward the same annihilation of self into which her sour, banal epistolary song had ultimately led his father.

The bleakness of this conclusion to *Searches & Seizures* is balanced by the qualified affirmation of the opening novella, and the two are mediated by the manic energy of the tour de force resolution of "The Making of Ashenden," itself a dramatization of language's ability to overcome the gravitational forces of formlessness and dissolution. None of the three is intended to represent an absolute statement or concluding vision, yet it is difficult not to find Main's reconciliation of the tension between self-expression and dissolution, between style and nothingness, the most convincing and resonant, perhaps because it most closely approximates Elkin's own response to these antinomies.

Main—"The Bailbondsman"—has a very clear notion of what the language his profession imposes upon him is and how he feels about it. "I'm called upon to make colorful conversation in my trade," he explains early in the novella. "Don't think I enjoy it. I'm a serious man; such patter is distasteful to me. When day is done I like nothing better than to ask my neighbor how he's feeling, to hear he's well and to tell him same here, to trade what we know about the weather, to be agreeable, aloof and dull. Leave poetry to the poets, style to the window trimmers. I'm old" (p. 25). What makes his occupation repugnant to him is not the highhandedness connected with his role as determiner of what felons will be set free, liberated back into their criminality, nor is it the strongarming he must occasionally resort to with fugitives who have jumped his bond; these are his exuberant means of "controlling the sluices and locks of ordinary life" (p. 105), his chosen way (to use a favorite term of Leo Feldman's) of "bearing down on the world." It is the rhetoric the job demands that he finds hateful, the obligatory use of "colorful rhythms" and "salty talk" a burden that nothing else in the trade can make up for, "not the viciousness or the seamy excitements or my collective, licey knowledge of the world" (p. 27). In the course of the novella Main's attitude toward his shoptalk, this "flashy grammar of body contact" (p. 118), changes considerably, language ultimately becoming the only medium of redemption he can know.

Main requires redemption for a number of reasons. First, his hard-edged, unforgiving bad man's perspective on the world has entered into a losing competition with an emergent cultural perspective characterized by humanitarianism, charity, and compassion; his own cherished ideals of impulse and revenge have been largely subordinated to the values of rehabilitation, sublimation, and order. This cultural shift manifests itself primarily in the fact that business is bad. The Federal Bail Reform Act of 1964 (which empowered federal courts to act as their own bondsmen, thus eliminating airplane hijackers, interstate kidnappers, and other federal criminals from the independent bondsman's rolls), the compassion-inspired legislation introduced by coalitions of social scientists, civil libertarians, and a left-leaning Supreme Court, and the increasing politicization of crime have all combined to reduce drastically both the number of felons available for bonding and the profit margin involved in bonding them. Main's Cincinnati colleagues discuss this situation at their weekly luncheon in Covington, Kentucky, agreeing that henceforth they will work in concert rather than in competition, facing adversity with a united front. In addition, they resolve to soften their hard-guy image by changing tactics: they will agree on a lottery system to determine which bondsman will get which prisoner, and they will talk any bail jumpers (upon whom they are empowered by law to use force) back to prison, rather than using violence. While they are formulating their democratically established concessions to the fact that "heart is winning the battle of history" (p. 56), Main is off in a Cincinnati museum, skipping the lunch so that he can study the teeth of extinct animals. He periodically visits this exhibit of the jaws of long-dead beasts, gaining inspiration and sustenance from the display of an untempered ferocity that he feels has fled the world. He examines the skull of a young jaguar, noticing that "skin still adheres to the palate, the concentric tracery as distinct and fine as what he touches with his tongue at the roof of his own mouth. It is teeth he comes back again and again to see, as if these were the distillate of the animal's soul, the cutting, biting edge of its passion and life" (p. 60). While his colleagues are fraternally agreeing upon policies of capitulation, then, Main is being nourished by an opposite vision, his sense of his isolate's integrity reinforced by the realization that the jaguar's palate is as singular in its detail as his own, "the cutting, biting edge" of his own "passion and life" confirmed as well by his recognition of its reflection in the jaguar skull's menacingly sharp teeth. It is from a world too sold on sublimation and too suspicious of impulse that Main wants most to be redeemed, his own drive for life finding no fulfillment in a culture gone slack with convenience, communality, and an incapacitating relativism.

The earlier Elkin protagonist whom Main most conspicuously recalls is Leo Feldman, partly because their irascible, uncompromising natures are similar, and also because they both assume positions mediating between law and lawlessness, Feldman supplying contraband goods and services through his department store basement, Main monitoring the passage of criminals off and back into the city streets. Both are also explicitly associated with older, more primitive worlds and civilizations: Feldman is linked with the severity of the medieval world, with "a distant, Praetorianed land, unamiable and harsh" (*ABM,* p. 42), while Main proudly and repeatedly invokes the memory of his Phoenician ancestors, a desert people whom he credits not only with the development of the bailbond but also with the invention of the oasis, innovations that, from one point of view, could be said to be one and the same. Their "horned, spiky skin," Main explains, "took the sunburn and converted it into energy," energy that they put to the services of resourcefulness, becoming "sand and water alchemists," "conservationists of the bleak," undauntable creators in the desert's arid wastes, "growing a world" (p. 7). The etymological relationship that links Phoenician to phoenix is, quite clearly, what Elkin has in mind in this description of the creation of oases from the desert's barrenness; it lies, too, behind his decision to give Main the nickname "The Phoenician," in anticipation of the character's ultimate rebirth from a condition of failed possibilities.

That condition is brought about in part by Main's displeasure with the law's increasing laxity toward criminals, but it has more to do with his overall disillusionment with crime itself. He offers a parable of that disillusionment ("My thoughts explode in words," he muses) to Crainpool, his secretary, appraising him of "the progress of a liver fluke through a cow's intestine to a human being." His account races the trematode's journey from cowflop to the blade of

Reading Stanley Elkin

grass in which it waits, "a befouled phoenix," for the appearance of the sheep whose liver it will attack and sicken, the sheep's poisoned excrement giving it still another bourn in which to await the arrival of the barefoot human offering his unprotected soles to its capacities for corkscrew penetration and spiral intrusion. The point of this delineation of " 'Nature's nasty marathon, its stations of the cross and inside job' " is that " 'What the liver fluke can do man can do. The fix is in, it takes two to tango, all crime's a cooperation. This I wanted to see. I've seen it, show me something else. Phooey. A Phoenician's phooey on it all.' " (p. 28). What disappoints Main, obviously, is the recognition that crime is communal, that even the liver fluke needs assistance in undertaking its nasty, instinctual break and entry; neither desire nor impulse is sufficient to liberate it from its dependence upon other living things.

Not until the late pages of the novella, however, is Main's comment (" 'This I wanted to see' ") clarified and the extent and meaning of his disillusionment with crime fully explained. He became a bailbondsman, we learn there, when he decided that "Crime was the single mystery he could get close to" (p. 106)—when it occurred to him that mastering the disciplines that address the most profound questions of the universe and of man was beyond his abilities, and that he must settle for a field in which the mysteries ("Who done it? What's the motive?" [p. 124]) are more manageable but no less obscure. His chosen field ends up disappointing him, leaves him bitterly asking his secretary, who has himself been a lawbreaker and jumper of Main's bond, " 'What does crime come to at last? Nothing. Crummy hornbook, lousy primer. Slim volume, Crainpool, pot fucking boiler, publisher's remainder. You taught me nothing, mister. And where did I get the idea that by getting next to aberration I could...' " (p. 124). Main's ellipsis might be completed with "make more sense of the world, understand the normal and the social by becoming expert in deviations from them." He had hoped, in other words, to find criminals as representative of primal, irrational human urges as he has found prehistoric animals' teeth reflective of the primitive impulses of those beasts, and he had convinced himself that the study of both could only reinforce his own raw hunger for life and help him to discover what that life is. He has, in the interven-

The Flashy Grammar of Body Contact

ing years, read all the words in crime's "slim volume," however, and he has had to recognize that crime is merely ordinary, that it reflects no "cutting, biting edge" of outlaw "passion and life" but represents only a dull, laughably circumscribable form of mystery that sheds practically no light on the larger mystery, the "Mystery that kept him going."

Although his experiences in the actual world have been supplying him with compelling evidence of crime's ordinariness, it takes a dream representation of this fact to convince Main (who had earlier dismissed dreams as containing "trivial enigma[s] we forget on rising" [p. 29]) of its indisputable truth. In his dream he witnesses the violation, robbery, and desecration of the tomb of a pharoah by two men whom he subsequently recognizes to be Oyp and Glyp, the only two criminals ever to have jumped his bail and to have eluded his attempts to recapture them. Outdoing the robbery of Tutankhamen's tomb (upon whose crime Elkin has modeled theirs), Oyp and Glyp not only destroy priceless artifacts in the chamber, spill the pharoah's invaluable unguents on the floor, and collect all that is portable; they actually exhume the pharoah himself, breaking through his sarcophagus, splitting his outer and inner coffins, penetrating his golden shell, and finally unwrapping his mummy so as to get at the riches it contains, pocketing not only rings and jewels but the pharoah's bandage-swathed heart as well.[13] The two are immediately apprehended by local authorities, and Main, who has witnessed the entire crime, follows them to court. Once they have been arraigned, Main feels obligated to try to win them their freedom once again, and he appears before the presiding magistrate to make his case. This effort compels him to argue what he has known professionally but has never before acted upon: the notion that even the most heinous crime is only ordinary, that even the violation of God's burial ground and the desecration of his corpse are merely mundane sorts of transgressions committed by common, banal men in—as Main puns—"under their heads" (p. 98). His argument fails to persuade the judge, but it does convince the dreaming Main completely. What Oyp and Glyp had come to represent to the waking Main was a romantic sense of crime as that which exists beyond the boundaries of civilized life, and of criminals as those who feed upon the experience

Reading Stanley Elkin

of extremity, those who press human limits to the edge and are ex-
alted by their daring defiance. His dream allows him to eloquently
and persuasively talk himself out of this misconception. In the
dream, the judge lets Oyp and Glyp go free; in waking from it, Main
understands that in fact, or perhaps only to him, Oyp and Glyp are
dead. The progression, as he sees it in the dream's end, goes like
this: they were "fugitives once from his scrutiny and control, then
from his intercession, and now from the earth itself. Fugitives from
the bullying freedom he needed to give them who till now could
stand between the law and its violators, having that power vouchsafed to him, the power to middlemen, to doodle people's destiny"
(p. 105). His dream oration leaves him bereft of the one remaining
absorbing passion of his life—the belief that the whereabouts of Oyp
and Glyp continues to be one of life's soluble mysteries, that they are
still out there, a two-ply exception to and repudiation of the ordinary.
The dream forces him to recognize that they have disappeared without a trace into the ordinary, that the ordinary has claimed another
source of his interest, his life, his passion. From this worst of all
losses he must be redeemed at the novella's close.

The ordinary and the exceptional are not the only contraries
that "The Bailbondsman" (and for that matter, the bailbondsman)
must reconcile if Main is to achieve his promised redemption. His
preferences in animals as well as his pride in his ancestors reflect his
attachment to the past, a partiality suggested, too, by his insistence
that his secretary act and dress like Bob Cratchit and that his own office duplicate exactly the look of a bailbondsman's office in film
noir. He objects to the present because it is only the present, the omnipresence of taste, style, and fashion attesting to its temporal one-
dimensionality, to its willing capitulation to the fact that now is only
and immutably now. Main is offended by contemporaneity as he is by
crimes generated by the law's permissiveness, explicitly linking the
two as he walks through Cincinnati's downtown shopping district:
"They spoke of the breakdown of law and order," he muses, "but
what a discipline was in these streets, what a knuckling under and ca-
tering to the times." The shops "burst with an egoism of the present
tense" (p. 76), the city is "pickled in taste" (p. 72), but Main has "no
taste, only hunger. I have never been fashionable, and it's astonish-

The Flashy Grammar of Body Contact

ing to me that so much has happened in the world. The changes I perceive leave me breathless" (p. 74). The rapidity of change has led him to conclude, "It's as if he lives trapped in the neck of an hourglass. Style, he thinks. As a young man he wanted it, hoped that when he awakened it would be there like French in his mouth. Now he sees it as a symptom of a ruinous disease" (p. 78). And so he walks the city streets, noticing the Easter decorations being hung in the trees ("long strips of gold foil in light rigid frames, exactly the size and appearance of bedsprings...inching their way the long length of the avenue like a golden blight" [p. 71]), morosely deciding, "It's too much for me—spring, style, the future" (p. 72).

His argument with the future is that he can't know it—it eludes him as Oyp and Glyp once eluded him, evades his "scrutiny and control" and thus "limits his power and his precious freedom" (p. 105). What he would know are those simple things that "a dopey kid of the next century could tell him," basic facts concerning the alignment of the major leagues, what songs become hits, who would be assassinated, what the new political slogans would be. " 'Everything I don't know and never will know leans on me like a mountain range,' " he tells his secretary, " 'It creams me, Crainpool. It potches my brain and rattles my teeth' " (p. 120). It threatens, that is, the symbolic locus of his "passion and life."

When he tries to foresee the future he is foiled by the unavoidability of contemporary analogues as well as the time-boundness of words, and he consequently becomes "depressed by language, the finite slang of his century....He needed new endings, new punctuation, a different grammar" (p. 108). He gets no new language, of course, but by the end his attitude toward the language he does have has changed considerably. The difference between his earlier feelings toward his rhetoric (his idea that "it was only a foreign language he had learned to speak, the flashy grammar of body contact, a shoptalk of which he is weary because no one has yet bested him at it" [p. 118]) and his subsequent, altered view is that he comes increasingly to mean what he says and to feel what he means. His addresses to Miss Krementz, a client, and Crainpool progressively reflect his willingness to use his "foreign language" as a medium through which to present his deeply felt concerns and fears. Neither of these

Reading Stanley Elkin

speeches is marked by an ingenuous simplicity, of course; both of them treat a variety of subjects, express a number of contradictory moods, and rely heavily upon rhetorical maneuver, their combined effect being to dramatize what Main is feeling more than to directly express it. For Miss Krementz he delivers an account of his life that is intended as an explanation of why he is refusing to post bail for her boyfriend. For Crainpool he expounds upon his frustration at not being able to know the future as a kind of prefatory explanation of his imminent banishment of his secretary back into fugitive status. Both monologues mix autobiography with business, as the habitual, indifferent shoptalk is gradually compelled to accommodate itself to more personal rhythms and more visceral concerns. This shift reflects Main's tacit awareness that language is the only means through which he can possibly resolve the primary tension underlying his personality—" 'who wired this tension in me between ego and detachment?' " (p. 120), he asks Crainpool—and the only agent capable of mediating between the other contraries that plague his life. Language, he comes to understand, is his only tool for mediating between himself and the world in the same way that he has placed himself "between the law and its violators" (p. 105). He recognizes, too, how crucial language is in resolving necessary conflicts between self and role.

This insight into the power of language is reinforced by Main's subsequent realization of the significance that language—what he calls his rhetoric—has had for him throughout his life. The two occasions upon which he mourns the success of Oyp and Glyp in evading his apprehension are both characterized by his image of the pair hiding in places so remote and forbidding "that the inhabitants have no language" (p. 62), or in exotic locales where they go undetected and undisturbed because "they don't speak the lingo" (p. 106). To escape him, Main's fantasies seem to suggest, the fugitives must escape the sphere of his language, perhaps even lose language as a social tool altogether, and leave behind the civilized world that empowers him to undertake his bailbondsman's role. Completely consistent with this sense of language's circumscribing powers is Main's realization that what has immobilized his other bailjumper, Crainpool, has been his rhetoric, the "foreign language he has learned to

The Flashy Grammar of Body Contact

speak" having "held [Crainpool] all these years, kept him in town while the Phoenician was out rounding up jumpers." The secretary has ultimately become a "connoisseur of the Phoenician's abuse" (p. 120). Main has used language, then, to give others freedom by arguing for and winning them the right to be bailed out, and he has used it to keep Crainpool and other clients where he wants them. Now he must use it to free himself from the pall that has descended upon his life, the feeling that "I could only recover with drugs the sense of my possibilities" (p. 67).[14]

He achieves his redemption through the monologue he delivers for Crainpool's benefit, a monologue that has as its primary object the discovery of a means by which he can "recover the sense of his possibilities," but that turns out to have been the very means for which he was searching. Main wakes Crainpool in the middle of the night to tell him that Oyp and Glyp are dead; then he pulls a gun, threatening to kill him because he jumped Main's bail years before. (When Crainpool objects that his eleven years of devoted service to Main has been restitution enough, Main responds that he is going to shoot him anyway because, as the law defines the relationship between bailed fugitive and bailbondsman, " 'You're the only man in the world I'm allowed to kill' " [p. 119].) Main's ensuing monologue careens from the description of his sense of life's loveliness to accounts of the latest scientific theories of " 'the universes. . . leaking into each other. . . this transfusion of law in the sky' " (p. 123) to his despair over the mundane facts of a future he can never know and the facts of a present he will never know, his ecstatic narrative culminating in the admission that, until now, " 'There was always someone to hunt. . . . A mystery I was good at. My line of country. But if Oyp and Glyp are dead. . .' " (He shoots at his secretary's hand, grazing him, and threatens to shoot again, sending the man into wild flight.) " 'LONG LIVE CRAINPOOL!' " (p. 125).

Main's secretary is being catapulted out into the world as a replacement for the now extinct Oyp and Glyp. His whereabouts will become the manageable mystery that Main may never be able to solve, but he will have the consolation of knowing it is soluble. Crainpool will provide Main with future opportunities for search, with reasons to remain interested in a world that is closing down all around

Reading Stanley Elkin

him. Propelling Crainpool back into the world is only the offshoot, the consequence, of a more significant movement Main undertakes (or, to use the collection's title, seizure he experiences). His mono- logue is based on the tacit assumption that the universe, for all its mysteriousness and inaccessibility to the human mind, must none- theless be perpetually confronted, must be attacked again and again with our only weapon capable of piercing its imperturbability and silence—words. In his peroration on new scientific discoveries about man and the universe, Main refers to the theory that " 'all life is merely four simple compounds arranged on a spiral spring of sugars and phosphates' " (pp. 122-23), his description recalling, and tacitly likening human beings to, the liver fluke, whose spiraling, foul pro- gress toward his goal he so patiently depicts in his parable of the communality of crime. The analogy's unavoidable implications are comically vulgar: if one must live in excrement in order to progress toward the ideal state of being, then one must indeed live in excre- ment, be it that which provides a temporary home for a liver fluke or that which is produced by a hyperarticulate bailbondsman. Or, to put the idea less scatologically, all of life strives toward some form of completion, some achievement of an ultimate which must be gained through the only means that the organism has at its command, be it the capacity for spiral locomotion or the ability to best everyone else with one's use of language.

The liver fluke is recalled here, of course, because of its explicit association with the Phoenix and with the novella's whole notion of rejuvenation. Its recovery from a state of torpor and paralysis prior to the sheep's arrival parallels Main's similar ascent from the despair of a world without possibility. The association of Main and the liver fluke with the Phoenix and the idea of rejuvenation is given rein- forcement in the novella's final image, which also reflects a resolu- tion of a number of the contraries that have undergirded Main's personality and have become central thematic antinomies. As he ex- its the hotel from which he has ejected Crainpool, Main looks around, lazily wondering where his new quarry might have fled: "East towards the railroad tracks? Or did he double back? To the street where he himself had walked that afternoon? Where the peo- ple were more like film stars than the film stars were, as everybody

The Flashy Grammar of Body Contact

was these days, handsomeness creeping up the avenues of the world like the golden bedsprings in the Cincinnati trees?" (p. 126).

The "befouled Phoenix" of a liver fluke, the "spiral springs of sugars and phosphates" that are all life, "the golden bedsprings in the Cincinnati trees"—all these are symbols of hope, possibility, life. The novella's final image adds the last requisite notion to the symbolic complex: the bedsprings are Easter decorations, suggestive of rebirth and redemption in the world. These "golden bedsprings" and the handsomeness with which they are associated recall the modernity that Main rejected earlier but embraces here, his restoration of possibility having reconciled him to the less subtle, more communal form that possibility can take for others—contemporaneity, fashion, the new and the now. By the end, then, he has come to accept (tentatively, at least) two of the three things he had earlier described as being "too much for him." Spring now has a personal, immediate meaning and no longer represents merely an inducement to meditations upon how little in his life is susceptible to regeneration. Style no longer seems "a ruinous disease" but has saved and restored him, his paroxysm of language having dramatized the realities of his situation and having led him to recognize that through the idiosyncratic, highly imaginative manipulation of language he can (for himself, at any rate) keep possibility alive in the world. (Crainpool, in fact, very nearly understands the point of Main's monologue, even if he does mis-anticipate its culmination. " 'You always have to have the last word,' " he complains, interrupting Main's speech. " 'You always have to do things big, don't you? Big shot. You'd kill me for nothing, for the sake of your style' " [p. 123].) The future has not been brought under Main's control, of course, but he has gained a small victory over it by exchanging a distant future in which incalculable and unimaginable things happen for a more immediate, more manageable future, one whose primary (and possible) object is the recapturing of a fugitive he has himself released.

On a number of levels, then, "The Bailbondsman" suggests that language allows us a few tentative victories over our circumstances, allows us to reconcile personal conflicts like those of ego and detachment, self and role, being and style, and even occasionally permits us to articulate ideas and images that will be, perhaps only sym-

Reading Stanley Elkin

bolically, perhaps only temporarily, redemptive. This is the argument of the most effective and impressive of the three *Searches & Seizures* novellas, and it is not in any way surprising that Elkin has admitted, "I, myself, am closer to Main than any other character [in my work]."[15] The upbeat conclusion of Main's narrative is not final in terms of its relation to *Searches & Seizures* as a whole, but it could be said to represent most accurately the deal Elkin has struck with language. Like Main, he has resolved to use language as his way of bearing down on the world, not because language will alter the future, but because it can occasionally be made to effect a seizure of the present. That the process is no less circular than that of seeking a fugitive whom the seeker has set free is a contradiction that Elkin, like his protagonist, has learned to live with. It is, after all, a gesture, and gestures are crucial. Dick Gibson could very well be describing Main's action of sending Crainpool out into the world to embody possibility when he presents this apostrophe: "Gestures, gestures, saving gestures, life-giving and meaningless and sweet as appetite, delivered by gestures and redeemed by symbols, by necessities of your own making and a destiny dreamed in a dream" (*DGS*, p. 331).

NOTES

1. Tony Tanner, *City of Words* (New York: Harper & Row, 1971), p. 19.

2. Richard Poirier, *A World Elsewhere: The Place of Style in American Literature* (New York: Oxford University Press, 1966), pp. 27, 39, 45.

3. The continuity between Elkin and his protagonist in *The Franchiser* is emphasized by Joan Elkin's cover drawing for the David R. Godine reprint of the novel. Her illustration depicts two men of not dissimilar appearance, one of them recognizably Elkin, the other, presumably, Flesh.

4. Elkin discusses the importance of the simile in his work and in his teaching in LeClair, "Elkin: The Art of Fiction," p. 86.

5. Ibid., p. 76, and Bernt and Bernt, "Stanley Elkin on Fiction," p. 15.

6. The prevalence of death as a theme in Elkin's fiction is a

central issue in the critical arguments of Larry McCaffery, "Stanley Elkin's Recovery of the Ordinary," *Critique* 21: 2 (1980): 43, and Francine O. Hardaway, "The Power of the Guest: Stanley Elkin's Fiction," *Rocky Mountain Review* 32: 4 (1978): 240-41.

7. Quoted from the dustjacket blurb on the Random House edition of *Searches & Seizures.*

8. When asked by Jeffrey L. Duncan what makes Push the Bully and Feldman admirable characters, Elkin replied, "Energy is what counts. It is what is on the good side of the ledger for Feldman and Push. Whoever has the better rhetoric is the better man, and since Feldman by and large tends to have the better rhetoric, he is as far as I'm concerned the more sympathetic character" (Duncan, "Conversation with Elkin and Gass," p. 61). In another interview Elkin admitted, "I stand in awe of the *outré*. Those characters in my fiction who are exaggerated seem, to me at least, more vital than the ordinary character, certainly more energetic. It's this energy that engines my work." (Sanders, "Interview," p. 132).

9. Elkin makes this point in the preface to *Searches & Seizures.*

10. The bear's language is "a classic aberrant syntax" to Ashenden's ears, but when transcribed it looks very much like Russian, a language not only symbolically appropriate to a bear, but one that putatively reflects human equality rather than social hierarchy, that suggests socialist homogeneity rather than cultural divisions and distinctions.

11. In addition to the thematic parallels linking the novellas of *Searches & Seizures,* the works also share a distinct technical similarity, one prevalent throughout Elkin's novels—the juxtaposition of first-person narrative with third-person interior monologue. Main narrates most of "The Bailbondsman," but some passages reflect a different perspective upon him and his activities; Ashenden narrates two-thirds of his novella, then gives way to a third-person account of his copulation with the bear; Preminger narrates the opening pages of "The Condominium," which takes the form of his habitation speech, but after this, save for snatches of indirect interior monologue, his story is presented in the third person.

12. Although neither so striking nor so evocative as the tomb theft scene in "The Bailbondsman" or the bear fuck scene in "The Making of Ashenden," Elkin's creation of the letters from Mrs. Riker to Preminger is itself a real triumph of language. The restraint

needed to pitch them perfectly between typicality and parody is observed throughout, and the unconscious banality of their composition is an effect completely achieved.

13. Howard Carter, the discoverer of Tutankhamen's tomb, describes the actual tomb robbery in *The Tomb of Tutankhamen* (London, 1923, 1928, 1933; rpt., New York: E. P. Dutton, 1972), pp. 59-62. Elkin's exaggeration of the theft makes Oyp's and Glyp's crime seem that much more unthinkable and unpardonable, thus making it that much more difficult for Main to convince the judge that theirs was merely an ordinary trespass, an average felony.

14. Leo Feldman experiences a similar depression in *A Bad Man,* doubting the sources of his own energies and deriding their products: "Ah, but how tired he was of his spurious *oomph,* of all eccentric plunge and push and his chutzpah only skin deep, that wouldn't stand up in court. . . . He was exhausted by his own acts of empty energy. Unambushable he was, seeing slush at spirit's source, reflex and hollow hope in all the duncy dances of the driven" (*ABM,* pp. 220-21). Feldman, too, longs for "new words, new lyrics" as antidotes for his dejection, but he finally escapes it only by being reconfirmed in his bad man's impulses by his confrontation with the land developer.

15. LeClair, "Elkin: The Art of Fiction," p. 84.

6

World without Simile, World without Story, Amen

The central role of language in the resolutions of *Searches & Seizures* reflects the extent to which Elkin has made his work's most conspicuous characteristic—what he terms "fierce language," "the aggression of syntax and metaphor"[1]—a subject and theme for fiction. It was, accordingly, at about the same point in his career that his public comments on the craft of writing began emphasizing the idea that fiction "gives language an opportunity to happen," is "a stage where language can stand,"[2] the work and the pronouncements alike increasingly insisting upon "the possibilities inherent in rhetoric."[3] "Let men make good sentences," he declared at the conclusion of "A Conversation with Stanley Elkin and William H. Gass,"

Let them learn to spell the sound of the waterfall and the noise of the bathwater. Let us get down the colors of the baseball gloves—the difference in shade between the centerfielder's deep pocket and the discreet indentation of the catcher's mitt. And let us refine tense so men may set their watches by it. Let fiction be where the language is. Let it *be* a language, as French is, or Bantu. And let it be understood that when we talk about fiction we are finally talking about the people who write it, about all those special talkers in tongues like Shakespeare or Faulkner or Melville or Gass. Let us enlist the Vocabulary, the Syntax, the high grammar of the mysterious world.[4]

Nowhere has Elkin articulated more eloquently what he thinks fiction is and what he expects it to accomplish, and nowhere has he more clearly stated the apparent contradiction underlying his entire

167

literary enterprise. To describe the pocket of a centerfielder's glove so as to distinguish it from that of a catcher's mitt is to undertake one kind of project; to make fiction a language unto itself is to do something else. Language calculated to discriminate visually between the colors of objects in the world is, after all, not the same thing as language released into freedom of invention, and the disparity between the representational objective and the more purely aesthetic or imaginative impulse is one of the major dynamics animating much of Elkin's later work. *The Living End,* which most deliberately adheres to the dictates of Elkin's "Let men make good sentences" pronouncement, attempts to resolve this opposition by forming a bridge between mimetic precision and aesthetic license. The nature of the bridge is suggested by Elkin's comment that "when we talk about fiction we are finally talking about the people who write it, about all those special talkers in tongues like Shakespeare or Faulkner or Melville or Gass."

What most crucially differentiates *The Living End* from any previous Elkin work is its want of a central protagonist. The omission is more than only technically significant. Elkin's first six books contain immediately identifiable protagonists, men who are not only the centers of interest but also the primary sources of extreme language. As numerous critics have noted, Elkin's protagonists are nearly all men who write or speak for a living,[5] and often professional necessity to express themselves provides a major rhetorical climax. Yet these protagonists are not the exclusive repositories of extravagant language, for Elkin has taken increasing delight in the presentation of minor characters possessed of rhetorical skills. "There are people in my work who may suddenly speak like Ph.D.'s or Ph.D.'s like slumlords, but this is simply a convention of fiction and drama," he told an interviewer. "Did the people in Elizabeth's court speak in blank verse? Did the children in the nineteenth century speak the way that children in Henry James speak? I allow every character my diction. And may it serve him better than it serves me."[6] The effect of this augmented choral ubiquity is to amplify dramatically the pervasiveness of Elkin's voice and vision; his style becomes increasingly omnipresent and, in *Searches & Seizures,* becomes all but inseparable from the themes as well. "The Bailbondsman," when viewed in

World without Simile, World without Story, Amen

these terms, comes to seem the central work of the collection—if not the career—in that it represents in analogue form Elkin's debate with himself about his style, one maligned by reviewers for being excessive and self-conscious. The novella culminates in the affirmation of that style as Main's/Elkin's means of imposing self upon world and of keeping mystery, possibility, alive in it. The style affirmed, Elkin proceeded in *The Franchiser* to examine the antinomies it contains (its precision and exactitude countered by its largely leveling, homogenizing tendencies), the novel acknowledging the heightened perception that the style embodies and enacts, as well as the continuity between its undifferentiating, simile-producing disposition and the symptoms of the protagonist's (and the author's) affliction. It is tempting to think that *The Franchiser*, dealing as it did with material so painfully close to Elkin's own experience, represented for him the obviation of the necessity to write protagonist-centered fiction, allowing him to replace character with a personal fictional language in his work, to substitute style (''the song the writer sings,'' as his dissertation has it[7]) for an author surrogate as the work's central concern. In any case, *The Living End*, a work whose development is thoroughly dictated by rhetorical purposes and that subordinates both character and plot to the exigencies of poetic extravagance, was *The Franchiser's* successor, the triptych reflecting a Stanley Elkin more confident of and more delighted by his style than ever before—so confident and delighted, in fact, that he was willing to entrust to it the restoration of vitality to the hoariest of imaginative terrains: Heaven and Hell.

What enables Elkin to recover this deadeningly familiar material for the purposes of fiction is, of course, his ability to ''spell the sound of its waterfalls''—his ability to visualize it, to render its reality through precise, highly imagistic language. That precise language depends, in its turn, upon an acuity of perception, a heightened vision of the world that is everywhere evident in Elkin's fiction but that takes on added and explicit emphasis in *The Living End*. If we could take his characters' attitudes toward their experiences of heightened perception as approximations of Elkin's feeling toward his own perceptive gifts, we would have to conclude that early in his career he was unsure why he was capable of perceiving the

Reading Stanley Elkin

world in greater detail and with more precision than anyone else. Jake Greenspahn, for example, is a grocer, not a poet, and when he is given the vision of a poet in "Criers & Kibitzers, Kibitizers & Criers," he seeks an explanation—and finds one. "Death is an education, he thought," recalling his son's recent death. "On the street, in the store, he saw everything. Everything. It was as if everybody else were made out of glass. Why all of a sudden was he like that?" (*C&K*, p. 9). He was like that, clearly enough, because Elkin has imagined him into existence, endowing him with mourning-induced powers of perception not incomparable to Elkin's own. A second protagonist whose profession only infrequently demands unusual rhetorical skills is Ben Flesh, but his speech at the closing down of his Fred Astaire Dance Studio, his address from the trademark bucket atop his Kentucky Fried Chicken franchise, his diatribe to Patty Finsberg while they are "in nature" in the mountainous outskirts of Colorado Springs, his "sex night" revelatory monologue, and all his other outbursts prove him yet another Elkinian examplar of perception and rhetoric. His extraordinary gifts of vision and articulation must also be accounted for, it turns out, and the explanation begins as he studies a hitchhiker he has picked up, intuiting all manner of characteristics about the man from superficial details of his appearance. Interrupting his own flow of insights, Flesh wonders, via Elkin's typical reflective consciousness mode of narration, "where did he [Flesh] get these ideas? how had vision come to perch on his eyes like a pince nez?" (*TF*, p. 215). The answer to his ponderings is never made explicit, but the inference is unavoidable: his visionary experiences and moments of rhetorical exhilaration are pathologically induced, each instance representing a further stage in the degeneration of the very nervous system that makes those perceptions possible.

Having dramatized, in *The Franchiser*, the terrible ambivalences involved in heightened perception, Elkin went on, in *The Living End*, to indulge and celebrate that visionary capacity. The work is largely propelled by an energy of invention and insight rare even among Elkin's endlessly imaginative literary performances. The first third of the volume's opening novella, "The Conventional Wisdom," is narrated in pedestrian, unforegrounded language that subsequently gives way to the simile-laden, intricately evocative prose style

World without Simile, World without Story, Amen

characteristic (if not more than characteristic) of Elkin. What accounts for the shift is the fact that Ellerbee, the central figure, has moved from life into afterlife upon his murder by a robber of his liquor store, and his lexicon has been considerably improved in the transition from one realm to the other. The angel of death who has ushered him into Heaven points out that when he was alive he had " 'a vocabulary of perhaps seventeen or eighteen-hundred words,' " and then asks Ellerbee, " 'Who am I?' "

"An eschatological angel," Ellerbee said shyly.
"One hundred percent," the angel of death said, [and, inviting Ellerbee to intuit the heavenly establishment's purposes in expanding his vocabulary, asks,] "Why do we do that?"
"To heighten perception," Ellerbee said, and shuddered.[8]

Heightening perception is, to be sure, a major means and a crucial end in all of Elkin's fiction, and it is not uncommon for the reader to experience a sympathetic shudder while adjusting his own perception to Elkin's expansive and precise vision. (R. Z. Sheppard identified this effect of Elkin's work exactly when he called *The Dick Gibson Show* "a brilliant approximation of what it is like to live with one's eyes and ears constantly open."[9]) The departure from terrestriality—the liberation from its givens and earthbound syntaxes—undertaken in *The Living End* allows Elkin to "give language the opportunity to happen" in a fashion less encumbered by the obligations of naturalistic coherence and consecutiveness than that offered him by the narrative strategies of any of his other works, the simple, proverbial features of Heaven and Hell and the general characteristics of their equally familiar inhabitants imposing the only real limits upon his literary inventiveness. *The Living End*, then, maximizes the opportunities for Elkin's poetic language to "upset the applecarts of expectation and ordinary grammar,"[10] by eliminating the naturalistic premises which partially dictate the surfaces of his other books and which inevitably contribute to the determination of their shapes.

There has always been a pronounced anti-naturalistic tendency in Elkin's work, a tendency variously expressed by his intentional blurring of narrative modes, his introduction of blatantly symbolic or

Reading Stanley Elkin

allegorical characters, his preference for outlandish plot situations, his penchant for looping, paralleling, and refracting temporal sequences, his conferral of eloquence on the most improbable characters, and his overall propensities for emphasizing expression over mimesis and for resolving his narratives through metaphor and symbol rather than through plot. *The Living End,* with its celestial beings and inconsolable inferno dwellers, its Lord on High and Holy Family, is a departure less in kind than in degree from Elkin's characteristic literary mode. The triptych allows him a freedom greater than any he had previously permitted himself, the "heightened perception" of the inhabitants of Heaven and Hell giving his expressive gifts free rein. It represents as well the work of a writer who has understood that "when we talk about fiction we are talking about the people who write it," and who, as a self-acknowledged "special talker of tongues," has resolved to make his own deliberately modulated, utterly crafted literary voice the subject and substance of his book.

In thematic terms, the novellas of *The Living End* address themselves to questions that Elkin's fiction has previously considered. The triptych is lent coherence and pattern through the presence in each section of desperate rebellious gestures undertaken by men who, although not consequently redeemed or restored from the absurd injustices inflicted upon them by a petty and capricious God, are nonetheless somewhat reconciled to their unearned sufferings as a result of their plucky, impossible revolts. Each novella takes for its title a familiar, platitudinous phrase; the titles of the second two works ("The Bottom Line" and "The State of the Art") are derived from the pool that gives the first novella its title ("The Conventional Wisdom"). It is worth noting that Elkin's original title for the volume was *The Conventional Wisdom,* because that title reflects the centrality of this notion to the entire triptych, isolating a thematic concern rather than merely hanging a name on the volume for the sake of a pun.[11] At the conclusion of the opening novella, Ellerbee, a Hell dweller for sixty-two years, realizes what the conventional wisdom means, and he describes it both as a preparation for the resolution of this section of the triptych and as a concept that will inform the following two novellas. "Everything was true," we are told, even the conventional wisdom, perhaps especially the conventional wisdom—that which made up heaven like a shot in the dark and imagined into reality halos and hell, gargoyles, gates of pearl, and the Pearl of Great Price, that had invented the horns of demons and cleft their feet and conceived angels riding clouds like cowboys on horseback, their harps at their sides like goofy guitars. Everything. Everything was. The self and what you did to protect it, learning the house odds, playing it safe—the honorable percentage baseball of existence. [p. 45]

The conventional wisdom, in Ellerbee's definition, means two different things, then: a place in the communal consciousness where such culturally conditioned images take root, and the reality in which Ellerbee, Ladlehaus, Quiz, Lesefario, and the other earthly protagonists of *The Living End* exist and have their being, the Hell, Purgatory, and Heaven in which they will, we initially assume, spend eternity. These two definitions converge and meet in the mind of God, of course, and it is against it and Him—against the conventional wisdom writ large and embodied in what Ellerbee will subsequently refer to as "the real McCoy Son of a Bitch God"—that they must stage their merely human, self-affirming revolts.

Since Ellerbee's rebellion is the most significant of the four undertaken by the central human figures of the triptych, not merely in terms of *The Living End* but also in terms of Elkin's characteristic aesthetic, it will be helpful to discuss the revolts of Ladlehaus in "The Bottom Line" and those of Quiz and Lesefaro in "The State of the Art" before concluding with an analysis of "The Conventional Wisdom." Jay Ladlehaus, the accomplice to the thug who robbed Ellerbee's liquor store and murdered its owner, is not a man accustomed to making significant gestures, for in life he had always been the bag man and co-conspirator, so innocuous an outlaw that he never acquired a criminal record despite a whole lifetime of crime. His strategy for endurance in Hell—insofar as his pain allows for thoughts of anything other than itself—is, not unlike Ellerbee's initial tactic, to lie low and be as unobtrusive a sufferer as possible. But an unanticipated visit from God suddenly propels him out of his cultivated anonymity and results in his being condemned to a new and singular form of punishment. God, in a good mood, entertains ques-

Reading Stanley Elkin

tions from the denizens of Hell, and is greeted by the taunting query, " 'Is there life before death?' " (p. 55). Outraged at this graffiti of a question, God erroneously holds Ladlehaus responsible for it, although someone standing near him had asked. Ladlehaus is singled out for unusual punishment not for asking the question but for his subsequent realization that "He makes mistakes," a blasphemy that prompts God to expel him from Hell and banish him to his grave, where he becomes the "only man in the long sad history of time ever to die" (p. 69)—the only man to spend eternity in a grave, rather than in Heaven or Hell. Here he gains a new adversary, Quiz, a caretaker of the high school track adjacent to which Ladlehaus is buried. Quiz hates the dead and is outraged that one of them is addressing him and begging to be disinterred; he gets his revenge by staging elaborate theatrical performances around Ladlehaus's grave. These are calculated to convince Ladlehaus that there is a civil war raging between the twin cities and, later, that he is only imagining that he is in his grave when he is actually in an intensive care ward of a hospital experiencing a coma dream as his family and physicians debate whether to pull the plug on him. Flanoy, one of the boys Quiz has hired to play a soldier in the Minneapolis–St. Paul war, finally discloses what Quiz has been doing to him, and the dead man takes the opportunity of God's presence at a recital being held at the high school to outwit both of his enemies.

God has appeared for the recital because He recruits musicians for Heaven at such events, to which He is drawn because of His love of music. Ladlehaus finds that he, too, loves music, but he hasn't recalled it during his time in Hell, has "forgotten harmony, the grand actuality of the reconciled. He did not remember balance. Proportion had slipped his mind and he had forgotten that here was where the world dovetailed with self, where self tallied with sympathy and distraction alike" (p. 92). In life the implementer of plans and never their designer, in death an inhabitant of a realm where connection, coherence, sequitur are absent, Ladlehaus is struck by his reunion with the "grand actuality of the reconciled" and inspired by it to make music the vehicle of his redemption, his notion of music as a mediator between self and world recalling Alexander Main's similar discovery of the purpose of style in "The Bailbondsman." Aware now

175

World without Simile, World without Story, Amen

that God is ever on the lookout for musicians with whom to staff
Heaven's orchestras and choirs, Ladlehaus waits until the Deity has
succumbed completely to the charms of a concerto and then suddenly shouts at Him, " 'Get [Quiz]. . .Get him! He's a composer!' "
(p. 95). God complies, smiting Quiz fatally; thus Ladlehaus is unbur-
dened of his tormentor and enabled to make his peace with the unusual terms of his death. He is grateful that he is interred where he
can be an eternal witness to "all the ceremonies of innocence the St.
Paul Board of Education could dream up" to hold upon the field surrounding his grave, and he is reconciled to spending his death "as
he had spent his life, accomplice to all the lives that were not his own,
accessory to them, accomplice and accessory as God" (p. 95).

In "The Bottom Line" the "snug coups of correspondence"
are the point. Ladlehaus's ability to manipulate God into ridding
him of his dead-hating nemesis represents what Dick Gibson would
call a "saving gesture." The grandeur of that gesture is vitiated,
however, by the fact that God has timed Quiz's death to coincide with
that moment in the recital when the children who had already per-
formed would be getting restless and need distraction. Ladlehaus has
manipulated God, in other words, but only with His cooperation. He
has, nonetheless, resigned himself to his plight and has even come to
affirm and feel nostalgic about the momentary mental impulse that
landed him in his grave. "A composer, he thought, I told Him [Quiz]
was a composer. Well, He makes mistakes, Ladlehaus thought
fondly" (p. 95), secure in the knowledge that a reiteration of the blasphemy that put him here can do him no further damage.

Similarly neutralized and assimilated into Heaven's infinite
plan are the rebellious gestures of Quiz and George Lesefario, the
central human characters of "The State of the Art," a novella dedicated primarily to the interpersonal conflicts of the Holy Family and
to the revelation of the mind of God the Creator. Quiz, precipitously
plunged into Hell upon his sudden demise, complains to his fellows
among the damned that he was slain—"Like someone ambushed,
snuffed by unions, eating in restaurants and rushed by hit men" (p.
99)—and that he suspects God is responsible. In Heaven, meanwhile,
God is having misgivings about His impulsive dispatching of Quiz,
and He turns to His Son for forgiveness. Christ not only forgives His

Father but sees to it too that Quiz's sufferings in Hell are abated and that he is finally translated to Heaven so that he might be brought before God as the culminating step in God's "perfect act of contrition." God refuses to offer Quiz repentance, but the incident nonetheless dramatizes how thoroughly He has lost control of His Kingdom, and how far His Son (Who loved being alive on earth, and Who holds His crucifixion death against the Father) is willing to go in opposing Him. It is a function of the volatility of Heaven that a spiteful, petty, unheroic man like Quiz can become the agent of its confusion despite the fact that he does nothing more to deserve this stature than what all the rest of the damned do: complain. Ever the unwitting insurgent, Quiz supposes that he has been raised up to Heaven because it was discovered that, in life, he had always stayed at YMCAs when he traveled.

A more hopeful and potentially heroic gesture is undertaken by George Lesefario, a clerk in Ellerbee's liquor store who had been gunned down in a holdup prior to the one in which Ellerbee dies. Formerly a fatalist who had decided that his life had no meaning, Lesefario concludes in Hell that "Death made no sense but it meant something" (p. 125). In order to prove this—or to make it true—he sets those suffering in Hell to timekeeping, persuading them that Quiz had left him the precise second, minute, hour, day, and year in an epiphanic moment immediately preceding his translation, and that they must continue to mark the time because "the meaning of death is how long it takes" (p. 128). What Lesefario is doing, of course, is appropriating eternal duration and translating it into humanly conceivable units of time, giving endlessness a human meaning. ("We can perceive duration," Frank Kermode argues in a pertinent phrase, "only when it is organized."[12]) Lesefario's heroism is similar to the heroism that Dick Gibson ascribes to Bob Hope, whom he sees as a man who "stands up in time and organizes it," filling it with jokes, thus conferring upon its meaningless passage a human dimension and a shape (*DGS*, p. 67).

However optimistic Lesefario's gesture, and however many of the damned agree to join in on the counting, it nonetheless ultimately leaves even its originator disenchanted and skeptical, partly because of the difficulties involved in keeping accurate time while

World without Simile, World without Story, Amen

ablaze, but also because one of Hell's elder residents convinces him that his scheme is no more useful and no less crazy than the "fad" Ellerbee started when he had the damned on their knees in the burning slime praying to God. Despairing of the hopelessness of eternal timekeeping and struck by the ancient denizen's argument for its futility, Lesefario gradually—and, as he subsequently realizes, tragically—loses count. What Lesefario doesn't know (he hadn't even been aware that Ellerbee was in Hell) is that Ellerbee's rebellious gesture had been at least partly successful, and that the old man's comparison of the two schemes, although not intended this way, implies that his counting project, had it been perpetuated, could have been effective within similar limits as well. Neither the old man nor Lesefario understands the insurrectionary significance of Ellerbee's apparently petitionary gesture, and the tentative triumph over God's eternal plan in which that gesture culminates.

Ellerbee's decision to rebel is not arrived at until late in the opening novella, when he learns the reasons for his transfer from Heaven to Hell shortly following his death. In life Ellerbee had been a decent, unselfish man, a responsible citizen who had supported the wives and children of employees injured or killed in holdups before he was himself murdered. At his death he ascends to Heaven, glimpses beatitude, and is summarily and without explanation dispatched to Hell. His initial response is to obey the injunction stamped into Hellgate's arch: to abandon hope, "and with it memory, pity, pride, his projects, the sense he had of injustice—for a little while driving off, with his sense of identity, even his broken recollection of glory" (p. 34). Because to compare his present agony with the happiness he had known in life and the bliss he had known in Heaven only exacerbates his suffering, Ellerbee initially resolves to "let them have all of it, his measly joy, his scrapbook past, his hope too," leaving him with "only pure pain, the grand vocabulary they had given him to appreciate it" (p. 35).

His strategy for minimizing suffering is defeated by the arrival of Ladlehaus. Ladlehaus's appearance compels Ellerbee not only to remember, but also to compare, and he is soon feeling anger at the injustice of the fact that he, the good man, was dispatched to death before his time, while Ladlehaus, a petty thief and crime's second ba-

Reading Stanley Elkin

nana, lived on past his hundredth year, enjoying an untroubled old age. Ellerbee tries to escape feeling once again, when Ladlehaus attempts to describe his wife's televised reaction to his murder and other earthly occurrences postdating his death, but he finally abandons his flight from the accomplice and his recollections, lying down in the river of molten lava and excrement that is Hell's floor. The legions of the damned crowd around this supine figure, imagining him to be dead, and he becomes aware of "their collective stench like the swamps of men dead in earthquake, trench warfare—though Ellerbee knew that for all his vocabularly there were no proper analogies in Hell, only the mildest approximations" (p. 39). Although he is raised from seeming death by a female denizen who handles his penis to prove that he still lives, his moment in the muck has not only convinced him that he retains his free will, but has also led him to discover the means through which he can—tentatively, at any rate— conquer Hell and outwit God's plan for it. While the onlookers encourage him to flee his pain and keep busy (Hell's conventional wisdom), Ellerbee kneels in the slime, prompting one of the tormented, then many at once, to see that he " 'looks like he's praying' " (p. 40). He begins by invoking the Deity as " 'Lord God of Ambush and Unconditional Surrender...Power Play God of Judo Leverage. Grand Guinol, Martial Artist,' " and once Ellerbee has compared Him to " 'an old man at a picnic' " and evoked His " 'zoned Heaven in Holy Escrow' " (p. 41), God responds, asking Ellerbee what he wants. " 'An explanation,' " Ellerbee replies, and the analogue upon which "The Conventional Wisdom" is founded gradually reveals itself.

As the novella proceeds, Ellerbee comes to be more and more explicitly identified with Job, that other good man whose undeserved and unaccountable sufferings lead him to reject the conventional wisdom offered by his friends. God appears as precipitously to Ellerbee as He does to Job, although Ellerbee, acquainted with the circumstances of his predecessor's audience with Him, is not to be put off with any argument for His awesomeness. Ellerbee wants no " 'Job job,' " he tells the Lord, turning the tables on Him by refusing to hear His "Where were you when I...?" taunts and insisting that what *he* wants to know is where *He* was when Ellerbee was being virtuous and moral, and why, having lived that kind of life, he has been relegated to Hell. He was damned, God answers in a fit of pique, because he failed to precisely honor the commandments— neglecting to honor his parents (whom he, as an orphan, had never met) at one point and taking God's name in vain at another—and because he thought Heaven looked like a theme park. That such petty trespasses can result in eternal damnation outrages Ellerbee, and he prays that God will close down Hell and eliminate the damned for- ever, a plea that prompts God to "light up Hell's blazes like the sur- face of a star" in His fury. His response is just what Ellerbee had anticipated, and he "wouldn't have it any other way. *He'd* damned him, no surrogate in saint's clothing but the real McCoy Son of a Bitch God whose memory Ellerbee would treasure and eternally re- pudiate forever, happily ever after, world without end" (p. 45). Eller- bee, quite clearly, recapitulates the point that Elkin had years earlier perceived Faulkner's Job figures to be dramatizing: "from the point of view of William Faulkner," he wrote in his dissertation, "the mod- ern Job comes off second best to the man who will, as it were, curse God and live."[13]

Elkin's Job confronts God and learns neither the infinite mag- nificence nor the incommensurability of the universe but the petty, doctrinaire moralism that permeates the creation and deprives it of all seriousness for him. At this point he realizes the full significance of the fact that "everything was true, even the conventional wis- dom," for the conventional wisdom has been proven to be the one and only ground of his being, a fantastic realm "made up like a shot in the dark and imagined into reality" but nonetheless solid, actual, inescapably *there* for him. This recognition leaves him with two choices: to continue to avoid exacerbating the torments of Hell by re- nouncing hope, memory, and identity, by living in it as Patty Fins- berg says Ben Flesh lives in the world—unattached, " 'even emptier-handed than the rest of us' " (*TF*, p. 210); or to accept it as the only world he's got, and to oppose its terms as he affirms its real- ity and assumes responsibility for his existence within it. Having watched Push the Bully "make do" with his "bully's sour solace" and his commitment to resistance, and having seen Leo Feldman come to the conclusion that he is not a "bad man" but a man who

Reading Stanley Elkin

affirms and loves his life, we are in little suspense as to what Eller-bee's choice, even in Hell, must be. Resolving to remain no longer Hell's isolate and alienated man, Ellerbee determines to find Ladle-haus, with whom he can share his irreconcilable impulses toward the Creator and His Plan, and with whom he can reminisce about Minneapolis-St. Paul, about his wife, May, and her TV interviews fol-lowing Ellerbee's murder, and about the life that the two of them lived in the Twin Cities.

"The Conventional Wisdom" succeeds on the same terms on which Elkin's other work succeeds—through the elaboration and re-solution of metaphoric (as opposed to philosophical or narrative) ten-sions. The metaphor that dictates the resolution of "The Conven-tional Wisdom" is metaphor itself, or, more precisely, analogy. Once Ellerbee has recognized that "there were no proper analogies in Hell, only the mildest approximations"—a discovery he must "die" to make—he has stumbled upon a central truth about the nether-world and the source of the torment it ceaselessly inflicts upon its in-habitants: Hell is what it is and nothing else. Like the "ultimate inner city" to which Ellerbee compares it when he first arrives, Hell represents the solid, inevitable, and unchanging, a reality as somber, unmediatable, and unassimilable as the moon. Into Hell's eternal im-mutability Ellerbee introduces the analogy—a simple, human rhe-torical ploy. Although it can neither douse the flames nor dam the excremental rivers that constitute the denizens' primary sources of torment, analogy can nonetheless subvert the netherworld's chaos by intruding relation and connection into it. To say that one thing is like another is to violate the informing logic of Hell, its ethos and meta-physics, which insists that all things are separate, irreconcilable, un-related, distinct and fixed. Thus, in turning to the analogy—by rec-ognizing the stench of the damned to be like something else, and by acting upon that knowledge—Ellerbee is repudiating his earlier pro-pensities toward solitude, passivity, and self-abnegation and moving toward the relational nexes that transcend (and to that extent defeat) the open-ended, eternal meaninglessness and inexplicability of Hell. Ellerbee rises from his figurative death to give the damned the gift of analogy, to prove to them that "the grand vocabulary they had been given with which to appreciate their pain" (p. 35) can be trans-

formed from an affliction into a means of counteracting Hell's oppressive irreversibility and fixity. He has succeeded, in other words,
in liberating the imaginations of the damned that they might have
the slight solace of mediating their torment with similes and analogies, thus altering modestly the changelessness of Hell, transforming
it, in language at any rate, from a realm of necessity to one of possibility, from a bourne of hopelessness to one of—albeit qualified—
hope. This explains why Ellerbee kneels in the muck (" 'Looks like
he's praying,' " comments one onlooker, exercising his rusty apti-
tude for simile); it explains, too, why God answers his summons,
struck as He is by analogies (" 'Lord God of Ambush and Unconditional Surrender' ") emanating from Hell, where there have been
"no proper analogies." God angrily denies Ellerbee's petition that
He close down Hell, but He has, in the process of explaining to Ellerbee the reasons behind his relegation to Hell, made of Himself "a
memory Ellerbee would treasure and eternally repudiate forever,
happily ever after, world without end" (p. 45). Analogy enables Ellerbee to outmaneuver God and to bring to Hell's formlessness and randomness a new relationality and human meaning. His discovery
allows him as well the anticipation of one of the few pleasures the
Underworld permits: "And one day he would look for himself in
Ladlehaus' glowing blisters" (p. 46)—one day, in other words, he
would experience the distinctly qualified but nonetheless real pleasure of having his own existence reconfirmed and affirmed by seeing
it reflected in the suppurating wounds of a fellow sufferer.

    That God is aware of the revolts carried out against Him by El-
lerbee, Ladlehaus, Quiz, and Lesefario is evidenced by His attempts
at coopting and mocking the three of them. He answers Ladlehaus's
challenge only in His own time and according to His own purpose,
even though he does come subsequently to regret having smote Quiz
at Ladlehaus's bidding. Quiz's rebellion is similarly dependent upon
divine intervention, his translation to Heaven being accomplished
not as a result of anything he did but because Christ willed it, and
because God could not or would not reverse a decision of His Son.
God manifests His omnipotence and invulnerability most un-
abashedly in relation to Lesefario's failed gesture of heroism, pick-
ing up on his counting scheme after its originator and his adherents

Reading Stanley Elkin

have abandoned it. His mocking reiteration of the count constitutes a crushing demonstration to the damned of Who the true Eternal Timekeeper is, and His declaring of an end to time so shortly after they ceased their counting multiplies exponentially their sense of self-betrayal and defeat. Only Ellerbee manages to successfully oppose God with no assistance other than His explanation of his relegation to Hell. His rebellion allows him to realize at once that he retains his free will even in Hell, and that he can use it to define himself in Hell's definitionless bourn as the unassimilable and uncompromised man, one whose torment is rendered bearable only by—to recall Push the Bully's formula—"the cabala of [his] hate, of [his] irreconcilableness" (*C&K*, p. 216).

Ellerbee's resolve to eternally repudiate God places him squarely in the ranks of those Elkin protagonists from whom assimilation is an impossibility and defiance a necessity, those who have "something...reprobate and unreconstructed" in themselves, as Boswell puts it, "if not the soul, then the will or the glands of [their] need" (*B*, p. 373). By defining himself through his opposition to the prevailing ethos, Ellerbee takes up the philosophical attitude that animates Feldman of "In the Alley" and Leo Feldman of *A Bad Man*[14] and Alexander Main of "The Bailbondsman," all of whom share Push the Bully's feeling that "There isn't any magic, but your no is still stronger than your yes" and would similarly affirm his declaration that "distrust is where I put my faith" (*C&K*, p. 215). Ellerbee's refusal to be reconciled is clearly an extension of the typical Elkin protagonist's commitment to resistance; this point—like so many in *The Living End*—is anticipated in Elkin's dissertation discussion of Faulkner's religious symbolism. Mink Snopes best exemplifies Faulkner's attitude toward God, Elkin argued, for Snopes learns that "men need not worry whether things work out for the best or not, that man is in an alien world, that he is to be tested, and that the source of the testing is a God who, despite his functioning as man's ostensible enemy, makes man's existence meaningful to him simply by giving him the opportunity to struggle, to resist."[15]

The Living End closes with God's annihilation of everything, a conclusion difficult to explain if we assume (as we have been assuming) that the life-affirming gestures of Ellerbee, Ladlehaus, Quiz, and

Lesefario represent the real thematic center of the triptych. The concluding apocalypse comes to seem more explicable and consonant and less gratuitously cynical if we follow John Irving's cue[16] and read *The Living End* not as a satire of Christian eschatology but as an allegory in which afterlife stands for life, the gestures of the various protagonists representing those acts that give life shape and make it meaningful.[17] Such a reading of the triptych necessarily alters the terms through which we perceive the God Who will shut it all down, certainly, His Judaeo-Christian deity aspect becoming minimized, rendered secondary to His representation of the ground of all being, the animating spirit of all life. He is aligned with and depicted as inseparable from the conventional wisdom because He is both the life we seek to understand and our attempts to understand it, both the existence we know and the complex of assumptions we have evolved through which to know it.

Elkin's personification of God in these difficult terms is clarified somewhat by his dissertation's explanation of the God Who appears in the pages of Faulkner's novels, where "we are presented with an image of God which is essentially sociological in character. One accepts the sociological slant, of course, but, peculiarly, the sociological projection, the Class God, as it were, turns out to be the God actually determining events."[18] God—the conventional wisdom—is true, then, to recall Ellerbee's phrase, because we believe Him to be true and thus make Him true, that truth becoming the medium in which we live out our days, formulate our sentences, and make our gestures. In this reading, consequently, *The Living End* comes to be seen as an allegory of life that ends in apocalypse because all life ends in dispersion and dissolution; the work's fiction is that such annihilation is general, universal, and simultaneous, rather than personal, individual, and temporally incoincident. This fiction is justified—if it needs justification—by the dramatic closure it permits and the linguistic extravagances it allows. By portraying God as both the source of all life and the embodiment of the intolerable restraints it imposes upon humanity's repacious will toward freedom, by depicting Him as a personification of all we know about life and of all that—because of that knowledge's conventionality and familiarity, its necessary limits—prevents us from finding out more,

Reading Stanley Elkin

Elkin manages to express in allegorical terms the same ambivalent attitude toward existence discernible throughout his work. It is the same ambivalence articulated in Meyer Feldman's epiphanic vision of " 'All the beauty...All the beauty' "[19] in the midst of a city's squalor, and the same that we find in Leo Feldman's ability to affirm his existence at the close of *A Bad Man* in spite of all "wars, histories, deaths of the past, other people's poverties and losses" (*ABM*, p. 336); it is the same ambivalence implicit in Ben Flesh's celebration of "the bouncy anthems of our firms, tears in *my* eyes in the face of all this blessed, sacred, smarmy hope even if I know, as I do know, what I know" (*TF*, p. 75), and the same ambivalence expressed by Alexander Main's contemplation of the mysteries whose solutions have eluded him (" 'Why is life so lovely? The night sweeter than the day, and the day more joyous than the night? Who alive can grieve?...Why doesn't desire die? Why is it that it's the one thing which remains intact, that has some fucking stranglehold on immortality?' " [*S&S*, p. 119]). It is the same ambivalence manifest in a number of other deeply felt monologues in Elkin's fiction, monologues made possible by the temporary suspension of the works' gravitational pull toward dispersion and dissolution so that the protagonist can briefly and sentimentally panegyrize the fullness and plentitude of existence. The God of *The Living End* is, in short, a personification of the impartibility of existence, a dramatization of the inseparability of life's terror from its trivia, its grandeur from its crap, its beauty from its loss. If His annihilation of everything on the closing page of "The State of the Art" doesn't elicit a shudder of anxiety from the reader, the allegory has failed, leaving *The Living End* nothing more than a cartoon version of Christian eschatology. The book is considerably more ambitious and effective than that.

Just before He relegates Heaven, Earth, and Hell to oblivion, God decides to reveal to the living and the dead the whys and wherefores of the creation. Once He has given them a brief review of the trials, punishments, blessings, and covenants He has visited upon humanity over the centuries, He finally explains why it was all necessary. Not so man would have free will, He assures them, and not because He " 'gets off on goodness,' " either; " 'It was Art! It was always Art. I work by contrasts and metrics, by beats and silences. It

was all Art. *Because it makes a better story is why'* " (p. 144).[20] For
Elkin, as for God, "it makes a better story" if things end apocalypti-
cally, and anyone who doubts the validity of this analogy need only
glance at the rear panel of the book's dustjacket, with its depiction
of Stanley Elkin ascending through clouds, or consider that God is
closing down the creation " 'Because I never found My audience' "
(p. 148)—a familiar and justified Elkin complaint. This final analogy
has its amusing overtones, of course, a fact consonant with the comic
purposes of *The Living End.* If it seems not completely compatible
with the triptych's alternative perception of God as the creator and
embodiment of the conventional wisdom, the point it allows Elkin to
express may justify the minor disparity. There is a good deal of evidence, in other words, that the value that underlies all of Elkin's
God's creation is a value that underlies all of Elkin's own creations
as well.

The most persuasive demonstration of the centrality of story as
a value in Elkin's fiction is not the plethora of stories incorporated
into his short stories, novellas, and novels; more compelling is the
frequency with which the resolutions of his works are dictated by his
protagonists' attitudes toward the relationships to the stories they
have to tell and the ones they act out. Leo Feldman learns through
his narrative of his relationship with Dedman that he is not a "bad
man"; the recounting saves him from despair and perhaps—if only
through inadvertence—from a fatal beating as well. Alexander Main,
who has won or denied men their freedom according to the narratives of their histories that he has chosen to present to judges and
magistrates, liberates himself by creating a story—the mystery of
Crainpool's whereabouts—that will keep alive his curiosity and rein-
vigorate his passion for life. Ellerbee decides that an aspect of his
opposition to God and His plan for Hell will be the exchange of stories of their shared past in Minneapolis with Ladlehaus, the gesture
in a small way subverting the Netherworld's purposed relationless-
ness. Then there are the protagonists for whom defeat, not redemption, is associated with story and storytelling: Dick Gibson, who finds
in middle age that the Franklinian paradigm he has attempted to live
out has left him distinctly unaltered, unmythic, and unreified, and
who responds to the nothingness he consequently feels surrounding

Reading Stanley Elkin

him by asking his listeners to fill it with their open-ended, meaning-less narratives, rather than himself trying (as his hero, Bob Hope, did) to impose a shape, a story, upon time. The deterioration of Ben Flesh's physical condition is clearly reflected by his self-betrayal in turning the circumstances of his hospital friendship with an RAF lieutenant named Tanner into a story for the edification of a man he doesn't even know at a gas station in Alabama, the narrative he deliv-ers helplessly replacing truth with a facile irony, accuracy with faked melodrama. Marshall Preminger's self-destruction is largely trig-gered by a banal and tawdry recounting of his father's death, nar-rated by a woman too blandly unimaginative to conceive what such stories can mean or do to their hearers, which he is powerless to insu-late himself against or assimilate. And, finally, Lesefario abandons the effort to "humanize time" in Hell "by giving it form," the "tick-ock" he has briefly imposed upon it (to use Kermode's model of the simplest possible plot) relinquished as "purely successive, disorgan-ized time,"[21] Hell's durational meaninglessness, reasserts itself upon his abjuration of his hopeful project.

The difference between having one's defeat or redemption asso-ciated with story is the difference between accepting the stories we have and knowing what stories we need. For Elkin's protagonists, the only redemption to be had is gained through pushing toward unac-customed stories and unfamiliar analogies, "the possibilities inher-ent in rhetoric" proving as real and as hopeful as any possibilities they are likely to encounter. The human mind's capacity for manipu-lating, creating analogies out of and devising relational matrices of plot between the words of the "grand vocabulary" we are given with which to appreciate our pain does not alter the condition of that pain, but it does provide the consoling effect of allowing us to de-scribe that pain to others, to make it seem sad, funny, metaphoric, significant. Language, analogy, story: these are the means through which Elkin's protagonists and his fiction attempt to intrude be-tween now and the annihilation to come the consolation of "the snug coups of correspondence" and the literary image of "the grand actu-ality of the reconciled" (p. 92). They will not transform the world that is their subject, but they will alter our perceptions of it, under-mining habitual thought modes by proving that "there is no conven-

World without Simile, World without Story, Amen

tional wisdom. The truth comes in 57 day-glo colors."[22] This point, of course, harmonizes the apparently divergent purposes of representational exactitude and aesthetic license in his work—this, and the fact that *The Living End* more completely than any of his previous books liberates the fictional voice that is (to borrow one of Leo Feldman's favorite terms) Elkin's way of bearing down on the world.

NOTES

1. Sanders, "Interview," p. 133.
2. Bernt and Bernt, "Stanley Elkin on Fiction;" p. 16.
3. Sanders, "Interview," p. 132.
4. Duncan, "Conversation with Elkin and Gass," p. 77.
5. See particularly Robert Edward Colbert, "The American Salesman as Pitchman and Poet in the Fiction of Stanley Elkin," *Critique* 21: 2 (1980): 152-58.
6. Sanders, "Interview," p. 141.
7. Bernt and Bernt, "Stanley Elkin on Fiction," p. 19.
8. Stanley Elkin, *The Living End* (New York: E. P. Dutton, 1979), p. 25.
9. R. Z. Sheppard, "Don't Touch That Dial!" review of *The Dick Gibson Show* by Stanley Elkin, *Time*, 1 March 1971, p. 82.
10. Sanders, "Interview," p. 133.
11. The book actually went through three changes of title, moving from *The Conventional Wisdom,* the title of Part I, to *The Bottom Line,* Part II's title, to *The Living End* (letter received from Stanley Elkin, 3 September 1978).
12. Kermode, *Sense of an Ending,* p. 45.
13. Elkin, "Religious Themes," p. 156.
14. The line of descent linking Ellerbee to Leo Feldman is evident if we compare Ellerbee's taunting prayer (" 'Lord God of Ambush and Unconditional Surrender' ") with the following prayer of Feldman's: " 'Lord God of hooked scourge and knotted whip, of sidearms and sidecar, of bloodhound and twoway radio, vigilant God of good neighborhoods and locked Heaven—lend us thy anger. Teach us, O God, revulsion' " (*ABM,* p. 228).
15. Elkin, "Religious Themes," p. 185.
16. John Irving, "An Exposé of Heaven and Hell," review of

Reading Stanley Elkin

The Living End by Stanley Elkin, *New York Times Book Review,* 10 June 1979, p. 7.

17. Elkin read Sophocles and Melville in similar terms, arguing in his dissertation that their work is "Godfearing, its hell the recognizable world, and its heroes, the gratuitously doomed, the playfully damned, walk up and down in it" ("Religious Themes," p. 367).

18. Ibid., p. 374.

19. Elkin, "The Sound of Distant Thunder," p. 57.

20. Alan Wilde cites these lines in arguing that the God of *The Living End* represents an emblem of modernism, a kind of Brooksian New Critical Creator. See his "Irony in the Postmodern Age: Toward a Map of Suspensiveness," in *Boundary 2: A Journal of Postmodern Literature:* 1 (Fall 1980): 35-38.

21. Kermode, *Sense of an Ending,* p. 45.

22. Sanders, "Interview," p. 133.

7

Lunchpail Mills
Meets the Epilogue Man

It is probably appropriate that a writer whose work assumes and dramatizes the basic changelessness of the human situation should experience, in the critical response his work elicits, a precise recapitulation of that very idea. What the reviewers of *George Mills* generally said about it was very much what reviewers had been saying about Elkin novels from *Boswell* forward: that it is "a lavish yet unsatisfying everything-goes-in variety show" and a "fabulistic free-for-all"[1]; that it is "disorganized," a novel whose author "stops whatever matter is at hand to tell us one shaggy dog story after another," thus substituting "sheet garrulousness for plotting."[2] Such familiar responses have this to be said in their defense: *George Mills* is not only Elkin's longest and most complexly organized work, but it also makes the fewest concessions to surface clarity, to narrative coherence and accessibility. Whereas the time frame of Elkin's previous novels spans at most the lifetime of the central character, *George Mills* covers some 1,000 years; whereas his novels prior to *The Living End* had all concerned single protagonists, *George Mills* deals with four distinct versions of the title character and elevates another character to the level of semi-antagonist as well; and, whereas *Boswell* through *The Franchiser* establish a consistent plot situation to which all of the works' incidents and anecdotes are traceable, *George Mills* consists of a number of story lines (seven largely separable strands, plus a number of vignettes and set pieces) that appear, on first reading, related to and integrated with each other in only the most tenuous ways. To argue that *George Mills* is not a novel that neatly resolves itself into aesthetic consistency and wholeness is one thing, but to present this characteristic (as many reviewers did) as a deficiency is to assume that Elkin was trying to write a well-made novel on the Cleanth Brooks model and somehow failed. This assumption, in turn, implies another one: that Elkin's fiction is perceived most fruitfully in the context of the modernist novel tradition, with its formal conventions and predominantly representational objectives. It has been my contention, to the contrary, that Elkin's fiction is more accurately perceived as a kind of bridge spanning two distinct literary modes—the traditional modernist novel (exemplified for Elkin primarily by the work of Faulkner and Bellow) and the postmodernist metafictional novel (Gass, Coover, Pynchon, and Nabokov the practitioners with whom Elkin's work and public statements have most consistently aligned him). The fact that these traditions meet and attempt reconciliation in Elkin's work demands further consideration in a treatment of *George Mills* for two reasons: first, because two recent critical discussions of Elkin's work have offered substantial reinforcing arguments for his placement between these two literary camps, and, second, because the book so effectively dramatizes the difficulties involved in and the discoveries that can result from the deliberate compounding of these two fictional modes.

In *Literature against Itself: Literary Ideas in Modern Society,* Gerald Graff includes Elkin among a number of writers who, in his view, manage to capture in prose the randomness and spontaneity of contemporary life without surrendering critical perspective to them. Impressed by the linguistic energy of Elkin's fiction as well as by its vivid, concrete detailing of the professional actualities through which so many of his characters define themselves, Graff cites Elkin as a writer who succeeds in reconciling a crucial involvement in the world he is depicting with the detachment necessary to that world's comprehension. Such an approach, Graff concludes, "restores that state of balance between unchecked fabulation and objective social realism without which fiction, in [Robert] Alter's phrase, must 'go slack,' degenerating into a trivial playing with the infinity of imaginative possibilities."[3]

Concerned less with espousing an ideal relationship between literature and society than with characterizing postmodernism and dis-

tinguishing it from its modernist ancestry, Alan Wilde produces
Elkin as a prime exhibit of metafictional tendencies tempered by for-
malist reflexes in two extremely insightful essays. In " 'Strange Displacements of the Ordinary': Apple, Elkin, Barthelme and the
Problem of the Excluded Middle,'' Wilde discusses the kind of fiction that falls somewhere between works of indicative address and
works of a more subjunctive mood or character, between realism and
reflexivity, between the sort of narratives that depict human experience and those that pose epistemological questions about the nature
and understanding of human experience. This in-between kind of fiction Wilde designates as "midfiction," and he characterizes it in
some detail. "Perceiving the world as neither objectively knowable
nor as totally opaque, making reference to experience without pretending to re-present it, such fiction,'' Wilde argues, "comprises the
tertium quid of current literature: experimentalism's poor relation,
realism's militant and rebellious heir, but finally, and most impor-
tantly, something independent of both—an integral, self-sufficient
mode of apprehending and expressing the world which, for want of
an adequate designation, continues to languish in the outback of
current criticism."[4]

What distinguishes midfiction from metafiction, on the one
hand, is its refusal to dispense completely with the representational
illusion; what distinguishes it from realism, on the other hand, is its
simultaneous and equally marked unwillingness to contain its materials within the bounds of probability and verisimilitude that realism
traditionally observes. Midfiction represents a useful classification
because it identifies, outside the familiar categories of realism and
metafiction, a kind of contemporary writing that draws sustenance
from each but belongs comfortably to neither. The two major risks
for the writer producing this kind of fiction are that his reviews will
tend to read like elementary lectures on the necessity of form in fiction, and the more serious risk that in his enthusiastic self-
emancipation from the critical and artistic precepts of modernism he
will prove himself deserving and needful of the pedagogic drill. (The
post–*Slaughterhouse-Five* work of Kurt Vonnegut is perhaps the
most familiar example of fiction that has succumbed too fully to the
excesses of imaginative freedom implicit in the repudiation of mod-

Reading Stanley Elkin

ernist literary imperatives.[5]) But there is much to be gained as well from staking out a kind of middle ground between the recognizable modes of fiction: a greater latitude of invention, for one thing, and an ability to achieve interstitial rhetorical effects inaccessible to writers working at the formal antipodes. A more significant attribute of midfiction, however, is that its midway position between forms enables it to mediate effectively between them, to establish a sort of dialogue between the themes and the techniques of the two modes. The moral and social questions that are realism's predominant concern cross with the technical and epistemological questions with which so much of metafiction deals. If the resultant admixture is less shapely than the modernist novel was, it is also more intensely reflective of the impartibility of existence, of the necessarily random but oddly unified, contiguous, simultaneous feel of lived experience.

That such a mode of fiction is perfectly suited to Elkin's gifts and artistic temperment is obvious. His imagination has, from the very beginning, chafed against the limitations that realism imposes, and yet the pervasive inflection discernible in his style—that of Americanized Yiddish, the idiom of Jewish comedy—could not be more earthbound, concrete, culture specific. But then the complexity and the baroque excesses of that style conflict with the necessary opacity of the narrative surface in realism, apparently diverting the reader's attention from world to word—until, through the odd inversion upon which Elkin's best work turns, it becomes clear that what is being depicted through this extravagance of syntax, diction, and simile are distinctly earthy, often grossly physical, simple, recognizable, fundamental human questions, situations, and problems. No American writer attempts with greater deliberation or risk to span the antinomies of contemporary fiction—form and freedom, verisimilitude and imaginative release—than does Elkin, his efforts at reconciling these contraries having gained him, among other things, a collection of wildly mixed, frequently contradictory reviews.

Those reviews became more contradictory and contentious in the early 1970s, when to the routine charge that the structures of Elkin's work are episodic, loose, too generously accommodating of heterogeneous materials was added the objection that his fiction had begun to subordinate plot and character to language, that he was sacrificing the mimetic assumptions that had anchored his previous work in the real to flamboyant flights of word play suspiciously resembling the baroque garrulousness in which he had previously indulged his protagonists. "The Making of Ashenden" represented Elkin's first extreme departure from conventional novelistic decorum, in part because it dealt with an utterly two-dimensional protagonist engaged in a distinctly fanciful quest, but also because the novella placed that protagonist in a highly improbable situation and then proceeded to depict the utterly fantastic sequel with a precision and detail worthy of the most uncompromising realist.

The Franchiser, similarly, mixed modes in its intermingling of the wildly implausible twins and triplets and their eccentrically fatal afflictions with the referentiality of the novel's cultural commentary and disturbingly mimetic description of the multiple sclerotic's symptoms and grim decline into ecstasy. In that novel Elkin managed to bring together the technical and the personal into nearly perfect balance, the ability of the set of metaphors suffusing the book to contain and reconcile all of its incidents, anecdotes, and concerns coalescing with Elkin's unavoidable identification with his protagonist to insure an equilibrium of aesthetic detachment and engagement, imaginative freedom and emotional involvement. The novel that most convincingly demonstrates Elkin's mastery of New Critical ideals of form in fiction writing, The Franchiser appears also to have freed him to abandon that mode in favor of a fiction that allows an even greater range of metaphoric and thematic improvisation. The Living End, which succeeded The Franchiser, is not a well-made novel or even a novel, the dustjacket designating it "A Triptych by Stanley Elkin." The purely imaginary landscapes of Heaven and Hell permitted Elkin to freely imagine, metamorphose, parody, fabulate, and joke, and if the book closes on a more final note than any previous work, the ending represents not artistic resolution but only arbitrary closure, the apocalypse as the writer/God's ultimate one-liner.

George Mills, which shares some of its predecessor's spirit of disengagement from the traditional strictures of literary form, does present itself as a novel, but not one in which imaginative extravagance has been very much curtailed by or sacrificed to the exigen-

cies of artistic unity. Nor has Elkin been particularly apologetic
about his novel's superabundance of plots, speeches, anecdotes,
stuff; much to the contrary, he has insisted that in writing *George
Mills* he came to the liberating realization "that I was a novelist, that
anything I say is a part of this novel *is* a part of this novel."[6] Elkin
doesn't amplify upon what confers relevance, consistency, congruence upon the divergent materials of *George Mills,* but the likeliest
medium of that correspondence of parts would have to be the language through which they are presented. Elkin's elaborately rhetorical prose unites and common-denominates the novel's multiformity
of voices, epochs, classes, and subjects, imposing a surface harmony
upon its discordant details. Despite its unifying influence, style proves inadequate to the task of holding together this deliberately over-
stuffed novel, and it becomes necessary to account for the excesses of
George Mills on alternative aesthetic grounds. In its incessant proliferation of extreme circumstances and exaggerated situations, *George
Mills* represents Elkin's most elaborate novelistic attempt at evoking
"the lost sense of wonder suddenly revived"[7] that he admired in
Faulkner's work, while the novel dramatizes simultaneously a protagonist for whom the experience of extremity inevitably concludes in
the restoration of a changeless, repetitive, spirit-defeating quotidian.
The novel depicts through a miscellany of narratives the conflict central to so much of Elkin's fiction: between extremity and the ordinary, between perceptions of existence that assume its progressively
significant shapeliness and those that take for granted its meaninglessly consecutive tedium. To read *George Mills* as a formless novel is
to read only Mills's half of the book, because for those around him
books, like lives, have the potential for being coherent, plottable, capable of resolution. What shape *George Mills* has derives from its extended and intensive examination of the form that books and lives
can be said to have, the novel using a succession of interrelated plots
to illustrate the inescapability and duplicities of beginning-middle-
end and to question the reality of character and the existence of fate.

The continuity between *George Mills* and Elkin's previous work
is reflected by his comment that he used to feel that if the present
project didn't "get it right," the next one would, whereas "this time
I think I got it right with *George Mills*."[8] One of the central themes

of the novel, for instance, is clearly anticipated in Dick Gibson's desire that his life resolve itself into shapeliness and mythlike self-containment, that his birthdays come to seem like "third act curtains in a play" and that external opposition mold his days into a redemptive and dynamic meaningfulness (*DGS*, p. 270). The disillusionment of these aspirations looks forward equally to *George Mills*. Ben Flesh is speaking in a similarly anticipatory spirit when he recognizes that "the lines of my life are beginning to come together, make a pattern. . . . It's getting on, the taxis are gathering, the limos, the cops are up on their horses in the street and I don't even know my lines—though they're beginning to come together—or understand the character." All he knows of himself, he confesses, is that he's "one of those birds who ain't satisfied unless he has a destiny, even though he knows that destiny sucks" (*TF*, pp. 134-35). In Dick Gibson's disappointed longing for a life lent order and consecutivity by a myth-incited dynamism and Ben Flesh's horrified recognition that the disease demyelinating his nerves is the only discernible configuration his personality has can be seen the general thematic antinomies underlying the "fabulistic free-for-all" that is *George Mills* and supplying the rules by which it is played.

George Mills is not, of course, so much a protagonist as a historical succession of protagonists, each one suffering under the identical curse of social immobility, a curse which the liege of the first Mills defines for all the rest. " 'Learn this, Mills,' " explains Guillalume, the son of a tenth-century nobleman whom Mills serves as stable boy,

"There are distinctions between men, humanity is dealt out like cards. There is natural sovereignty like the face value on coins. Men have their place. Even here, where we are now, at large, outside of place, beyond it, out of bounds and offside, loosened from the territorial limits, they do. It's no accident that Guillalume is the youngest son for all it appears so, no more accident than that you are the horseshit man. It isn't luck of the draw but the brick walls of some secret, sovereign Architecture that makes us so."

Whereupon the first George Mills mourns for the terrible heritage he has yet to bequeath to his descendants, grieves "for the Millsness he was doomed to pass on, for the frayed, flawed genes—he thought blood—of the second-rate, back-seat, low-down life, foreseeing...a continuum of the less than average, of the small-time, poached Horseshit Man life."[9] Thus begins for the generations of Mills males, as Elkin elsewhere puts it, "a thousand years in the typing pool."

Each Mills has two things to pass on to his son, then: the doom itself, and the knowledge of it. Each son (for the fatality dictates that each Mills have but one son, no collateral offspring issuing from the centuries of Mills marriages) must respond to his heritage as best he can. The first Mills, upon learning of the familial destiny, resolves never to have children and thus to prevent his line's perpetuation, but Guillalume reminds him of a wench pregnant at the manor whose condition has already precluded that dodge. George Mills XXXXIII (a native of Britain alive during the reign of George IV) seeks to circumvent the doom by raising himself above it, by follow-ing the example of those thousands of his era who had managed to parlay the reform bills, patronage, and hard work into social ad-vancement, into entry into the suddenly burgeoning middle class. His efforts to curry the favor of the English monarch, however, only get him exiled to Turkey on a mission the hazards of which he can't suspect and in flight from which he bears his burden of fate to the land of opportunity. This Mills's grandson hopes initially to circum-vent the doom by moving his family from Milwaukee to Florida ("fleeing Corinth" is how that he thinks of it), but he ultimately re-signs himself to "the myth victim's delicious condition, squeezed dry of force to change his life, with, at the same time, his eye on all the eleventh hour opportunities which could change it for him" (p. 175). This Mills's son—the novel's principal protagonist—can't be certain whether his parents haven't managed an eleventh-hour eva-sion of the family doom, for he deserts them immediately upon learning of a prophecy foretelling his mother's pregnancy with the daughter who will variegate the line and consequently void its curse. But late twentieth century Mills acts very much as if the doom is still in effect, declaring himself "saved"—immune to harm or conse-quence, impervious to the larger excruciations of existence—as the distillation and culmination of ten centuries of Mills peripherality, anonymity, and insignificance.

Lunchpail Mills Meets the Epilogue Man

What interests Elkin most in all of this is not the occasion it provides for the mimetically detailed depiction of lower-class life
through the years; the Millses' blue-collar condition is merely the
symptom of their fate, and this fate and its meaning most intensely
engage Elkin's imagination. There is something ultimately paradoxical and strange, after all, about a fate that decrees changelessness, a
destiny that dictates nothing but more of the same. While still a boy,
the first George Mills comes bitterly to this truth when he is forced
to compare the deep-dyed and various colors of the aristocratic life
with another, faintly hued tapestry. Brought from the stable to his
lord's house for the first time on an errand, young Mills gapes at a
quartered arms displayed above "a hearth so wide and deep they
could have burned villages in it,"

the bright shield as mysterious to me as the position of the stars, one
who only having heard of honor suddenly confronted with it . . . star-
ing up at honor's manifest lares and penates glowing like primary
color on the very shape of Honor. . . . And oh, the dyes, the dyes! No
such colors in nature or in life. No sky so blue nor blood so red nor
grass so green; the lineage repudiate to Nature; candescent even in
the measly taper'd dark, the fuels they burned the oils of unicorns or
the sweet fierce heroic burning breath of the gilded rampant animals
themselves perhaps! [pp. 27-28]

Astonished at this visual lesson in the convergence of values
with chromatics, and dumbfounded by the preternatural bright-
nesses of nobility's true colors, Mills turns his attention to a tapestry
that reflects nobility's perception of his world. He notices immediately that this is not like a picture in church, because there are in it

No saints with halos like golden quoits above their heads, no nim-
buses on edge like valued coins, not our Lord, or Mother Mary, or allegory at all, but only the ordinary pastels of quotidian life. A
representation, in tawns and rusts, in the bleached greens and
drought yellows of high summer, in dusty blacks and whites gone off,
in blues like distant foliage. Everything the shade of clumsy weather.
There were gypsies in it and beggars. There were honest men—
hewers of wood and haulers of water. Legging'd and standing behind
their full pouches of scrotum like small pregnancies. There were
women in wimples. Ned and Nancy. Pete and Peg. It was how they

Reading Stanley Elkin

saw us—see us. Shepherds and farmers. Millers, bakers, smithies.
Mechanics with wooden tools, leather. Pastoral, safe, settled in the
tapestry condition of their lives, woven into it as the images themselves. [pp. 28-29]

Mills objects that the tapestry doesn't reflect him or his descendants
because it conveys no sense of their resentment, nothing of the
"something sour in their blue collar blood." But this is merely his
way of considering the source, of recognizing the unavoidable patrician tendency to romanticize him and his lot; otherwise, the tapestry
not only dramatizes his condition for him—it also defines the metaphoric terms of that condition for the novel as a whole. Mills and his
posterity are not to live amidst primary colors, colors that exceed
nature's own or symbolize the magnificence of humanity's aspirations, the purity of its ethical abstractions; theirs will be the hues of
natural compromise and attenuation, of seasons on the wane. More-
over, their lives will be marked by nothing mysterious; no mythology
will redeem them, no allegorical scheme will be adumbrated by their
days and ways. All that they could be said to symbolize is
themselves—themselves and their ability to perpetuate themselves,
which the "full pouches of scrotum like small pregnancies" simile
deftly summarizes. Save for that, their surface is their substance, the
mundane, quotidian world the only one they and their descendants
will ever know.

Such, then, are the deprivations to which the Millses and their
lot are born. But perhaps the cruelest and most painful deficiency
they must suffer is the absence of adventure, growth, tension—in a
word, plot—in their lives. Circumstances seldom ripen for them, and
they almost never have anything on the line; their potential for
change is negligible because they so infrequently experience the
conditions that foster change, and dramatic occasions are as alien to
them as are Jacuzzis and downstairs maids. Purpose, will, self-
assertiveness—these are qualities their superiors have, and in the
service of which Mills and his kind are often dispatched as instru-
mentalities. It is in carrying out their superiors' designs that the
Millses come closest to experiencing extremity, to knowing for themselves the old thrill of opposition, the distraction of conflict and resolution.

Lunchpail Mills Meets the Epilogue Man

The novel's three major narrative units each dramatize a Mills vicariously participating in an adventure precipitated by his betters; he travels to an exotic location ("the border towns," "somewhere off-shore") far from the civilization that has defined his meniality, only to be returned there again.

In the first of these, Mills I sets out for the Crusades in the serv-ice of Guillalume, but the two take a wrong turn and end up in what would someday become Wieliczka, Poland, where they are put to work in a salt mine. (Mills's job, that of talking his horse around a great central shaft in the mine's core, is one of the novel's many em-blems of the Millses' possibilities for advancement in the world.) Es-caping the mine, they travel back toward Northumbria, and when they encounter a pack of barbarians impatiently awaiting the arrival of the Word, Mills (because these infidels expect that the message must be "the last shall be first") is compelled to become the evangel of pacifism, of civilization and submission to authority. " 'I have come to tell you...*Not*...to hit,' " he exhorts them, " 'God hates hitters. He thinks they stink....Hitting isn't good. Yes, Lord. Thank you, Jesus.' " Thus begins the other Crusade, the one led by "God's blue collar worker," and although Mills apparently fails to proselyt-ize them into compliance with what he offers as the Lord's second imperative (" 'God wants you...to take the stableboys who shovel your horseshit for you and make them princes. Just after not hitting that's what He wants most' "), he nonetheless comes accidentally to know, for the duration of their journey home, what it is to wield power, "what it [is] like to be Guillalume" (p. 41).

Mills XXXXIII is launched into intrigue and adventure early in the nineteenth century. George IV mistakes a character reference written for Mills by a squire as the work of the king's Stuart oppo-nents; thus he dispatches the supposed seditionist to Turkey bearing a gift calculated to enrage the recipient, the Ottoman Emperor-in-waiting, and to consequently ensure Mills's protracted absence from England. For his punishment, Mills is summarily conscripted into the Janissaries, an elite and brutal Turkish fighting corps whose charge, Mills learns, is as much to suppress the Turkish populace as it is to defend it against enemies. He and a companion contrive to flee the Janissary ranks and to find sanctuary in the Emperor's pal-ace, where they are taken for, and taken on as, eunuchs in the sul-

Reading Stanley Elkin

tan's harem. Mills settles comfortably into this asylum ("Complacency, lassitude, getting used to things," he thinks. "The piecemeal slide of the heart. All submissive will's evolutionary easement" [p. 429]), until the threat of his exposure as an intact male and the fear of consequent castration compel him to save himself and his posterity. Pure luck rescues him, finally—luck and his ability to manipulate the protocols that the powerful use to keep the powerless in place. Mills escapes Yildiz Palace because he fortuitously happens upon the corpse of a royal relative and because he understands the complex Turkish mourning rites and the hierarchial ceremonies of notification appropriate to such occasions. "It was all protocol," Elkin's narrator explains,

Because you couldn't draw two unprotocol'd breaths in a row in this, or, for Mills's money, any other Empire either, which was why he'd granted to God what everybody agreed belonged to God—the Sign, the providential deign-given Sign, which was only careful planning, knowing one's onions, the known onions of protocol. . . knowing that the first to learn of a royal's death had the right to strip the bed, signifying not only grief but continuity too, and not only grief and continuity but the grief part absolutely of the highest, purest order, pure because often as not removed from all consanguineous ties and arrangements, the shrill, pure grief of subjects, bystanders, citizens— good clean taxpayer grief! [p. 442]

By observing the prescribed death duties of the Ottoman Empire, Mills provides himself with the opportunity to flee the palace and find sanctuary in the British embassy, the ambassador subsequently securing for him passage on a ship bound for America. Like Ellerbee in The Living End, Mills XXXXIII outwits his oppressor by turning the oppressor's own forms against him; like greatest grandfather Mills, he experiences briefly what it means to initiate action rather than merely to respond to the actions of others, learns what it means temporarily to rise above his family's habitual station and to exercise what another precursor of his—Push the Bully—calls "force."

It is only appropriate that the descendant of the man convinced that he had been saved by "God's Sign" should feel himself similarly saved, in a state of grace, immune to serious consequences. (He believes, in other words, "that nothing could ever happen to him, that he was past it—anticipation and interest and concern and disappointment and injury, and glory too" [p. 297].) But contemporary Mills has nonetheless to experience an adventure of his own, a sequence of casually related events that temporarily changes his life and alters his position. The patrician with whom he becomes involved is Judith Glazer, the daughter of a wealthy St. Louis family; she hires him to accompany her to Mexico, where she is to receive laetrile treatments for her pancreatic cancer. Once in Mexico, his employer has him drive them to the Ciudad Juarez barrio to dispense alms to the poor, hoping that a starving Mexican will murder her for her money and thus give her the consonant, significant death of a martyr. When this fails, she leaves vast sums of money lying about the motel suite that she and Mills share, tempting him to kill her for it. But he declines to cooperate, and the two resign themselves to watching her submit less dramatically to cancer, which her treatments have succeeded not at all in retarding. Initially her companion and gofer, Mills gradually becomes the woman's nurse, not only feeding and washing her but making himself an expert as well in her pain, "reeling off for them, the nurses and doctors at the clinic, Judith's infinite symptoms and impressions with an impressive and devastatingly authentic Siamese collaterality" (p. 249).[10] Judith's death puts Mills out of work, but it also allows him the temporary elevation of being a pallbearer at her funeral, the dead woman having insisted, much to her family's dismay, upon Mills's participation. So Mills takes his place beside immaculately turned-out executives who own banks, newspapers, and NFL franchises, and together they bear Judith to her grave. The funeral over, Mills is dismissed, charged, in effect, with resuming his "yokel's back bench condition" (p. 307).

The progression that these avatars of Mills, and the adventures they undertake, adumbrates is obvious enough: tenth-century Mills is *Homo religiosus,* man subjected to the spiritual, rendered servile to faith; nineteenth-century Mills is *Homo politicus,* man diddled by and subjugated to statecraft and the exercise of power, protocol; and late twentieth century Mills is *Homo psychologicus,* man enslaved by the personal, in thrall to the internal realities of another human be-

Reading Stanley Elkin

ing. In each instance Mills must master a set of conventions, protocols, processes, learning as well the relevant lexicons so that he too
might articulate and proselytize for them; in each instance he is being confronted for the first time with the conventions and sequiturs
that exist above and beyond his own horseshit shoveling, carriage-
hacking, dispossessed-family-evicting experience.

The basic antinomy dramatized by the Millses' adventures—
that of randomness being confronted by form, of life viewed as a
meaningless duration encountering life viewed as a pattern of consequences and a progression of significant, transformative occasions—
represents familiar territory in Elkin's fictional landscape. In ''A
Poetics for Bullies'' Push pits his instincts against the proprieties
and civilized games of John Williams, the paragon whom he mocks
for being a ''model of form''; in *A Bad Man* Feldman opposes the
warden's prison system with his own innate need for disruption of sequiturs in the name of self-aggrandizement; in ''The Bailbondsman'' Main counters what he perceives as the overlegalization both
of the law and of bailbonding with his jaguar's-teeth ethic and self-
generated forms of possibility. What differentiates the Millses most
strikingly from these earlier protagonists is their inability to impose
themselves upon reality, to successfully—as Feldman puts it—''bear
down on the world.'' They, like Marshall Preminger of ''The Condominium,'' are men possessed of inadequately developed senses of
self, men capable of generating energy sufficient to produce resentment and anger at their positions and conditions, but not enough to
change them. These protagonists' lives are most accurately described by a spiritualist whom the young late twentieth century Mills
encounters: '' 'It's an astonishing fact, George, but the truest thing I
know,' '' he explains to the boy. '' 'Our lives happen to us. We don't
make them up. For every hero who means to cross an ocean on a raft,
there are a hundred men fallen overboard, a thousand who find
themselves in the lifeboat by accident' '' (p. 179). Push, Feldman,
and Main do manage, to some extent, to make their lives up, to transform will into personality and to create relatively consistent selves
out of the scraps of their need. But more of Elkin's protagonists—
the narrator of ''Cousin Poor Lesley and the Lousy People,'' Bertie of
''The Guest,'' Dick Gibson, Marshall Preminger, and the Millses

Lunchpail Mills Meets the Epilogue Man

among them—fail, to a lesser or greater extent, in much the same way that James Boswell confesses hat he has failed: "You have to make a life, however grab-bag or eccentric," the protagonist of Elkin's first novel comments, "there has to be routine, pattern. I've failed there. Something about my life gives my life away, something improvised and sad" (*B*, p. 294.)

One of the crucial dualities in Elkin's fiction consists in the distinction between two basic protagonist types: on the one hand, those whose lives, in part through their own efforts, describe patterns, reflect congruences and consonances, and are cumulatively meaningful; on the other, those whose lives are random, openended, merely and meaninglessly successive—those whose lives reflect, as Bertie's does, "the fool's ancient protection, his old immunity against consequence" (*C&K*, p. 125). The protagonist who most effectively encompasses both sides of this duality is Ben Flesh. Recognizing that "he had no good thing of his own" and that "the best thing for him would be to place himself in the service of those who had," Flesh sets out "to discover which men's names were for sale" so that "he can buy them and have that going for him" (*TF*, pp. 49-50). Living his "franchised life under the logos of others" (p. 252) briefly lends Flesh the illusion of selfhood, allowing him to make his itinerary of franchise stops "what he had in lieu of life" (p. 245). But gradually the pattern of his franchises organizes itself into the very image of the disease that is dulling his ability to distinguish between sensations, the America he has helped to create (and whose projected shape is as much of a self as he has) proving so homogeneous that its differences are "as absent, as blasted away as the tactile capacities of his poor mother-fuck fingers and his lousy son of a bitch hands" (p. 245). The pattern he had contrived to give order and meaning to his life, in other words, turns out merely to imitate the essential physical dissolution that is his fate, multiple sclerosis revealing itself as the configuration both of his personality and of his cultural ideals. Paresthesia is his portion of destiny, then, " 'Poetic justice, symbolism. Irony and fate,' " Flesh complains. " 'Life's rhyming couplets, its punchlines. The goblins that get you when you don't watch out-...What form does, what made us what we are today' " (p. 120).

From *Boswell* through *George Mills* Elkin has been interested

Reading Stanley Elkin

in the designs his characters' lives do or do not describe, and no-where does he address this central theme more explicitly than in that first novel. "Something happens," Boswell contends early in the work, "It's a life principle. Wheels turn. Conditions ripen" (*B*, p. 33). But he subsequently reverses that judgment, admitting, "Almost fondly I remembered that old foolishness, a faith in the thermodynamics of forever ripening conditions. But that was in another physics.... Conditions do not ripen. Things do not happen. Nothing happens. We're like poor people on Sundays. We're all dressed up with nowhere to go" (pp. 105-6).

Which brings us back to Mills. It isn't as if things don't happen to this composite Mills protagonist, of course, but what are the ulti-mate consequences of his adventures? By contrast, Guillalume re-turns to Northumbria to learn that his elder brothers have died in Palestine, thus clearing the way for him to succeed his father as lord of the manor; Bufusqueu, Mills's companion in the sultan's harem, decides to remain in that "strange sanctuary," agreeing to submit to emasculation because " 'it's part of their dress code' " (p. 439); and Judith Glazer moves from life into death, discomfiting friends and relatives with mischievous pranks en route. For Mills's consorts in adventure "Something happens. Wheels turn. Conditions ripen"— or at least shift, change, allow for unexpected resolutions and result in altered circumstances. Mills's fate, conversely, is that whatever happens to him will in no way alter his essential condition; he must emerge from every experience untransformed and unconverted, the situations of urgency and extremity he has known in the end only re-storing him to himself and to his ignominious position in the world. Late twentieth century Mills makes a last-ditch effort to cast off the family doom and salvage something from his Judith Glazer experi-ence when he tries to play her family's claim to her estate off against her husband's claim to it, both contending parties believing that a sympathetic deposition from him is essential to the success of their suits. But his attempt to bear down on the world, to manipulate its power levers to his own advantage, fails when a tangled skein of cir-cumstances finally renders his testimony irrelevant, and he is conse-quently left with just another Millsishly profitless, Millsishly meaningless experience. The only point that this or any of his other adventures could be said to dramatize, in fact, is another Boswellian notion recorded in Elkin's first novel: "People do not change," Boswell argues, "I am no believer in epiphanies. What we are is what we come to. We are stuck with ourselves. Rehabilitation is when you move into a new neighborhood, but some furniture travels always with us, the familiar old sofa of self, the will's ancient wardrobe, the old knives and spoons of the personality" (*B*, p. 220).

The real haves and have nots of *George Mills* are not to be identified simply according to their wealth or social position, then—for all of its ostensible interest in classes and class fates, there are few novels less seriously Marxist in intent than this one. To be fortunate, elevated, superior, in this novel's terms, is to live a life dynamic in form, a life possessed of meaning, connection, and consequence, one marked by development and evolving circumstances, by the opportunity and potential for change. To be lowly, on the other hand, is to live in a "tapestry condition" of stasis and fixity; it is to live a becalmed life in which tension, drama, and the prospect of change are missing. (To have adventures is, of course, to be temporarily released from this life of meaningless, patternless durationality, and Mills XXXXIII is particularly responsive to their pleasures, to briefly living "within some rhythm of action and respite which were as much the physical laws of adventure as ebb and flood tides are the governing physics of the seas" [p. 400]. But the unaccustomed tension of the adventurer's life abandons him once the adventure has ended, the mythic passage having proved untransformative, and he is obliged to pick up where he left off, shoveling dung or removing dispossessed families or—in the case of George Mills XXXXIII— taking his family doom off to the land of social mobility, only to discover that he can't rise there either.) The lowly are not only deprived of coherent, consonant lives: they are also victimized by the very forms they lack, subjected to the customs and proprieties through which their betters hold them in place. If Mills XXXXIII is able briefly to manipulate the sultan's protocols and late twentieth century Mills can use an understanding of the law to maneuver the disputants for Judith Glazer's estate, their efforts win them only a restoration to their "pastoral, safe tapestry condition."

What most clearly distinguishes the one class from the other in this novel, finally, is the fact that the elite have meaning on their side—it is their province, their possession, their right. The elevated are so accustomed to congruence and relation in all things that they react violently against the slightest manifestation of the casual, the random. Judith Glazer's psychiatrist sums up this point for all of the patricians of *George Mills* in his eulogy for the dead woman: " 'the patient insisted that everything have meaning,' " he explains.

"I mean the patient demanded that everything *have* meaning. She had no tolerance for things that didn't. 'Tom and Jerry' cartoons drove her up the wall, and she couldn't understand why ice cream came in so many flavors....She could be phobic about fillers in newspapers. As a matter of fact, during her worst years, she wouldn't even read a paper. She couldn't take in why the stories weren't connected, and it terrified her that an article about a fire could appear next to a piece on the mayor. She was the same about television. She couldn't follow a story once it was interrupted by a commercial. Variety shows, the connections between the acts." [p. 308]

Although Judith Glazer's commitment to meaning takes an extreme form, it nonetheless typifies the extent to which the novel's nobility insist upon relation and connection, and the extent to which they feel that the commonality's diversions—cartoons, newspapers, TV dramas and variety shows—violate that essential decorum. The contrast between these polarities—between the elite, with their resolution-tending, peripetia-producing, meaning-suffused lives, and the plebeians, with their random, unstructured, arbitrarily open-ended and pointless experiences—represents the central organizing dynamic of *George Mills,* its presence providing much of the novel's tension and thematic coherence. Late twentieth century Mills's relationship with the novel's semi-antagonist recapitulates this thematic dichotomy in *George Mills*'s final chapter.

It is tempting to think that Elkin introduced Cornell Messenger into the novel in response to a feeling that the Millses' similarity of character was making them seem too schematized, too much the illustration of an idea to deeply engage the reader's sympathies. In any case, it is significant that Messenger resembles Elkin in a number of important particulars (he is the son of a costume jewelry salesman, has published fiction, teaches at a university, has suffered a heart attack, prefers marijuana to alcohol, and is suffering the loss of his hand-eye coordination), and that he has an all but obsessive need to articulate, verbalize, to turn world into word. "He was contemptuous of whatever quality it was, not sincerity, not candor, not even truthfulness finally, that compelled his arias and put words in his mouth," we are told in a description that closely approximates Elkin's sometime attitude toward his own literary gifts. "It was as if he had felt obliged to take the stand from the time he had first learned to talk, there to sing, turn state's evidence, endlessly offer testimony, information, confession, proofs, an eyewitness to his own life who badgered his juries not only with the facts but with the hearsay too" (pp. 70-71). The primary testimony he has to offer upon his first appearance is "the griefs"—"remotest mourning's thrill-a-minute patriotics, its brazen, spectacular, top hat, high-strutting, rim-shot sympathies" (p. 71). He grieves ostensibly for the muscular distrophied children whose Labor Day telethon he weeps through each year, but their affliction is really only a substitute occasion for him, an excuse; what he is really mourning is himself and his possibilities, grieving over the "blight on his generation" that renders him and his friends burned out, ineffectual, hopeless, and reconciled to death before they have even reached the age of fifty. The cancer diagnosed in Judith Glazer, the wife of his university's dean, is an additional cause of his despondency, as are the nervous breakdown of another friend, the affair that threatens to break up two more friends' marriage, and the difficulties that his son, Harve, age fourteen, has had in mastering the alphabet and getting the point of jokes. He weeps, then, for the randomly meaningless reversals people suffer, and for the general loss of faith in people's abilities to respond constructively and effectively to these setbacks. " 'As if,' " he complains early on in the novel, " 'problems could ever be solved. I mean if anything's wrong it's wrong forever. You can only make things worse' " (p. 217).

Messenger presents this complaint to the late twentieth century Mills, the two having met over the dying figure of Mills's father-in-law. (Their meeting is the result of Judith Glazer's machinations, it being one of her favorite forms of mischief to play "mad politician"

Reading Stanley Elkin

by intermingling the classes and serving as a conduit of gossip between them, conveying the soap operas of each to the other as a way
of keeping things bouncing.) Secure in his state of grace, Mills pa-
tronizes Messenger and his sorrows, but he resolves nonetheless to
avoid this man who has already begun to force intimate revelations
about the upper classes upon him. What discomfits Mills in the
manic bulletins about the East St. Louis contingent and their trou-
bles (which Messenger will continue to deliver throughout the remainder of the novel) is that they remind him of similar disclosures
he had been obliged to suffer when, as a boy in Cassadaga, Florida,
he had been made into a sort of confidant and confessor by the local
spiritualists. Thus he listens to Messenger's obsessed reports, recognizing that they are "like the devised sequences and routines of the
Cassadagans. Because he was something of the straight man now
too, the old Florida Follies Kid. Thinking: you don't ever grow up.
Nothing changes, nothing. Certainly not your character" (p. 455).
What these spiritualists had confided in him were the tricks of their
trade, the contrivances and sleights-of hand, the "pattern of [their]
magician's preemptive sequences" (p. 145) that enabled them to
seem to contact the dead and to move objects telekinetically. Their
message had been that what appeared to be evidence of a supernatural reality was only the ordinary after all, their sequences only seeming to preempt the inescapable quotidian. Throughout most of the
novel this is the gist of Messenger's messages as well.

The last fifty pages of *George Mills* are dominated by two related and intricately interwoven subjects: Mills's attempt to wrest
some material advantage from his Judith Glazer employment by
seeking to conspire with one of the two contending litigants, and
Messenger's continuous updates on the disposition of his elevated
friends' woes. In a nearly classic example of dramatic reversal, Messenger's hopes rise as Mills's diminish, the former's good news
about Judith's husband and his friends representing distinctly bad
news so far as the latter and his objectives are concerned. Eventually
a revitalized Messenger visits Mills, weeping now not for the griefs
and the hopelessness and the insolubility of problems, but over the
confidence—" 'all that Special Olympics confidence, all that short-
range, small-time, short-change, small-scale, short-lived, short-shrift,

small-potato, small-beer fucking confidence' " (p. 479)—that allowed his friends' and relatives' woes to be resolved, overcome, eliminated. Buoyed further by subsequent improvement in his group's
situation, Messenger pays Mills a final visit, cruelly regaling him
with a vision of the world that has little relation to Mills's own experience of it. " 'How do you like the way things work out?' " Messenger wants to know.

"How do you like this idyll vision, this epithalamion style? How do
you like it the game ain't over till the last man is out? How do you
like it you can dig for balm? That there's balm and joy mines, great
fucking mother lodes of bower and elysian amenity? How do you like
deus ex machina? How do you like it every cloud has a silver lining?
What do you make of God's pastoral heart? How do you like it
there's pots of gold at the end of rainbows and you can't keep a good
man down? How do you like it ships come in and life is just a bowl of
cherries? How do you like it it isn't raining rain you know, it's raining violets? What do you make of it every time I hear a newborn
baby cry or see the sky then I know why I believe?" [pp. 501-2]

The blight that Messenger—the self-proclaimed "epilogue man"—
had ascribed to his generation as if it were a supernatural doom is
long forgotten; in its place are the patterns, the sequences, the sequiturs that make lives and popular songs work—and work out.[11]
  Which leaves Mills and his sequiturless mode of being. By novel's end Mills has had to abandon even the consolation that the one
myth he had allowed himself afforded, the pattern of patternlessness
that had been the family fate proving as illusory an ordering principle as any of the other myths the Millses had contrived to make sense
of their perpetually drama-deprived, resolution-lacking, significance-
defying lives. " 'I ain't saved,' " he confesses to a church congregation he has been invited to address in the novel's closing scene, his
sermon recalling the first Mills's tidings of civilization to the Cos-
sacks, " 'I spent my life like there was a hole in my pocket, and the
meaning of life is to live long enough to find something out or to do
something well. It ain't just to put up with it. . . . Hell, I ain't saved,'
he said, oddly cheered, 'Being tired isn't saved, sucking up isn't
grace' " (p. 508). This realization frees him to believe that the pre-

diction of one of the Cassadaga spiritualists had been correct—that his mother had been pregnant with a daughter when he abandoned the family, and that her existence (he imagines that, wherever she is, she is doing well) has nullified the family doom for good. Consequently, he feels "relieved of history as an amnesiac," and thus he is able, in the novel's last line, to affirm his solidarity with those men and women in the congregation whose servility and anonymity are personal and individual rather than familial, the " 'Brothers and sisters' " he acknowledges here reflecting merely a slightly revised estimation of his own self-admitted irrelevance, submissiveness, and peripherality.

The temptation to too readily identify Elkin with Messenger and Messenger's upbeat resolution is strong. (Hasn't Elkin always enjoyed punning on popular song titles? Isn't one of Ben Flesh's most appealing ideas the notion that "lyrics are the ground of being"?) But against it stands Elkin's concession that Mills's salvation credo is derived from his own experience, from his own recent feeling that "I'm safe, you see. . . . It will be death by natural causes, multiple sclerosis, pneumonia, stuffing the stomach. . . . I don't believe that anything can happen to me, either. I believe I'm in that sort of state of grace."[12] Both Messenger, "the epilogue man," and Mills, "the horseshit man," are projections of their creator, clearly enough, and his earlier fiction has provided additional corroboration of Elkin's ability to view the world as at once meaning-imbued and randomly meaningless, possessed of resolutions and open ended, deserving of celebration and repudiation, inspiring hope and dictating hopelessness. *George Mills* offered Elkin much greater latitude for sounding out the opposed voices of the ambivalence so central to his vision of things, and through a prose reminiscent of Faulkner yet distinctly his own he was able to fashion a work that is at once a complex fable of meaning and non-meaning and a compellingly dramatic readdressing of the thematic antinomy pervading his fiction. While still in his boyhood, late twentieth century Mills recapitulates that antinomy as he waits for a Cassadaga spiritualist to put him in touch with the sister-to-be, whose predicted birth will break the chain of male Millses and thus undo the curse they have borne. "He knew his place in history," we are told, and was waiting to be shown an infant ghost whom he would not be able to question because she had no vocabulary. It was an ordinary afternoon in his life. In Cassadaga. Where ego did not exist. Where it merged with bereavement, where grief was the single industry. Where children grieved. And soon his sister would be there. To give him a message. Which he thought he had already guessed. That there were no ordinary afternoons. That not just houses but the world itself was haunted. That death was up the palm tree. On the hoarding. In the square. It was an ordinary afternoon. [p. 176]

The closing scene of *George Mills* at the Virginia Avenue Baptist Church strikes a note similar to that upon which a number of Elkin works conclude. Mills's reflections upon having a sister, and his consequent belief that the family doom has been nullified, is rendered equivocal by one of his passing thoughts as he contemplates her. Recalling the Xerox machine repairwoman he had briefly believed her to be, he remembers the uniform she wore and associates it with the pads he wears in his family dispossession work, pads donned "not out of deference to the furniture of the poor... but...[to give] the illusion of deference, keeping myself safe from splinters, blood poison, the rough, unvarnished and nail-studded underneaths of a black man's dining room suite" (p. 507). Mills admits that it isn't plausible that he has a sister; he admits, too, that he never returned to Cassadaga to learn whether he had one. But he insists upon believing in her nonetheless, hoping that this long shot will come through, as did the even longer one that saved his ancestor in Turkey a century earlier. The idea of a sister is padding, then—it is a deliberately assumed form of protection against reality's splinters, against the mind-poisoning possibility that the doom has not been cancelled, that the fate will never be lifted. Mills's embracing of this illusion unites him with the members of the congregation he is addressing, who place their faith, as he does, in some *deus ex machina* that will intervene to lift them out of the lower-middle class. In designating them "brothers and sisters," consequently, he is not only affirming his solidarity with them, but is simultaneously, in declaring them his siblings, evoking the very situation that would liberate him from their ranks, freeing him to rise above them. On this paradoxical note the novel closes.

Mills's closing affirmation also unites him with those characters in the novel—the clients of the Cassadaga spiritualists and Judith Glazer among them—who place their faith in last resorts and last-ditch hopes, who want to believe that the boundary separating life and death can be breached through seances or that death sentences can be reversed by laetrile treatments. His sermon dealing with "the sad intricacy of things" unites him as well with other Elkin protagonists whose narratives conclude upon their deliberate adoption of illusions, their choosing of saving fictions over intolerable truths. Bertie of "The Guest" gladly embraces the unearned role of thief when the alternative is to confront the rapidly accumulating evidence that he is no one at all; Danny in "Cousin Poor Lesley and the Lousy People" knows that life is "a pile of crap...It's no deal at all" (*C&K* p. 237) and escapes it by pretending to be mentally unbalanced and having himself committed to an asylum, signaling the ruse to the story's narrator by "a broad wink in the wild and knowing eye" (p. 238). Bailbondsman Main artificially creates a fugitive for himself with whom to replace those who have retreated to places so remote that his language can no longer retrieve them, while Ben Flesh knowingly experiences his disease-induced euphoria as real joy, perceiving the blink-bulb neon panorama of a Birmingham motel strip as the ecstatic culmination of his vision rather than as the geographical configuration of his illness, the shape that multiple sclerosis, when imposed upon the land, takes. These are all works in which (as Elkin described the stories he selected for *Best American Short Stories 1980*) the central "sadness is suddenly mitigated, or even retracted," in which "the character, acting on his own, suddenly lets go," or in which "the sadness is not repudiated at all but actively embraced in some higher emotional game of razzle-dazzle performance and shell game dexterity." "Isn't reprieve literature's last act anyway?" Elkin continues, "Isn't it some notion of acquittal or deliverance that off and on vouches for our condition and consigns our lives?"[13]

The three Elkin works in which such reprieves fail to materialize have in common their protagonists' relinquishment of redemptive illusions briefly before the conclusions. Ladlehaus and the other denizens of Hell in *The Living End* lose count, thus forfeiting the change to impose human meaning upon Hell's timelessness and upon the apocalypse that God is soon to declare. At the close of *The Dick Gibson Show*, the radio man has abandoned his wild hope that Behr-Bleibtreau will reemerge to "focus the great unfocused struggle of his life," it having become clear that there is no mythic elevation in store for him, but only "an interminable apprenticeship that he saw now he could never end" (*DGS*, p. 331). And finally, in the bleakest denouement Elkin has written, Marshall Preminger gives up his lifeguard role at the condominium pool, and with it any hope of accommodating himself to the ordinary communal world of his neighbors. Mrs. Riker's banal epistolary confession of complicity in his father's death convinces him how thoroughly he is the son of his lonely, lusting dad; once he has read it, "All hope left him. He understood her reluctance [to appear at his apartment]; he understood everything" (*S&S*, p. 303). In "The Condominium," understanding leads to nothing but despair; self-knowledge inspires nothing but the urge toward self-destruction that Preminger obeys.

These three conclusions deny utterly any benefit to be gained from the relinquishment of one's source of hope, nor does any of them suggest that the process of disillusionment, of learning the truth, is ennobling or uplifting. In the monologue cited above, Dick Gibson continues, "It did no good to change policy or fiddle with format. The world pressed in. It opened your windows" (p. 331). Early in his career, Elkin tended to affirm the experience of having one's windows opened: Jake Greenspahn is clearly a better man for having learned of his son's human frailties in "Criers & Kibitzers, Kibitzers & Criers," and a number of other protagonists in the early stories (Ed Wolfe, Richard Preminger, Feldman, and Push the Bully) similarly benefit from their last-moment epiphanies, their confrontations with the truth of their situations and conditions, as does Leo Feldman in *A Bad Man*. From *The Dick Gibson Show* forward, however, having one's windows opened becomes a markedly more ambivalent experience, one that leaves one protagonist hopeless and demoralized and that prompts another to leap through the opened window to his death.

As Elkin abandoned his early disposition toward social realism, his attitude toward the relationship between reality and fiction

Reading Stanley Elkin

shifted significantly, his protagonists increasingly repudiating a knowledge of the truth in favor of consciously adopted fictions that make life supportable, vital, susceptible of hope. In affirming that he has a sister, George Mills is declaring solidarity, finally, with art itself, with what Elkin has called "the beautiful cool comfort of a language that makes it all better, the soiled history, the rotten luck." Elkin understands that these "rhetorical sacraments" may bear no more necessary relation to reality than does Mills's sister fantasy, and he admits in his *Best American Short Stories 1980* introduction that the resolutions achieved by the stories he has selected are only "art's and language's consolation prize." He knows, at last, "that it won't work, that it can't last, that inversion and magic and series and transcendence and saying something twice aren't enough, that in real life they would have to print a retraction. But I'm easy. I love my remote virtue. I'm moved by my morality. *I enjoy my heart.*"[14]

NOTES

1. Josh Rubins, "Variety Shows," review of *George Mills* by Stanley Elkin, *New York Review of Books*, 16 December 1982, p. 14.
2. Leslie Epstein, "Generations of Horrible Fun," review of *George Mills* by Stanley Elkin, *New York Times Book Review*, 31 October 1982, p. 30.
3. Gerald Graff, *Literature against Itself: Literary Ideas in Modern Society* (Chicago: University of Chicago Press, 1979), p. 238.
4. Alan Wilde, " 'Strange Displacements of the Ordinary': Apple, Elkin, Barthelme and the Problem of the Excluded Middle," *Boundary 2: A Journal of Postmodern Literature* 10:1 (Fall 1981): 182.
5. "Let others bring order to chaos," Vonnegut exclaims in *Breakfast of Champions*, "I would bring chaos to order, which I think I have done" ([New York: Delacorte Press/Seymour Lawrence, 1972], p. 210).
6. William Gass, "Adventures in the Writing Life" [interview with Stanley Elkin], *Washington Post Book World*, 10 October 1982, p. 10.
7. Elkin, "Religious Themes," p. 49. In his foreword to a collection of stories and novel excerpts titled *Stanley Elkin's Greatest*

Hits (New York: E. P. Dutton, 1980), Robert Coover emphasizes this objective of Elkin's work, citing this phrase from the dissertation in explaining that Elkin "relates rhetorical intensity—what he calls 'heroic extravagance'—to a vision, a reach for significance, a spiritual connection to mystery," the deliberate heightening of language intended to "recover 'the beauty that sleeps in the vulgar' " (p. x). Larry McCaffery's "Stanley Elkin's Recovery of the Ordinary," published in the same year as Coover's foreword, offers a similar explanation for Elkin's "expansive, energetic prose" (p. 50).

8. Gass, "Adventures in the Writing Life," p. 11.

9. Stanley Elkin, *George Mills* (New York: E. P. Dutton, 1982), p. 10. Subsequent quotations from this edition are cited in parentheses in the text.

10. The narrative of Judith Glazer's death from cancer in Mexico is counterpointed with Mills's Delgado Ballroom narrative, in which he recounts the circumstances under which he met his wife. The purpose of the juxtaposed narratives is to point up a contrast between Mills's gaining control over his body, socializing and legitimizing its urges through courtship and marriage, and Judith Glazer's loss of control over hers through disease.

11. The analogue that Alan Wilde uses in previously cited essays to illuminate "The Making of Ashenden" and *The Living End*—that of defining the works' central tension as a conflict between modernist and postmodernist impulses—proves equally applicable to *George Mills*. Considered in this light, the elite of the novel are aligned with modernism, with the triumph of form over chaos, with the values of hard-won reconciliation and struggled-for resolution. (Messenger, whose journey from "leaking griefs" to "weeping for the confidence" enacts the ideal heroic modernist passage from nihilism through ultimate connection, identifies himself with the movement by repeatedly mock-paraphrasing one of modernism's signature epigrams, " 'The horror, the horror, eh Mills?' ") Mills, conversely, represents the lowered expectations and unheroics of the postmodernist vision with its accommodations to the ordinary world, survivalist ethic, and acceptance of randomness and contingency. According to this reading, Mills's grace is merely a symptom of his decision that he need never again oppose, contest, or commit himself to anything, his reversal suggesting a repudiation of this commitment to a defeatist postmodernist ethic.

12. Gass, "Adventures in the Writing Life," p. 11. Whereas

Reading Stanley Elkin

early in his career Elkin reserved all autobiographical comments to interviews, he has recently begun publishing essays which amount to personal memoirs. See Stanley Elkin, "Why I Live Where I Live," *Esquire* (November 1980): 108-11; Stanley Elkin, "Where I Read What I Read," *Antaeus* 45/46 (Spring/Summer 1982): 57-67; and Stanley Elkin, "Turning Middle Aged," *Washington University Magazine* 54:1 (Spring 1984): 15-17.

13. Elkin, "Introduction," *Best American Short Stories 1980*, p. xiv.

14. Ibid., p. xix.

Index

Alter, Robert, 45, 190
American dream, 53, 57
Anderson, Sherwood, 88, 98n
Apple, Max, 21, 22, 25, 33, 191
Auden, W. H., 8
Auerbach, Erich, 33

Bargen, Doris, vii, 17n, 130n, 131n, 133n
Barth, John, 8
Barthelme, Donald, ix, 8, 21, 22, 25, 33, 49-50n, 191
Beckett, Samuel, 8
Bellow, Saul, ix, 27-31, 33, 190; *Adventures of Augie March*, 27; *Henderson the Rain King*, 27; *Herzog*, 27; "The Old System," 27; "Seize the Day," 27; *The Victim*, 36
Brooks, Cleanth, viii, 190
Brooks, Mel, viii

Campbell, Joseph, 57, 59, 65, 66, 68, 82
The Catcher in the Rye, 134
Colbert, Robert, 187n
Coover, Robert, ix, 23, 33, 36, 136, 137, 190, 215n; "The Cat in the Hat for President," 21; "Foreword," *Stanley Elkin's*

Greatest Hits, 215n; *Pricksongs and Descants*, 22; *The Public Burning*, 136

Didion, Joan: "The White Album," 113, 132n; "Why I Write," 9
Doctorow, E. L., 35

Eliade, Mircea, 54
Elkin, Stanley: "crossover," 105-6; cultural narcissism in fiction of, 82, 85-92, 95, 102, 103; debt to existentialism, 5, 27, 50n, 138, 188; debt to and departure from Jewish-American novel tradition, ix, 27-49; diaspora metaphor, 41-47, 53; disease as metaphor, 112, 113, 131n, 132n; "expanding universe," 120, 121, 124, 125, 130; father-son relationships in the fiction of, 41, 64-66, 96n, 144-53; influence of Saul Bellow on, 27-31, 190; influence of William Faulkner on, 12-17, 19n, 64-65; metafictional impulses, 25, 35, 136-39, 189-95; and the ordinary, 21-24, 37, 42, 48, 49, 55-59, 157-58, 191, 194, 208, 215n and

217

Index

Index

A Note on the Author

A New York native, Peter J. Bailey holds an M.A. from the Johns Hopkins University Writing Seminars and a Ph.D. from the University of Southern California, where he completed a dissertation on Stanley Elkin's fiction. He teaches American literature and fiction writing at St. Lawrence University in Canton, New York.